Adrift

TRISTAN JONES

Adrift

THE BODLEY HEAD

LONDON SYDNEY

TORONTO

To Lugd, Govannon, Taran, Riannon, and
Dadga of the Caldron: Survival, Defiance, and Dreams
—for Those in Peril and to the memory of
James F Andrews, who was as bright and steady
a guiding light to me in my distress as is
the Bishop's Rock to many a desperate mariner.

Ar y diwedd y mae barnu.
You must judge at the end.

YR HEN GYRYS O IAL, A WELSH BARD, *The Red Book of Hergest,* A.D. 1397.
LUGD, GOVANNON, TARAN, RIANNON, AND DADGA ARE THE OLD CELTIC GODS
OF WALES, THE GODS OF LIGHT, CREATION, THUNDER, AND HEALING,
RESPECTIVELY. DADGA WAS THE GODDESS/GUARDIAN WHOSE CALDRON WAS
THE FORERUNNER OF THE HOLY GRAIL.

CONTENTS

Shag'd

On My Way Rejoicing

FOREWORD

In 1938 my first sailing skipper was Tansy Lee (1866–1958). Out in the North Sea, on a filthy night in a roaring gale, I asked him why he didn't work ashore.

"I did once," he told me, "back in 1880—I was fourteen, same as you are now. I spent a month ashore, harvesting, but the farmer didn't pay me."

"What happened to you?" I asked Tansy.

"What happened?" he replied. "I was rag'd, bag'd, shag'd . . . and went on me blessed way rejoicing! You wants to stay at sea . . . watch your step ashore. . . . That's where all the real problems are!"

*   *   *

No time traveller or intelligent being from another planet (if there ever were any such beings) would find Western shoreside "civilization" as strange as I found it when I interrupted thirty-seven years at sea. Twenty-two of those years had been spent in small ocean-sailing craft, mainly alone and with meager resources, as I have described in *Ice!*, *Saga of a Wayward Sailor*, and *The Incredible Voyage*.

The names of some people in this book have been changed to protect them, also those of some places and some of the dates. In the political climate of Uruguay and Argentina, this is still necessary. May the day soon arrive when it won't be.

Lisbon, London,
and New York

May–December, 1979

Adrift

Rag'd

A wand'ring minstrel I—
A thing of shreds and patches,
Of ballads, songs, and snatches,
And dreamy lullaby!
My catalogue is long,
Thro' ev'ry passion ranging,
And to your humours changing
I tune my supple song!
I tune my supple song!

FROM "A WAND'RING MINSTREL I," *The Mikado*,
W. S. GILBERT

So fare thee well my darling,
And a thousand times adieu,
For we're outward bound from the Holy Ground
And the girls we all love true—
We will sail the salt seas over
'Til we return for sure—
And still we'll live in hopes to see
The Holy Ground once more—
FINE GIRL YOU ARE!
(You're the girl I do adore)—
And still we'll live in hopes to see
The Holy Ground once more!

FROM "THE HOLY GROUND," A NINETEENTH-CENTURY SEAMAN'S
BALLAD. THE HOLY GROUND WAS THE RED-LIGHT DISTRICT OF THE
SCOTLAND ROAD IN LIVERPOOL, WHOSE LANDOWNER WAS THE CATHOLIC
CHURCH.

Tangos and Tears

. . . and after you've sailed within spitting
distance of the ruins of Tiahuanaco—what then?

IN the 60,000-mile voyage just ended as this book begins, I
had taken an ocean-going craft as close to the heavens as
may be done until man finds water among the stars. I had set
a challenge to the future, but in every way that a man can be
broken, I was almost broken.

After a tremendous haul to smuggle my twenty-one-foot cut-
ter *Sea Dart* through Peru from the Pacific coast and across the
Andes Mountains, I at last reached Lake Titicaca in 1974—and
found myself trapped on a body of water almost three miles up
in the sky. Originally I had intended to haul the boat back down
from the lake to the Pacific shore of Chile, and then to refit her
and sail across the ocean to Australia, but the way through Chile
was now blocked by the revolution that toppled President Allende.

On the lake, I was sailing on a shoestring, forever short of
money, in an area where political upheaval and violence are
endemic, where the cold and the shortage of oxygen make any
kind of physical effort an agony.

I had three choices: I could stay on the lake and starve; I
could abandon my vessel and make my way, somehow, back
home to Britain; or I could carry on with *Sea Dart* across the
continent. I chose the last. A mariner could do no other. (The
whole adventure is given in *The Incredible Voyage*.)

The descent from Lake Titicaca to the headwaters of jungle
rivers that lead to the Atlantic Ocean meant struggling across
what is still one of the least explored areas of the last "dark
continent."

In August of 1974 I set off to complete the crossing of South America. First the boat was hauled through what turned out to be an abortive military coup in the capital city of Bolivia, La Paz. Then we journeyed over unbelievably rough tracks across the Corderilla Real, rising to heights of almost five miles above sea level, then down to the furnace-hot Chaco Desert, where our ancient truck gave up the ghost.

After a hand-and-muscle haul of some miles through the scrub to the piranha-infested headwaters of the Paraguay River in the green hell of the Mato Grosso, *Sea Dart* was navigated by Huanapaco, my Quechua Indian mate, me, guess and God through the seemingly limitless jungle swamps—a devilish maze of tortuous, stinking water traps alive with malicious life and the screams of sudden death—until, almost dead with hunger and despair, we broke out into the clear pampas of Paraguay. From there we descended, wended, strove and bashed our way down twenty-five hundred miles of mostly uncharted hazard-strewn rivers, through the hellish, mosquito-ridden green maze of the Paraná River delta and so out into the Plate Estuary, at Buenos Aires, Argentina.

We arrived at Buenos Aires, by the grace of God and a sternwind, on Christmas Day 1974. We were, both of us, Huanapaco and I, both proud and humble in our achievement and our poverty. We were both conscious that we had placed ourselves among the Incas and the Conquistadors, not to pillage the land of gold and souls, not to show that we were "supermen," but to guard our word and our trust, each to the other—and both to his own conscience and the vessel.

*　　*　　*

I first met Hagan the following January in the Coco Bar on the Calle Florida in Buenos Aires, soon after I had arrived in the port. After sending Huanapaco back to Bolivia by air, I didn't have much money left, so to go inside an air-conditioned bar—out of the stifling, muggy heat—was a rare treat.

The Coco Bar was in the red-light district. It was a place where a seaman could go and know he would not be ripped off by a bargirl nor mugged outside if he had one "over the eight," for Maggie Collins would make sure that one of her "boys," the bouncer or a porter, would take the man safely back to his ship or his hotel. Maggie was an elderly Irishwoman who had long before married an Argentinian seaman and moved out to Buenos Aires with him. She was now a widow who kept a motherly eye on her regular patrons, some of whom had been coming back to her bar, between their voyages, for over thirty years. Maggie was very friendly to me, and by the end of January I was invited to chalk up my dues "on the slate" until I should be paid for some of the writing I had submitted to editors in various parts of the world.

On this particular afternoon the southern summer sun was making a baker's oven out of the anxiety-ridden city of Buenos Aires. Argentina had been put under a "state of siege" by Isabel Perón two months before. The crowds of weekend shoppers and strollers, in from the sprawling suburbs and the countryside around the biggest city in the southern hemisphere, preening and flirting on the Calle Florida, did not make me, a down-at-heel exile, feel any the more content with my condition, and Maggie Collins's place was like a haven in a storm. There the very basics of human dignity could be taken for granted. There I could speak English. The use of any language but your own, for any length of time, seems to retard your conversational age. It doesn't matter how fluent you are; another language can never allow you to express yourself as precisely, as accurately, as your own. Even in North America, to hear British-English is to me a pleasure; in South America it was a sanity-saving relief.

" 'Lo, Captain." Maggie always called me that. I usually don't like the title, but Maggie was such a dear soul I hadn't the heart to protest.

"Top o' the day, Maggie." I looked briefly around the bar. There were a couple of younger seamen, obviously Scandinavians, betrayed by their blond, almost white hair and the rapidity of their drinking (Germans and Dutch are usually pretty steady drinkers). Then a couple of older men—maybe ship's officers or petty officers—and, standing alone at the far inner end of the bar, a tall, gaunt man of about forty-five with fair hair and red beard, and an infinitely sad air about him. He did not look at me as I studied him, although I knew that he had already gauged me as I walked into the darkened bar. At first I put him down as another seaman, but then his clothes denied this, for they were of South American cut and his waistcoat and tie were a little too formal for a European to wear on such a hot afternoon. Now and again he glanced nervously at the door as someone walked in or out.

I accepted a beer from Maggie, glanced at the lone stranger and quickly rubbed the side of my nose, in sign language asking her if he was a cop. Maggie laughed. "Irish," she murmured. "Irish-Chileno."

"Cheers," I toasted Maggie. She turned to the Irishman.

"Mike," she called, loudly.

The lone man looked up from his glass of wine and smiled. He was Irish all right, no doubt about that.

"Come and meet a fellow Celt," said Maggie, as I moved over and shook Hagan's hand while Maggie introduced us. It's a fact that the further away from Ireland the closer the Irish and the British, especially the Welsh, identify with each other. Except in the United States, that is. There, the hardness of the American experience, piled on top of racial memories of the Great Famine, have made many (but by no means all) Irish-Americans into rabid Anglophobes. In South America it's a different tale, probably because the Irish went there as foremen or Army and Navy non-commissioned and commissioned officers, especially in Chile, Argentina, and Uruguay. This meant that when they arrived they were already close to the top of the heap instead of at the bottom, as in the United States.

"Pleased to meet you—have a drink," responded Hagan. He had the same precise, yet not affected English as most South American–born Britons. Buenos Aires has the biggest British-descended population of any city outside the English-speaking countries, and most of them, the older ones, anyway, are fluently bilingual.

"Hear you're from Chile," I said. "How are things now?"

"Haven't been there in eighteen months," volunteered

Hagan. "Only got out by the skin of my teeth." The idiomatic phrase stumbled out clumsily. "That bastard Pinochet . . ." He stopped talking abruptly as the door opened and an Argentinian Navy sailor walked into the bar.

It took me about a week, over several encounters in Maggie's bar, to piece together Hagan's story. He was the son of an Irish petty-officer in the British Royal Navy who had married a Chilean girl of Irish descent. He had been employed as a foreman in a copper mine in Northern Chile and had been a trade union organizer. When the 1973 military revolution led by General Pinochet deposed the elected Socialist government of Salvadore Allende, bloody murder had been the order of the day. Hundreds of left-wingers (in Chile that meant anyone who was not an outright Fascist) disappeared, were shot, imprisoned, or exiled indiscriminately.

Hagan had been one of the lucky ones. Warned by the mine management, he had hidden out in the mountains of Chile for a year, before, seeing that a counter-revolution was out of the question, he had crossed the frontier into Argentina. The story which he told me of the struggle over the five-mile-high Andes peaks by the last starving stragglers of anti-Pinochet resisters deserves a book to itself. Finally they entered Argentina and, avoiding the Peronist government forces, handed from one ERP (Argentinian People's Revolutionary Army) cell to another, they had reached Buenos Aires. Now, Hagan was lying low, living mainly on small handouts from ERP friends and on Maggie's "slate."

Three days after I first met Hagan he turned up with a woman of about twenty, whom he introduced to me in Spanish. Roberta was also a Chilean refugee and spoke no English. She was dark, of Spanish descent and almost as tall as me, about five feet nine, and she came from Santiago, the capital of Chile.

It was Roberta who broke the news to me around mid-February that Hagan had been arrested and was now in Villa Devoto Prison under questioning by the Argentinian military authorities.

"What do you think they will do to him, Roberta?" I asked.

Roberta passed her hand over her throat, "Avellenada," she said, naming the cemetery where *desparecidos*, "those who disappeared," were buried in trenches by a bulldozer. Then she murmured, "Or send him back to Chile . . . who knows?"

"And if Hagan is sent back to Chile?"

Roberta passed her hand again over her throat, then she said one word. *"Seguro."* For sure. She shook her head. Her hair was cut short, like a boy's.

We walked out of Maggie's bar into the bright sunlight on the Calle Florida, and threaded our way through the strolling crowds, mostly well dressed, mostly well fed, mostly haughty and posing, both of us knowing that under this surface circus Orwell's 1984 was already here in Argentina. Over the Andes, the land of Chile was undergoing an even worse nightmare. There, the only human rights were the rights to starve and to die, or to buckle under to strutting bullies.

"I'm getting the hell out of Argentina, Roberta," I told her.

"Where will you go?"

"I don't know yet. Depends on the state of the boat. Maybe I can get to Brazil, but if not, at least to Uruguay."

Sea Dart was in no condition to sail anywhere at that time. During the hell-trip through the Mato Grosso and down the raging Paraná River, her keel-bolts had been strained when she had hit the rocks so often, her mast had been weakened by colliding with so many tree branches, her lines and sails were rotted and her wooden hull and deck had opened up so much with alternate freezing cold and seething heat that I could see as much daylight through her opened seams as I could through her portholes. Added to this I had no stores and very little money. It would take at least three months to get her ready to sail. Now I was on the military "wanted" list as a known associate of "terrorists" and "illegal aliens."

"Can you take me with you?" Roberta pleaded.

"Sure, but I have to work on her—I can't shift her for a few weeks yet. What about you, do you think you can lie low that long?"

"I can try. I have some contacts up in Rosario. They might put me up for a while. How can I keep in touch with you?"

"Through Maggie. When you get fixed up in Rosario, send a letter with your address," I told her.

At the corner of the Calle Lavalle, two military policemen were waiting, scanning the crowd. We slowed down even more. Roberta hissed, "I'm taking off." She gave me a quick kiss, a mere brush on my beard.

"Good luck, *amiga*," I called as she disappeared back down the Calle Florida.

Roberta never got to Rosario. A few days later Maggie told me that she had been arrested at the main railroad terminal by the military police and taken to the big detention jail at Villa Devoto.

"They'll send her back to Chile," Maggie told me, "as sure as God made little apples."

We were both quiet then; we both knew what that entailed. If Roberta was lucky it would mean twenty years in a concentration camp. She had been a registered member of the Chilean Socialist Party. Here in Argentina, after ten years of harsh military government, with eighteen thousand known political prisoners and thousands more who had disappeared—the *"desparecidos"*—and murders occurring right and left throughout the country, it was bad enough, but in Chile the beast was really on the loose. For anyone like Hagan and Roberta there were only two possibilities in Chile; base survival or death.

The military ("order") moved to take over from Isabel Perón ("law") on March 5; I was arrested in the street on March 14 and held for identification for three days in Station 13 of the Buenos Aires *prefectura* under vile, filthy conditions, in a cell only fifteen feet square along with fifteen other men and youths. There I witnessed the military police kick a boy's eye out as men retched and cowered against the bars. Through the cell window, if we stretched on tip-toe, we could just see a statue of Simón Bolívar—the Liberator.

All the while this was going on, terror piled on terror, the

portenos of Buenos Aires, the bourgeoisie, strutted the streets
in their effete finery or drove along the boulevards in their
European and American cars. No matter though some of them
had hardly enough to eat, they were all dressed up like pea-
cocks, the men stern and macho; the women haughtily glanced
from under their stiff bouffant hair-dos and diamonds twinkled
on their fingers as the heart of Argentina—men and women,
boys and girls—was tortured and violated by brutal thugs only
yards away, behind the thick gingerbread walls of the *prefec-
turas*. Outside those walls, the insane, sadistic extremists of the
Argentina Anti-Communist Alliance grabbed their victims—in-
tellectuals and leftists, the innocent along with the "responsi-
ble"—and burned them alive and screaming in abandoned cars
along the roads to La Plata and Rosario. Every night the left-
wing Montoneros did the same. Not just isolated incidents, not
just a few victims. *Dozens* of them, every night, and bombs
went off in the sprawling suburbs every few minutes of the day
and night, and people died in agony every minute and still the
vacant-eyed parade of coxcomb elegance went on up and down
the Calle Lavalle and along the Pueyrredon and Libertador
avenues.

I was lucky; the city police confused me with a seaman from
one of the big cargo ships and released me before the political
police got around to me. As soon as I was out on the street I
made for the dockyard, where *Sea Dart* was anchored by the
Club Nautico.

In Argentina, as in practically all the police dictatorships I've
experienced, there seemed to be very little cooperation between the different branches of the police and the armed forces.
In fact, at that time, early 1975, there were about eight different
forces, including the Army, the Navy, and the Air Force, as well
as the various police forces, operating separately and, it seemed
from the street, against one another. Admiral Emilio Massera's
Navy was mellower than the other forces, much more disposed
to democratic government, much less rightist than the Army,
Air Force, or the five police forces. The main Buenos Aires

dockyard was like an armed Naval camp, and no soldiers were allowed in. Under the sympathetic eyes of Argentinian sailors, I hauled up *Sea Dart*'s anchor, hoisted her ragged sails, and limped west along the coast to the small fishing port of Olivos, about eight miles along the shore.

I had visited Olivos a week before to spy out the land, and knew that there was no guard there during the day. On the way along the coast I took down and stowed away the British ensign and slapped some white paint over the name and port of registry on the stern. Now she was reasonably disguised and, from a distance, would not stand out among the fleet of similar small sailing craft moored in Olivos harbor, among which I berthed her.

I had not cleared customs and immigration to take the boat out of Argentina. I dared not, in case the political police might arrest *Sea Dart*. I said nothing to anyone when I left Buenos Aires and when I arrived at Olivos, and no one inquired about me or the boat. In 1975, in Argentina, only policemen asked questions.

In April, I started to get *Sea Dart* ready in Olivos to voyage to Brazil, even though I had no money to buy her new lines and sails, of which she was in dire need. I cleaned out her bilge and painted it, I took down her mast and strengthened it by inserting a steel pipe to take out the distortion, and I painted her topsides, all gray so as to not let her stand out in the crowd. I was also busy at the typewriter in the evenings, by the light of my oil-lamp. It was stuffy in the tiny cabin, for I'd had to shut the hatch and curtain the ports so that the soldier on guard at night could not see that someone was onboard. I wrote seven or eight short stories and articles during my hiding in Olivos, and sent them to sailing magazines in different countries. Of course I dared not write about my predicament at the time, for who knew if the article might be published while I was still in hiding? I wondered, as I sent a lad to mail the manuscripts (I dared not go to a post office—they were all watched by the military), if the readers of the stories would ever know under what conditions, in what anxiety, they were written. Cramped in a small, damp, hot cabin only six feet wide by eight feet long by four feet high.

I had been to the British Embassy in Buenos Aires, a closely guarded, fortresslike building. I had not reported my arrests or my troubles. If I had done so the officials would only have advised me to leave the country immediately. How could I go without my *Sea Dart?* How could I, after all we had been through on the long voyages to date, abandon her? I might as well be asked to cut off my limbs. The embassy officials were kind and courteous to the "crazy old sea-dog" (*quite a character, actually, old chap*), and they never dreamed that I was on Isabel Perón's bully-boy's wanted list as an associate of Chilean trade unionists.

*   *   *

I spent May 8, my fifty-first birthday, reconnoitering Nazi war criminal Martin Bormann's house. I had met Karl, one of the gardeners from the villa. He was a German-Argentinian secret leftist whose grandparents had immigrated to Argentina sixty or so years before. He had been looking at the boats in the harbor, and I had fallen into conversation with him. I had told him that I was Peruvian, but it was soon obvious he knew better. At any rate he confided in me, after we had drunk tea a few times onboard at my invitation, and beer a few times ashore at his, and told me that a Nazi bigwig was living close by. It took him a couple of weeks to get around to mentioning the name Bormann. Karl told me that the old Nazi had been in a nunnery, in Santa Cruz, Bolivia, for the past year or so, undergoing treatment for a heart ailment. Now he was back in his villa, which sat only a hundred yards from the presidential palace at Olivos. This I had to see, so Karl and I strolled through the English-looking, tree-lined streets of the suburb, looking very casual. In my tatty clothes, sunburned as I was, I would arouse no suspicion. Karl and I headed for the villa, *chez* Bormann.

Oh Johnny came over the other day,
Way, Rio!
Oh Johnny came over the other day,
For we're bound for the Rio Grande!

He told what the Old Man had to say,
Way, Rio!
He told what the Old Man had to say,
For we're bound for the Rio Grande!

That sailors is tinkers and tailors is men,
Way, Rio!
That sailors is tinkers and tailors is men,
For we're bound for the Rio Grande!

FROM "RIO GRANDE." A HALYARD OR WINDLASS CHANTY FROM THE MID
EIGHTEEN HUNDREDS, IT IS ONE OF THE MOST PLAINTIVE MELODIES. IN IT,
THE WORD *Rio* IS PRONOUNCED "RYE-OH."

Rio Grande!

BORMANN'S VILLA was medium size by Olivos standards, which means quite big by any other. It was built, like so many other villas in the area, in the English Tudor style, and I reckoned it must have had at least fifteen rooms, though it was difficult to see very much, as the house was surrounded by trees, thick bushes, and a ten-foot-high barbed wire fence. About six feet inside the first high fence was another, about eight feet high, and this was evidently electrified. The grounds-man told me that there were four armed guards inside the grounds, always on duty, and I saw for myself that there were four Argentinian soldiers patrolling outside the grounds.

I reckoned then in my notes that it would require at least twenty well-trained men, plus probably an armored car or a small tank, to even get inside the front door of Martin Bormann's house. I walked back to the port telling myself *"The hell with it—why worry about some ancient, ailing has-been from the forties? The devil will look after him soon enough."* Besides, I had enough problems of my own in the here and now. What was one "war criminal" among thousands?

By mid-July I had received enough money from selling my writing to be able to stock the boat, but again I dared not go to the authorities for an exit permit. So I determined to wait, now that it was mid-winter, for a foggy night, and then creep out of the harbor under the noses of the heavily armed soldiers at the harbor entrance. This I did, a risky business, for the soldiers were trigger-fingered. In the dead of night I made for the Uruguayan shore of the Plate Estuary, by miracle not spotted, and by morning was bowling along nicely toward Montevideo, the port-capital of Uruguay, about five miles offshore, in one of the narrow channels which lace the otherwise very shallow mud-banks of the Plate. In mid-forenoon one of the sudden high storms from the south—*pamperos* they are called—blew out of the blue and drove *Sea Dart* onto the rocky coast of Uruguay, even though, in despair, I had anchored well offshore. By a superhuman effort, I had jammed sails between the boat and the rock she was pounding, and at least kept her afloat, even though she was badly holed about the stern. Then, when the storm eased off, I somehow sailed her into Montevideo Harbor and drove her up onto a mud-bank, exhausted, in both triumph and disaster.

There was no possibility of making repairs effective enough to sail *Sea Dart* home within a year, and it would take me that long to earn enough money to do the job properly. There was hardly any possibility of earning any money except by writing magazine articles, and that takes time—both the writing and the payment for it—so I took yet another risk. I smuggled ashore, through the dockyard gates, under the noses of the military police, some of *Sea Dart*'s gear: her sextant, charts, outboard motor (ostensibly heading for repairs), mooring lines, and even her rubber dinghy. These I sold to a "fence" for about one-third of their true value. This provided enough money to live on ashore until I could earn the rest of my air-fare home— I was short of about $250.

In July, I made arrangements with the Houlder Brothers shipping line for *Sea Dart* to be shipped home onboard the steamer *Hardwicke Grange*. It was understood that I would pay the shipping company in England.

Having seen *Sea Dart* onboard the ship, well bowsed down, safe, I now had only myself to worry about. I had found a room in a cheap boarding house in the red-light area of Montevideo. During the day the huddle of narrow streets looked quite respectable; the madams sat out on their window balconies and some of the girls (and boys) shopped for food in the tiny butcher's shop at the corner or the greengrocer's a few doors down, while other girls (and boys) took the sun up on the flat roofs. During the night, after ten o'clock, the electricity went off all over the city. This, the government-run papers said, was

an economic necessity. Then all was quiet in the area. But between six o'clock and ten in the evening, the narrow alleys and
the bars all around were a scene which would make Times
Square look like a Church of England convocation. Then the
putas and *putos* were out in force, dressed to the nines. The
sailors and fishermen turned up and soon the street was loud
with shouts and song and guitars and the barrel organ on the
corner while the bribed policemen looked the other way. My
room overlooked most of this, and while it was not the ideal
place for writing and meditation, at least it was grand for entertainment, and the food in the cafés all around was dirt cheap. I
could write during the day and, after a meal, I could sit at my
window and watch the theater below and all around, or, if I felt
like exercise, I could walk up to the main city square, only
blocks away, and sit in the park for a couple of hours. In this
way, I thought, I would await the arrival of payment for stories
I had sent to France and Australia and the United States. Then,
when I had enough money, off I would go, back home. It was
about time, for I had not been in Britain since my three-month
sojourn seven years previously. Being broke in a small boat far
from home is bad enough, but being broke ashore is far worse,
and especially in a place like South America, with little possibility of work to be found.

The days and nights passed by in this way. On occasion I
visited the Yacht Club in the main harbor, on the off-chance
that there might be some work there, perhaps repairing a boat
or delivering one. Each week I went to the club, and on the
second week I fell in with luck. Señor Cardona wanted his
sixty-foot powerboat taken to Rio Grande do Sul, in Brazil, in
the first week in August. I would need to do some work on the
boat before I sailed, so Señor Cardona gave me the keys, and it
was arranged that I would find a crew of two to assist me. The
fee I would be paid amounted to three hundred dollars. This,
then, was enough to get me back from Rio Grande to Montevideo by bus, and then to pay the remainder of my air-fare to
Britain. I was elated.

I would have to return to Montevideo, for I had not yet been paid for all the gear I had sold out of *Sea Dart.* This was due at the end of the month, after the middleman had sold the gear and gained his profit.

The next evening, in a mood of celebration, I went to a cinema to watch a (heavily censored) Fellini film. Everyone was frisked on entering, but by now this had become mere routine to me. I sat through an hour of the savagely cut movie, then, disgusted, left. As I emerged from the cinema I saw a familiar shape on the sidewalk opposite, walking slowly along. I stared, then ran across the road to get a closer look—and found that I was looking at the back of Roberta's head! I walked along hurriedly and grabbed her arm. She turned and seized my hand. "I've been looking for you all over the city," she cried quietly.

"Wait, Roberta," I replied. "Follow me a couple of minutes until we're out of the lights." I started off toward a dark patch.

"Dios mio," was all Roberta could say. Seeing her *was* a chance in a million, I felt—but said nothing. It was as if I had been directed to this place by some unseen hand.

But I wondered to myself as I walked a few paces ahead of Roberta, *"What the hell now?"* I was doing quite well in Uruguay. I had written six stories and the payments were slowly coming in. I had a job which would soon ensure that I could get back home to Britain; I had not been bothered by the police here . . . I stopped. Roberta caught up.

In the dark Roberta grabbed my hand again and shook it. "Tristan," she almost shouted, "I've been looking for you all over the place!"

"Ssh, steady, Roberta," I muttered. "Walk slowly and tell me what happened."

"The ERP dynamited the wall at Villa Devoto prison; a hundred and twenty got out. The military death squads are on the loose. There are thousands of *desparecidos* . . . they're dynamiting the bodies . . ."

"Hagan?"

"Yes, he got out. He's in a bad way. He got a bullet in his ankle. We managed to get him into a car and he's at Mar del Plata now, hiding out . . ."

"Hell."

"Yes, he's recovering all right, but he needs to get out of Argentina, fast . . . he can't go north by land—everything is watched." Roberta rambled on, "The death squads are using helicopters, too, for *las comidas para las pescas.*"

"Fish food?"

"Yes, they take the *desparecidos* up, bound hand and foot, over the ocean, slit their bellies"—Roberta passed her tightly closed palm swiftly from her waist to her chest—"and throw them down into the water. That way they won't float, see?"

We crossed the main square as the electric street lamps flickered and went out and four Army trucks came to a halt, spewing armed soldiers out onto the sidewalks. We strolled on trying to look nonchalant, like two lovers—or a father and daughter—and soon were through the gateway into the old quarter of the city, comparatively safe from questioning. As we walked down the cobblestone street to the red-light area and my room, Roberta asked me, as I knew she would, "Can you help Hagan, Tristan?"

"My boat's gone back to England, Roberta." I looked at her. She was much thinner, much paler than when I had last seen her only four months before. "Anyway," I asked her, "how did you get over here?"

"Fishing boat," she said. "Friends." There were dark shadows under her eyes.

"Can't they get him out?"

"They can get him out of La Plata, but it's very risky to try to bring him ashore here in Uruguay. The coastal patrols are very busy checking, and if he isn't on the crew list, they'll arrest him and send him back to Argentina. The authorities there will . . ." She left the rest unsaid. We both knew that Hagan would be shot on sight in Argentina.

"When do you go back?" I asked Roberta.

"In the morning, early," she replied.

"Right. Come up to my place. I'll work something out. I'm delivering a powerboat to Brazil in a few days. We'll work out a rendezvous for your fishing boat and meet you at sea. I'll take him up to Brazil as one of the crew."

The rain started to spatter just as we reached Señor Rodriguez's boarding house. The dead, quiet, darkened street awaited the tread of the watchers.

*   *   *

I made the rendezvous for August 7. I had the sixty-footer ready for sea by August 5 and delayed sailing a day on the excuse that I had some business to clear up at the British consulate. *Conchita*, the powerboat, was very well built and fitted with two twelve-cylinder Paxman diesel engines. Once out of Montevideo I explained what we were about to do to the two Uruguayan fishermen, both in their early twenties, whom I had engaged as crew. They would receive twenty dollars each for keeping quiet, which they agreed to eagerly. Twenty dollars is a lot of money when one's annual earnings work out to five hundred dollars.

The rendezvous was for noon at longitude 55 west, latitude 36 south, and *Conchita* was there, heaving and pitching in the stiff South Atlantic swells, an hour before the fishing boat showed up. The wind was southerly and cold. The sea was too rough for the two vessels to come alongside each other, so the fishing boat lowered her dinghy, into which three people clambered, and soon they were rowing over to us. When they came closer I saw that both Roberta and Hagan were in the frail craft, and also a fisherman, rowing.

Soon Hagan was onboard. He was in a bad way, pale, haggard, and unable to stand, so that my two crew had to support him and walk him down the companionway to the saloon. Not easy, for he was a big man.

"You coming, too, Roberta?" I called, as the fisherman held the dinghy off.

"No, I'm going back," Roberta cried.

"Come on . . . you'll be safer in Brazil!" I shouted against the rising wind.

"No, they need me here!" she replied. Then she turned to

the rower, who started pulling at the oars, away from *Conchita*. In the southwest the sky was darkening with the threat of a *pampero* windstorm. The Plate Estuary, or anywhere near it, is no place to be when the *pampero* whistles up. There was no time to lose. *Conchita* had to take off for the open ocean as soon as possible.

Although the vast flat pampas of Argentina were well out of sight over our western horizon, about a hundred miles away, we could see the rising soil-dust being swept up into the sky, as if the devil were sweeping Argentina clean. Across the gray winter sky, like a latitude-line drawn across the heavens, from our east to their west, a great long cloud, shaped like a cigar (hence it's name: *cigarro*) was rolling itself like a huge, dirty blanket. All around us the sea was as "snot-green" as James Joyce ever saw it in Dublin bay, and the old southerly wind, all the way from Antarctica, was clutching at our oilskins, bringing tears to our eyes.

The little fishing boat dinghy was rising and falling, rising and falling, disappearing behind the rolling hills of cold Falkland current water, while the fishing boat itself, two hundred yards away, steamed slowly, head to sea, slashes of silver-white spray streaming from her bluff bows while astern of her, wheeling, rising and dipping, the ever hopeful seabirds followed her, as if they were tethered to her by invisible leashes, and searched her empty wake.

I balanced on the side deck of *Conchita* and watched the tiny dinghy slowly grow smaller and smaller, until it was a mere blob appearing at intervals on the crests of the seas. This was my first sally into the deep ocean for well over a year, since I had taken my fateful step ashore on the Pacific coast of South America.

As I stared after Roberta I recalled, in flashes, all the misery and suffering that I had witnessed on my journey through that God-forsaken continent. I saw in my mind's eye, again, all the poverty and dirt and starvation, all the phony macho strutting and posing, all the bullying and violence, all the five jails I had

been in, all the senseless, stupid, sadistic cruelty, all the cow-
ering servility and panic and blind anxiety, all the *waste;* then
I gritted my teeth and looked around me, all around the storm-
laden sea and sky and I gloried in my surroundings, and I knew
that, at that moment, I would not choose to be anywhere else
on earth, nor anyone else on earth, nor in any other company. I
stood there for a few moments as *Conchita* pounded up and
down in the steepening seas and gave thanks to all the powers
that be that I had survived to see again the majesty of the ocean,
which takes not one iota of notice of the power and wealth of
mere men, but demands only her dues and gives back a harvest
fuller than landsmen can ever imagine. She makes all people
who love and respect her, *monarchs* within themselves.

I waved goodbye to a very brave woman and turned to the
wheel.

When we were well clear out into the ocean, one of my crew
took the helm and I went below to see how Hagan was doing.
He was sitting on the saloon sofa with his wounded leg up.

"God, am I glad you turned up!" he averred in English.
"There's all hell on the loose."

"Rough, eh?"

"They had me hooded and chained for five days. I had three
sessions in the 'operating room' . . . they were laughing and jok-
ing and—"

"The what?"

"The 'operating room'—that's what they call the torture cell
—they use electric cattle prods and force 'em," Hagan searched
for words, then said, "up your bottom . . . then switch on. I got
that—I don't know—maybe a dozen times and the 'submarine'
I don't know how many times, I blacked out."

"The submarine?"

"They submerge you in the prison cesspool—it's a big concrete tank full of sewage—Christ!"

There was silence for a moment. Then I said, "I've put you
down on the crew list. You can land in Brazil, no problem. What
concerns me is what happens to you then."

"I've some money with me, enough to go from Rio Grande to Sao Paulo by bus. Once I'm there I'll be okay. I have an address to go to there. I'll be all right in Sao Paulo."

I poured a cup of coffee for Hagan. "And then?" I asked him.

"Try to get to the States, I suppose."

"How about Ireland?"

"That's another idea," he murmured, without enthusiasm.

"How's your foot?" I asked him.

"I'll see a doctor again in Sao Paulo," he sighed, creasing his face. "The thing that distresses me most is Roberta not coming with me, but she wouldn't hear of it. Her father's in jail . . ."

"Why do you do it, Mike?"

"Do what?"

"Keep fighting against those bastards." I gestured to port, to the west.

He looked up at me, his blue-green eyes firmly on mine. They were like the eyes of a child but surrounded by furrows of suffering, creases of pain. "I'm only struggling to stay alive," he explained.

"But all this stuff with the ERP in Argentina. You know there's a lot of bloody fanatics among that lot . . ." I rejoined.

"No more so than on the other side," he interjected. "And anyway, like I said, I'm only struggling to stay alive. I was a shop-steward in Chile, for Crissake, Tristan, can't you get it into your head what that means? All I ever wanted was to get a decent living wage and working conditions for a bunch of poor blighters who've never had them. All the other side wants is to make bigger and bigger profits every year. People . . . nobody can live like animals anymore, Tristan. Not even the Indians of the Atacama Desert. No more. They know that there's something better, and they're determined to reach for that something better . . . someday . . . someday . . ." Hagan sighed and rested his head on his hand.

After a moment of silence Hagan looked up at me. "Anyway," he demanded, quietly, "why the hell are *you* here? Why have you come six hundred miles out of your way to get me out of a . . . mess? There's no money in it."

I put my tea mug down carefully on the violently bucking saloon table. " 'Cos I like it," I said.

I turned as I climbed the companionway ladder. Hagan leaned back, grinned at me, and shook his head slowly as I winked at him and turned again to climb up to the wheelhouse.

On the passage up to Rio Grande (although he was seasick for the first few hours), I found Hagan to be even better self-educated than our previous conversations had indicated to me. We spent many hours discussing the merits of authors, English-language and Spanish, from Agatha Christie to Caradoc Evans, Unamuno and Ortega to Rubén Darío. We also talked politics from a South American angle. I came to the conclusion that Hagan was much closer to Tom Paine than he was to Karl Marx. All this man had struggled for was, quite simply, protection from tyranny and a fair day's pay.

Conchita arrived at Rio Grande three days later, and Hagan and I landed soon after we were entered in by the Brazilian customs. I took him to the bus station by taxi. "Here," he said, as we shook hands. He pushed an envelope into my hands. "A little memento from the boys," he said, as he hobbled to the bus.

Unthinking, I slid the envelope into my pocket and helped him up the steps into the bus, then waved him off. As I turned away to trudge back to the waterfront (no taxis on an economy budget), I felt for the envelope and pulled it out. I wiped the dust, blown by the hard wind, off my face, and opened the envelope. There were ten American twenty-dollar bills! A small fortune.

I split one hundred of the windfall dollars with my two crew. It was not they who informed on me back in Argentina, of that I am reasonably sure. It was probably someone from the Argentine fishing boat and I hope his soul rots in hell. It must have been someone from the Argentine boat, for the authorities never did find out where Hagan was landed, and six months later he finally got to Ireland, where he later became a citizen.

I myself arrived overland back in Montevideo, after a very long and tiring bus ride from Rio, on August 15. It took the

Argentine and Uruguayan police forces five days to connect Hagan's escape with *Conchita* and me.

*   *   *

The security police broke in the door at 5:00 A.M. I woke to see three submachine gun muzzles pointing straight at my head and to hear a gravelly voice say softly in Spanish, "Move and you're a dead man." He was so close that it may have been garlic that woke me and not his voice.

The gravelly voice gradually formed itself into a thickset figure in the dirty light from the one bulb in the hallway. He was wearing a white canvas hood, slitted for his eyes, and a natty blue pin-striped suit. Gravel-Voice held an automatic pistol, pointed directly at my left eye. "Stay absolutely still," he ordered, almost gently.

The three uniformed policemen lowered their guns and moved to search the room. As they did so I could see Señora Rodriguez, the landlord's mother, standing in the hallway, quaking and crying, wiping her tears away with a corner of her black shawl. The *Policia de Sequridad*—PoSec—cops, two quite young, in their early twenties, and one, short and fat, in his fifties probably, went at the search with a will, pulling the drawers out of the sideboard, scattering my clothes and writing gear all over the floor and throwing the coats out of the wardrobe. The little fat one found my case under the bed. He opened it. Empty. He pulled out a knife and ripped the linings of the case, then tore the lid off and threw the pieces out into the hall. All he said was *"puta!"*

The finished manuscript of a short story I had written for a French sailing magazine was inspected now by Gravel-Voice while Fatty held his machine gun muzzle against my ear. Not being able to make out French, Gravel-Voice rammed the manuscript into his overcoat pocket. Fatty spat at the window, which was still closed. A gob of green phlegm dribbled down the pane.

"Get up slowly," Gravel-Voice said. "Very slowly." I got up, naked. Señora Rodriguez turned her face away.

"Get dressed—slowly," said Gravel-Voice.

"What's this about?" I asked. They were the first words I had spoken since I had been awakened.

"Shut up, you gringo pig!" Fatty rammed the gun-muzzle up hard under my ear, making my head ring, at the same he kicked me hard in the balls.

Ten minutes later we were entering the Liberdad (Liberty) Prison, me handcuffed and in leg shackles, almost doubled over in pain. As we walked into the main door, Gravel-Voice said, "Take a good look at the sunrise, gringo; it's the last you will see if I have my way." "Fuck you," I said, quietly and in English, but with his hood and all the noise from a dozen chattering PoSec thugs around us, he probably didn't hear me. If he had, and had understood, I wouldn't be here now writing this account.

"Where's Hagan?" Fatty demanded, as one of the younger cops forced half a liter of olive oil down my throat. I shook my head. Fatty kicked me on my left knee with all the force of his boot. I fell to the floor. Gravel-Voice grabbed me by the throat and jerked me upright again, then the two younger cops hustled me to a cell.

"Where's Hagan?" Another boot on the right knee, this time from Gravel-Voice. "*¿Donde está Hagan?*"

"*No se. No conosco Hagan.*" I don't know, I don't know Hagan. A fist in the face from Fatty. "Where's Hagan?" The dirty cell walls spun.

Silence. A kick from Gravel-Voice, with the flat of his sole on the small of my back. My knees almost gave way.

"Where's Hagan?" A smashing left hook from Fatty, and I slid to the floor in darkness.

*　　　*　　　*

A few hours after being beaten up by Gravel-Voice and Fatty I came to in the Montevideo Liberdad jail cell. I was lying in a pool of stale urine. I had plenty of time to reflect on how things had gone. Five days, in fact. Five days of painful meditation, for I was alone in my cell. Five days and nights broken only by shouts, shots, and screams from outside (God only knows what was happening out there) and by the arrival of greasy soup and a hunk of bread shoved into the trap door once a day. Five days wondering if I, too, would become a *desparecido.*

There was no furniture in the cell, only a filthy mattress on the even filthier floor. In one corner of the cell was an open sewer outlet. Above it, on the wall was a water faucet. But no water came out, and consequently my predecessor's excrement was piled up in a stinking, dried out, monumental pyramid about two feet high. The one window in the cell was about nine inches square and set at the top of the wall, about ten feet up. There was no way of seeing anything outside the cell. The only exercise was pacing the cell up and down, swatting flies and mosquitoes and reading the scrawls on the walls.

"Goodbye Maria, hello death!"

"*Viva las putas!*"

"Diego was here ten months—may the governor of this prison die of cancer *del culo!*"

"Ramirez is a traitor and is hereby sentenced to death—Guido."

"Guard Sanchez is a *maricón!*"

"CS58 has three days to live and I will live forever!" ·

"Long live the people!"

I paced the cell for hours at a time, reciting poetry to myself —Shakespeare, Donne, Milton, Byron, Tennyson, Wilde—hobbling painfully around and around with my bruised knees, repeating to myself again and again that these bastards were not going to get me down . . .

On the fifth day, in the afternoon, a guard opened the door and ordered me outside. By this time I was severely weakened by the diet. I staggered out into the hallway, which was almost as dirty as the cell I had just left. "Get cleaned up—there's a faucet over there!" the guard ordered. I did as he shouted, almost losing my breath as the cold water sluiced over my head and down my back. Then I stood up and smoothed my hair with one hand. "This way!" ordered the guard. "Look lively. There's an Englishman here. He's got your release, you lucky *hijo de puta.*" He shoved me forward.

The visiting room was a complete contrast to what I had seen of the rest of the jail. For one thing, its walls were sparkling white. It had furniture. Its floor was scrubbed clean. There was no shit-smell.

A young man of about thirty was sitting in a chair. Sandy hair and mustache, tweed coat and trousers and an old school tie. My heart leapt to see him. He jumped up, grabbed my hand, and gave me a cigarette.

"Got some terrific news for you, old chap," he announced as I lit up.

"My pleasure!" I wheezed, wondering that he had negotiated my release so soon.

"Yes, fantastic isn't it?" he burbled. "Really surprised everyone at the embassy and the club!"

"Surprised? Club?"

"Of course, you wouldn't know, would you?" the embassy official said. "India's all out, 120 for 6! Terrific game—best cricket they've seen at Lords for the last few years!"

But give him his due. He had me out of the prison the next morning, with all charges dropped.

Much later I heard that Roberta was arrested in 1976, in Córdoba, Argentina, and was *desparecido,* "disappeared under custody." So far as I know she has not been heard of since, neither by her friends nor her family. She is only one in thousands. Her memory is all the more precious for that. To this day I cannot hear a tango played without remembering her and many others like her.

*   *   *

The Montevideo middleman, to whom I had "sold" my dinghy and compass and other gear from *Sea Dart,* settled up with me soon after. Of course he screwed me out of a hundred dollars, but that mattered little to me. There was nothing I could do about it, and anyway, with the hundred dollars that Hagan had given me I had (just) my fare to London. Apart from that I had only an old pair of torn jeans, a frayed shirt, an oilskin jacket, a broken pair of deckshoes, most of my notes, and my battered old typewriter—but I had my fare to London! After seven long, hard years' absence I was going home! And I was doing it *myself*, by my own efforts.

We're going home—I heard them say,
Oh fare thee well, oh fare thee well,
Our orders came from home today—
Oh fare, oh fare thee well.

FROM AN EIGHTEENTH-CENTURY HALYARD CHANTY

Show Me the Way to Go Home

T HE SWEDISH JET, huge and almost empty of passengers (there were only three of us from Rio de Janeiro on), seemed to me, straight from years of existing on bare essentials, to be the embodiment of Western affluence, power, and profligacy.

At Rio we off-loaded almost all our passengers—shy, polite, neatly dressed maids for the Brazilian *nouveaux riches*, elegantly dressed, overweight wives of military government officials, Uruguayan, Argentinian and Brazilian, going to and from shopping sprees. There were a few harassed-looking regular businessmen, most of whom had spent the flight flogging their brains through thick piles of official-looking forms, and the usual half-dozen drug-smugglers found on practically any South American international transport, as usual trying to look *incognito* in their neatness, their expensive leather jackets, their thick gold rings and their hard, confident, knowing eyes.

The plane held over for an hour at Rio. I went into the waiting area to send a postcard to Roberta, so that she would know I was safely out of Uruguay. There I glanced at the passing parade. There were few signs of the real Rio, few hints of the disease-infested *favelas* that sprawl over the bare, waterless hills only a couple of miles away.

Only a few groups of peasants, mainly in family huddles, were reminders of the world outside. They looked cowed in these unfamiliar surroundings, stiff in their Sunday best clothes, the men with their black fedoras at awkward angles and the women in clashing colors, all sunburned, all silent, all staring, as I myself stared, at the alien affluent in their tight-assed white pants and Gucci sandals. Third-world major airports are microcosms of the social structures around them, except that the numbers are reversed; very few of the under-privileged are found there, but milling hordes of the fortunate few—who do not have to expend all their creative energy in wondering where the next few days' food is coming from—are always there to decorate the lounges and deceive the unaware. In Rio airport there were few indications of the millions of hopeless lives being wasted in the *favelas* all around us.

The smartly uniformed cop at the exit, smiling at the girls passing, almost made me forget that the police execution gangs were busy, all around us, tracking down anyone who dared to raise the slightest mutter against the government, to put them to death without even arrest, much less trial.

Here was only the Rio of Copacabana beach, the *carrioca,* the Mardi Gras and the arms of the concrete Christ outstretched in, so far, futile benediction atop the Sugarloaf Mountain. Plastic chairs and plastic walls and plastic ceilings and a lot of seemingly plastic people with probably plastic souls wrapped in the evidently plastic cocoons of their make-believe plastic world.

The only relief that I could see was in the faces of some peasants and a few youngsters, mainly of a Northern appearance, who, from their eyes, their complexions, and their travelling gear, seemed aware perhaps that the night breeze was whispering outside, calling from the ocean, that the moon was in her third quarter and that Orion's Belt was ascending from the eastern rim of the world.

Suddenly my inner vision changed and I remembered the other end of Brazil; that miserable huddle of huts, San Lazaro, on the banks of the mosquito-clouded black-muddy Rio Apa, and the glazed eyes and corpselike faces of its inhabitants; faces without hope, without intelligence, without future, *over there.* I peered through the west window of the never-never lounge and gazed at the dark horizon, beyond the airport lights—*over there*, a thousand miles and more *over there*, in the Mato Grosso, over the barren scorched hills and over the silent peons laboring for pittances, over the dreary, steaming wastes of marshes, over the thousands of square miles of thin, soggy shallow soil, fit only to support a murderous jungle—San Lazaro!

Then my thoughts wandered away further to the west to where the coca-stupefied Quechua and Aymara shivered in the thin, cold air of the high Andes; and even further west to the ramshackle cardboard *barrios,* miles upon miles of them, that cling to the skirts of Lima, the oldest whore in South America, and to the millions of souls who, somehow, eked out their lives in squalor which would make an American pig-breeder blanch. South, I thought of the ground-down people of Chile. A quick glimpse further south, in the direction of more established terror, official and unofficial, throughout Argentina, Paraguay, and Uruguay, where a person's life was no more valued than was his shadow on the bloody ground.

And north, the morass of Ecuadorian officialdom's venality, and the grand Mafia manor of Colombia, with the biggest harlot-training ground and staging post on earth—*Buenaventura!* East through the Army-run marijuana fields of Colombia, on over the newly rich, pompous, gluttonous, arrogant ruling clique in Venezuela, on down over the reverse-racist hells of the Guianas—and back to Brazil and the airport lounge. I took one more look at the parade of pretense, the incredible charade all around me, then turned on my heels to re-board the plane, to cross another Rubicon.

There was a quiet, seething rage in me at the thought of the crass stupidity of that callous, blind minority of South Americans who were, and still are, crucifying their peoples on the altars of two opposing political systems to neither of which their peoples have, nor ever will, belong, so long as the Pacific Ocean laps the shores of Atacama, so long as the South Atlantic caresses the beaches of the pampas, so long as the ghost of the Manco Capac strides the mighty Andes, so long as the winds of the world whip the bitter rocks of the Horn!

So long, South America! So long.

*   *   *

"Fasten your seat belt please, sir."

"Er . . . oh . . . what did you say, miss?"

"Fasten your seat belt, please, we are about to take off . . ."

"Oh, yes, thank you, miss . . . I was dreaming . . ."

"I hope it was a pleasant dream, sir."

"Er . . . yes . . . actually it was . . . very pleasant."

The Swedish stewardess was tall, slim, blond, blue, blue eyes. She smiled.

"What did you dream of?" she asked me.

"I dreamed that I was already home, in a good pub, with a pint of beer . . ."

"You are English, sir?"

"You might say that."

"Ah . . . I thought for a minute . . ." She hesitated and glanced again at my rags as I sat in the lone splendor at the rear of the fuselage. "I thought you might be . . . er . . . well, perhaps some kind of a sailor . . . but of course . . ." she breathed hesitantly.

"You might say that, too, miss," I grinned at her.

For a moment the stewardess looked puzzled, then she smiled again. "You are lucky on this trip," she said. "We have eight people to look after only three of you."

"Sounds like the Strand Palace Hotel," I joked. "Home away from home!"

The Swedish girl laughed and walked away down the aisle. I closed my eyes again. The twinkling diadems of lights—thousands upon thousands of them strung all around Rio harbor—below us as we climbed into the night sky did not keep me at the plane windows, for I had seen Rio in the dawn, from the ocean. The memory of that stupendous sight is one of my greatest treasures.

As our plane climbed higher and higher, banking to the east, I suddenly knew that we were over the sea. It was as if I could sense her, luring me back to the life that can only be lived without pretense, where there are not short cuts, no smart moves, nothing but the right way and the wrong way. I imagined I could hear the ocean seas murmuring as they concertina'd on the continental shelf—"*What have we here? What have we here?*"

In my last moments of consciousness, before I fell asleep, I reckoned that we were now almost a hundred miles out over the ocean. A hundred miles? It would have taken a day and a half to cover that distance in *Sea Dart!* No wonder those people at the airport seemed so remote from reality—so blasé in their seemingly unthinking acceptance of technological miracles. No wonder they looked as if they never had a dream in their lives, nor as if they could ever have any connection with anything as mundane as a hairy caveman blinking at the stars.

My thoughts wandered back to the sea. In my mind I could see her, far below, thousands of feet below us, as we paced through the stratosphere like canned gods. Below, every sea— all the oceans seas were calling. I felt that they were calling me back, and yet how could that be? The sea shows no sign that she knows anything about mankind. We cannot carve wide swaths out of her, nor huge monuments. A thousand of us can ride over one square yard of her in a day, yet when we have passed she shows no sign that we even exist. Out of sight of any vessels, the sea appears today exactly the same as she did ten billion years ago. It is as if mankind had never been.

Then why this pull, why this longing? The sea is faithless, fickle, downright cruel and wicked at times, and yet she has a voice which commands us—she does not appeal (this is no love affair), she commands, and then, if we should falter, she changes her tune and sings her siren song to that audacity which is one of our saving graces and which may yet gain us salvation for all our grievous faults. When the face of the ocean darkens and her anger rises, when all our strength and even hope is gone, then she takes our audacity, which we must render up as our ultimate sacrifice, and she plays with it as a baby plays with a teething ring, to throw back at us or not, depending on her whim, depending on how she gauges our awareness, on how she measures the staunchness of our hearts. None of the shoreside pomposities, none of the affectations, none of the wealth, none of the power, none of the sex appeal, no *machismo*, none of the "beauty," none of the "talent," no family tree matters to her one iota. She knows only the true and the false; she recognizes only the very basic virtues and values.

*   *   *

"Here we are, sir." The Swedish attendant broke into my reverie. "Thank you, miss." Plastic fork . . . plastic knife . . . plastic tray . . . Hmm. . . . plastic sole, too. . . . wine's not bad. Corbiere (vision of the Pyrenees seen from the canal basin at Castelnaudary). Later. Put on earphones. Channel five. Tchaikovsky "Sympatique." Marvellous. Bloody marvellous. Close eyes . . . I thought of the ocean down below, again. How many times had I crossed it? "Let's see now . . . yes, twenty-three. Thrice in big ships and thrice flying, counting this flight. That's a lot of ocean miles under sail. Small craft, too, very few of them over thirty-five feet. Why did I do it? To earn my bread in many cases, but in others just for the hell of it.

"Oh, come on, now, there must be something more to it than that. What about the sense of achievement?" I asked myself.

Yes, there's that too, but it's not *my* achievement, understand that. It is not my individual achievement. It is part of a process in which everyone who ever lived is involved. It is the successful use of certain techniques and skills, mostly learned from the experience of others, to capture and use natural blind forces. Not yet to tame them, that is for the future. To be part of the process. To be part of the eventual conquest of the universe. To be a tiny particle in a stream of knowledge and skill and effort and power. To know and realize my own presence in the thrust of man to the stars.

I looked through the window at the sky. Deep ebony astern, a-sparkle with stars. Below the plane wing, seemingly motionless, streamed the straining hound-clouds of the southeast Trades. Ahead, a shy promise, a touch of dawn; light, creamy gold over the eastern horizon. We were like giants striding the dawn in the heavens. Already I could sense Africa, far ahead, lying supine over the curve of the world, hot, heavy, passive, waiting (but not for me).

"Did you enjoy your meal, sir?" the stewardess asked me.

"Splendid. Thank you very much."

I donned my earphones again and leaned back. Ravel's "Bolero."

What other reasons had I had for living my life as I had done?

The need for freedom—geographical freedom—was one, although I knew full well before I ever started the small-boat voyages that life in a world as tiny as the average sailing craft would mean many more self-restraints, much more self-discipline, than was the case ashore. Even if I were sailing with another, in the crowded confines of a small craft the smallest fault in someone else can be magnified out of all proportion. A certain habit, even the way you twitch your eyebrow, for example, a stutter, or an accent can fray the nerves of your companion to the verge of murderous intent.

I knew full well that the sea is both isolating and confining. Out there you are on your own, confined to your own resources. There is no doctor, no chemist, no dentist, no lawyer, no mechanic, no grocer, no policeman, just down the road. There is no limitless supply of fresh water, no magical light or heat, or let-up from heat, at the touch of a switch. There is no relief from concern for the well-being of one's vessel, either at sea, on passage or in haven. There is no escape from care at sea. There is only a change in cares.

And yet, and yet . . . we came from the sea in the first place. We smell, we even *taste* of the sea: taste your tears and taste salt water, taste your sweat and every low-tide jetty on earth is rushed into the knowing of your senses. Knowing and feeling this, consciously or not, it is at sea that the overwhelming knowledge comes to us that we are, each one individually, a particle of the whole of the world and the universe. We *are* the sea and the sea is us. And yet she is not. Her nature is paradoxical. She does not flagellate us with the shoreside fears—loss of status, loss of looks, loss of level. On the sea there are only two levels—on the surface or under. And she does not care on which level we are. Her demands are very simple, and in that way, and only in that way, is she kind. So it will be in space.

The top-man at sea, the king of all, is—and this is not to deprecate him—the one who most successfully lives on his wits. Money at sea means only such things as corned beef and a spare mainstay and a bolt of sail canvas. Away from the land, show the sea a whole hull full of gold and she will, if you have shown her the slightest shortcoming, broach you to and send icicles of fear stabbing into the very center of your heart and beat you down to the level of the lowest grovelling coward, so that you will know yourself, as she knows you, for what you are. And yet, and yet . . . be honest with her and she will make you a sovereign within yourself, for the sea, the maddening, wayward sea, is always beautiful to those who sail with respect for her. She enfolds a craft in a little world of grace and simple goodness. And so, as time goes by, it is harder and harder for the sailor to leave her, to step into the—to him—ugly world of the cities; and thus, unless he is an adept old hand who can deftly and swiftly put a round turn and two half hitches on his heart, breaking for the sea, his tendency to the bottle or an early death.

For voyaging at sea, good health (and that is mainly in the mind) and a sense of humor, and to not be shy of work are necessities. You must be willing and able to rouse yourself and look after yourself, to cook for yourself and to sleep as the weather demands and not as you will it. You must have the intelligence to be able to consider all the phenomena of the sea —the wind, the tide, the currents, the fetch, the buoyage, the chart, the sailing directions, the vessel's rig, the vessel's position; you must be able to deal with a hundred facets of the one problem—at once. What is the problem? *To get the craft from A to B in good fettle.*

The elements and their demands on you will turn you into a conservative. The values you learn at sea—your concern for life and the well-being of your fellow creatures—turn you into a defiant rebel against unjust impositions, against senseless obstructions raised and maintained by power-seekers and power-holders for the sake of their own aggrandizement and gain. Thus the almost schizophrenic duality of the true seaman's attitudes. Thus his innate respect for law and order—to a certain point. Thus, if a law is stupid he will be among the first to break

it. Thus, if a law enforcer bullies, he will be the first to resist.
But he is no halfhearted treader of any center-line. Let the
injustice persist and he will cry to the high heavens, a scream
of defiance for every lash-weal on the bent backs of his prede-
cessors through the ages.

O poor old Reuben Ranzo,
Ranzo, boys, Ranzo!
O poor old Reuben Ranzo,
Ranzo, Boys, Ranzo!

They say he ain't got no money,
Ranzo, boys, Ranzo!
They say he ain't got no money,
Ranzo, boys, Ranzo!

He came in onboard a whaler,
Ranzo, boys, Ranzo!
He came in onboard a whaler,
Ranzo, boys, Ranzo!

Reuben Ranzo's a good old sailor,
Ranzo, boys, Ranzo!
Reuben Ranzo's a good old sailor,
Ranzo, boys, Ranzo!

Spare a penny for Reuben Ranzo,
Ranzo, boys, Ranzo!
Spare a penny for Reuben Ranzo,
Ranzo, boys, Ranzo!

"REUBEN RANZO." POOR OLD REUBEN TURNS UP IN A DOZEN DIFFERENT CHANTIES. THE NAME RANZO SEEMS TO COME FROM "ALONZO," BUT THIS IS NOT CERTAIN. THIS IS A HALYARD CHANTY, EARLY NINETEENTH CENTURY.

Landfalls

"EXCUSE me sir, please fasten your seat belt, we are about to touch down in Monrovia." A different hostess now, this one shorter, with dark hair and dancing eyes.

I fumbled with my seat belt and watched through the window as Africa, green, black, gray, silver West Africa thrust up her palm trees at us like a woman thrusting up her belly. There was a slight bump, a quiet screech, a slither, and a light rumble, and we had crossed the Atlantic. In seven hours we had done what would take *Sea Dart*, taking into account weather, currents, and sailing-routes, eleven weeks!

There's the second cause for another duality in the modern sailor's make-up. He voyages in a small craft at an average speed of a man walking at a fair pace. Five to six miles an hour. He voyages over a continually moving surface, that is, moving up and down, with his vessel heeling over at an average angle of 45 degrees from the vertical and all the while dropping down and rising up an average of five feet every four seconds; fifteen times a minute; nine hundred times an hour; 21,600 times a day. On a voyage from Rio to Monrovia I would have dropped up and down over one and a half *million* times in eleven weeks! The sailing mariner voyages in conditions very similar to those in which men voyaged five hundred years—two thousand years ago. Many of his charts were drawn up arduously by courageously devoted men over 130 years ago. His volumes of *Sailing Directions* were first written up well over two hundred years ago, and much of it is still in the language and terminology of that time. The consequence is that after months and months of sailing alone with only navigational aid from these men of the past three centuries, a small craft sailor may tend to identify with those long-dead men and to even assume some of their characteristics. It is very easy, rounding the Cape of Good Hope, to get into the frame of thought that must have been in the minds of the fifteenth-century Portuguese navigators who first rounded that perilous point. Thus he voyages in time as well as in space.

And he does this, and lives with this, in a world where we can simply sleep and dream our way across an ocean in a matter of hours!

Suddenly the wet airfield runway around the plane sprang to life as a truck pulled up and a dozen Liberians jumped to the ground and ran to service the plane. There was something about those blacks ... they *did* sing and they *did* move rhythmically and they *did* grin up at the plane ... of course, they were at home there. The palm trees on the fringes of the airport looked rather second-hand and weary, as if they were tired of the rainy season. Then the rain pelted down again and hid the palm trees and the African grins of welcome, signals of a common existence, and we inside the plane were once again sealed off from the world.

I read a magazine and had breakfast as we flew north. I felt like a beggar having a snack in a rich man's house. The maid-hostess smiled sympathetically each time she passed. At least my clothes were clean and shipshape, even if they were a bit tattered, and I'd trimmed my beard for the occasion, but some stray haunting from the Mato Grosso and the Argentine jails must yet have been in my eyes, for the hostesses were a mite too solicitous ... or was it my age? I must have looked at least seventy. And felt it. Every day of it.

We were winging high above the Sahara now. A great orange splurge across the surface of the earth, featureless. The sky, as it curved to the horizon all around us, turned from deep blue to green, to yellow, to orange, then dark purple. A solid sea of sand beneath an upturned bowl of color, it seemed too perfect to be natural; too artificial, too contrived.

The first hostess was back on duty now.

"Did you say you were a sailor, sir?" She sat beside me. I

could sense her femaleness. "I have a brother at sea. He is navigating officer onboard an oil-tanker."

"Oh, I'm nothing as grand as that, I'm afraid. Just small craft, you know, sailing boats."

"Really? And where have you sailed?" Her English was precisely perfect, though she looked anemic after the bronzed complexions in South America.

"All over the place."

"That must be lovely, to sail over the sea. Do you go alone?"

"Sometimes, and sometimes with other people."

"It must be heaven. Do you prefer to sail alone?" she asked.

"Depends on the trip."

"How do you mean? You mean that if the weather is rough it is good to have other people near?"

"Oh no, quite the reverse. If the weather is rough then I'm thankful I have no one else to worry about but myself."

"But when it is fine weather and the sun is shining on the sea?"

"Ah, then . . . then I want to *share*."

The hostess smiled broadly. "I will bring you coffee if you like," she said, standing up. "I like to share, too."

"I'd prefer tea, please, if you have some."

"Tea, of course." She left me alone again, thinking of Europe waiting to our north, and beyond . . . the scepter'd isle in a silver sea.

I had only two dollars in my pocket, but that mattered little to me. I was going to be safe from storms and terror and anxiety. My pulse quickened. Just for a while, to be safe. After that, who knew? Who cared? To be in my own land, with my own people, *safe*, for even a short while, would be enough to restore my exhausted body, mind, and spirit.

As the lunch trays were collected we were striding, as if we were wearing seven-league boots, across the Atlas Mountains of Algeria. Beethoven's Fifth was hallowing the air on the music system. "*Very appropriate*," thought I as I craned my neck to look forward through the window, for a sight of the Mediterranean Sea and perhaps the Balearic Islands. A landfall? A seafall? Then I considered to myself how very different is a landfall from the moving deck or rigging of a small sailing craft. How different the voyage, how different the landfall and how very different, how much more rewarding the arrival, than was this being freighted about like a biscuit in a box.

The way in which land is discovered from a small craft has a curious, dreamlike quality to it. Generally (unless in fog or rainstorm) the land does not suddenly stand into view, nor does it reveal itself gently out of the vastness of the horizon. Rather, it appears at first almost as a figment of the imagination; it is there and yet it is not there, a mirage, a slight shadow, a subtle change in color in all the grays and blues, like a coy wraith ascending reluctantly from the curve of the ocean edge. Suddenly, with heart-stopping charm, for one magic moment the land is there, then, just as suddenly, it is gone again, shyly, like the promise of spring in the northern skies when the sun breaks for the first time through the March clouds. For long anxious moments to every eye onboard it is there—it is not; it is yet another cloud —it is not; it is a darker haze among all the others—it is not; and then, triumphantly, gloriously, the cry rings out (even, at times, on single-handed craft), *"Land ho!"*; and we know that humanity is once again all around us, and we and the ship become different again, tiny particles of something much greater.

Onboard the jet airliner, crossing a continent was like turning the page of a giant stamp album. I did not feel that I was travelling at all, but that I was being transported. (Yet I was thankful for that.) I reflected how the most difficult landfalls in a small sailing craft are those made on coral islands in the tropics. My mind went back to the landfall of African Islet in the Indian Ocean. Just one palm tree on the islet, one old, weathered palm tree, which shook in the monsoon wind like a highland bull at the challenge, and when I was sure of it, when I knew that it *was*, that I had found this small object in all the vastness of the ocean, then, in humility I had bent my head and remembered how small, how infinitesimally small I was.

On this giant people-conveyor it seemed that the time of arrival was of little importance. We would be guided in on invisible beams to our destination. How different to mariners in small craft, where so much has to be taken into consideration, where usually no one at the destination knows of your approach.

I remembered how, in the tropics, on coral coasts and islands, for example, dawn is the best time to arrive in a harbor, when approaching from the east, for then the low sun is at your back and will make the coral heads and outcrops glow emerald green below the azure surface of the sea. If approaching from the west, then the best time is an hour or two before dusk, for the same reason.

In the temperate zones the best time to approach and enter a strange haven is at night, for then the navigation lights and buoyage will guide you in much easier than the dull gray light of day.

Of all the landfalls from the sea, the most thrilling are the lonely ocean islands. Easter, St. Helena, Tenerife—the high islands. A sensitive mariner can sense the high, steep islands long before he sights them, for the sea transmits a backwash that changes the rhythm of the waves and that sends a thousand different emotions singing through his heart. After days or weeks of one steady rhythm, only changing with the wind, suddenly there is a hesitation, a pause, as if the sea were breathing at an increased pace, and we know the land is there, ahead of us. Invisible, but *there*.

But for me to compare the plane-passenger experience with the magic of arrival under sail was futile, for there was no comparison. As a passenger on a plane you sense none of the gradual approach whereby you become part of the place to which you are bound, already, before you even sight the first mere smudge of the landfall ahead. There was, for a passenger, little of the uncertainty. None of the skill of entry, none of the bone-bred art, craft, and guile of arrival in a strange, foreign port; none of the dozens of hazards that the mariner knows await him as soon as he hears the cry "Land ho!"; rocks and reefs, currents, eddies, overfalls, races, sunken wrecks, sudden, vicious

katabatic winds sweeping down off the hills; and also none of
the tremendous sense of achievement when the boat is tied up
alongside. To successfully enter a port for the first time in bad
weather is the ultimate orgasmic experience, as the Freudians
say. "Like being on the vinegar strokes for a dog-watch," as the
sailors have it.

Thus my meditations, until suddenly the blue of the Mediterranean was below the plane, and I crossed the cabin, so I could
look out to the west, to inspect like a celestial being, the coast-
lines below us, so well known to me. There was the course we
took in *Fanny Adams,* with Deaf Henry and Closet and Pete
Kelly (described in *Saga of a Wayward Sailor*), and way over
there, gleaming in the sun, the Sierra Nevada Mountains of
Spain, our landfall of Europe. Quickly I crossed the cabin again
to look through a starboard window. There was Ibiza, spread
out below as if in a school atlas. I searched for, and plainly saw
the Ensanada Hondo, where my sloop *Banjo,* (the second of my
three *Banjos*), had been sunk in 1968. Then, even as I searched
the tan islands of Ibiza, Formentera, and Majorca for haunts of
years before, the south coast of France had swung into view,
and in a few minutes more the Alps were motionless, yet growing, away ahead.

*   *   *

The first sensation I had of feeling like a foreigner among my
own people was at Basel airport. It was six years since I had
been among them. The waiting lounges were jammed pack full
of British holidaymakers returning from Southern Europe.
They appeared well fed, sloppily dressed in good quality casual
clothes, the older ones all seemingly in good health, and they
mostly had that quiet cheerfulness that accepts God as a Briton,
the younger ones carefree and happy. Once I, sitting quietly
drinking in the sights and sounds like a desert survivor at an
oasis, became accustomed to hearing their regional accents, it
seemed to me that they were talking a great deal in catch-
phrases, the sense of many of which completely escaped me.
Later I learned that these were—I cannot say learned—they
were absorbed from television. They were a lively crowd, very

friendly to one another and (after Argentina, miracle upon miracle) polite and well mannered. I sat there quietly, watching them with affection and gratitude, all of them. A few of them glanced at me more intently than most. I must have looked like a scarecrow in my tatty jeans. But there were no insolent stares, no despising my appearance. I was proud to belong to the same race as these folk. But I spoke to no one.

The BOAC plane, much smaller than the Swedish plane from Rio, left Basel in the evening.

"Been on 'oliday, then?" asked the man who sat beside me in the plane. He was about my age, fifty, but of course he looked much younger than I. He wore a corduroy jacket, gray slacks, and the almost obligatory brown shoes. His sharp nose was slightly blistered, as if the smoke from the pipe between his teeth was too hot. His wife, gray-haired, plump and suitably bronzed, sat across the aisle from him, chatting merrily with another middle-aged woman.

"Sort of," I replied.

"Spain?" He asked.

"Rio," I said. I thought that to have said "South America" would have been too pretentious. I imagined I might just as well have said "the moon."

"Lovely place," he said, "me and the missus went there the year before last. We were there ten days." He thought for a moment. "Packaged tour it was. Cost a packet, but I'd won a few hundred pounds on the football pools, so I thought, well . . . it's only once in a blue moon, innit?"

"I s'pose so," I replied. It truly was as if someone were speaking to me in a foreign tongue.

" 'Ow long were you there, then?" asked Corduroy, as he delved into his wife's bag, across the aisle beneath her feet.

"Oh, a couple of days," I replied.

"Me and the missus didn't like it all that much," he said. "It was too 'ot for us."

"Me too."

"What?" he demanded.

"It was too hot for me, too," I said.

Corduroy opened his paper and fell to reading.

Although I could see nothing outside the plane, I knew when we passed over the white cliffs. I knew when the green fields of Kent were below us, and long before we banked for our final approach I had felt the first pulses of London as clearly as I would have felt the hesitation in the rhythm of the sea at the first backwash of the undertow from an unseen island in mid-ocean. Silently, with a gratitude beyond words, I made every landfall.

It was raining and almost 2:00 A.M. when we touched down at Heathrow airport. I stepped out into another lounge almost exactly the same as the one at Rio, only bigger. There were no hungry stares from peasants, only a sprinkling of chubby-faced Pakistani travellers who looked prosperous in their suits and colorful saris. I was home!

Earth has not anything to show more fair:
Dull would he be of soul who could pass by
A sight so touching in its majesty:
This city now doth like a garment wear
The beauty of the morning; silent, bare,
Ships, towers, domes, theatres, and temples lie
Open unto the fields, and to the sky;
All bright and glittering in the smokeless air.
Never did sun more beautifully steep
In his first splendour valley, rock, or hill;
Ne'er saw I, never felt, a calm so deep!
The river glideth at his own sweet will:
Dear God! the very houses seem asleep;
And all that mighty heart is lying still!

Upon Westminster Bridge, WILLIAM WORDSWORTH

Home and Dry!

THERE WAS no problem about delay at the baggage carousel at London airport; I had no baggage, only my logbooks and typewriter, and I carried those with me. There was little delay, either, at the money-changing booth. Two dollars equaled one pound and a small amount of change. The new decimal coinage looked very un-British to me. By the time I had paid the one pound subway fare to the West London Air Terminal I had just my fare from Charing Cross station, on the other side, of the city of Westminster, to Blackheath and the home of my good friends, Peggy Middleton and her husband, Alec.

I had first met Peggy and Alec while they were on holiday in Spain in 1965. Peggy had been a London county councillor and was the champion of the oppressed everywhere. Small, chubby, ebullient, forthright; few bullies escaped her scathing wit. Alec, lean, gaunt and deadly serious, a scientist at the National Coal Board, was a relative of the great English novelist Thomas Hardy. Under his mournful outer demeanor, Alec was highly literate.

I had corresponded with Peggy and Alec for a few years, and last time I had been in London Peggy had put me up for one night (I would impose on them no longer), just long enough for me to get my bearings. Since heading from the West Indies to South America in 1973, however, I had lost touch with them, although I had sent a short postcard ahead of me from Montevideo, saying that I was on my way.

Friends are precious indeed, but how much more precious they are when they remain steadfast friends over years of absence from one's company, when the bond is held firm only by fragile words in letters. I had discovered Peggy and Alec quite by accident. The only regret I ever had about their friendship was the thirty odd years of my life before I had met them.

It was dawn when the first "underground" train reached the Earl's Court Terminal. From there to Charing Cross station was a good four-mile walk. As I paced along the Cromwell Road the day was lightening. The wind was in the east. I must have appeared a little strange to the early morning workers—the charladies and the milkmen—in my yellow oilskin jacket and tatty jeans, sunburned to the complexion of an East Indian, but I comforted myself that London had seen many stranger sights. I certainly did not feel any stranger than London looked to me, so clean and swept and tidy and the people so pale, cheery and polite, and the *unarmed* bobbies (yet I automatically crossed the road to avoid them. I was still avoiding passing policemen on the street a year later, a legacy of South America).

It was six o'clock when I reached Westminster Bridge. I walked onto the bridge and leaned against the parapet, to rest awhile and think about my situation. The River Thames was at half tide up and the seabirds were slowly winging their way upstream, gliding on the easterly breeze following the tide. I was tired (it had been an eighteen-hour flight) and a little hungry, but the sight of Big Ben and the great union flag slowly moving in the early morning breeze atop the houses of Parliament, and the red double-decker buses crossing the bridge were consolation enough for any shortcomings in my inner state.

Sea Dart was due to arrive in England that very day, at the port of Newhaven, on the south coast. I would see Peggy, borrow my train fare down to Newhaven, arrange a mooring for *Sea Dart* and, staying onboard her, make Newhaven my base until I had earned sufficient money to refit her. I would probably be able to find work in Newhaven, perhaps on the docks, until we could again put to sea.

As I pondered, cheering myself by degrees, a tug with a line of dumb barges astern passed upstream, under the bridge. I watched the red ensign on the tug's stern. Then I peered downstream, to where I could just make out the hazy shape of *Discovery*, Robert Falcon Scott's ship, where she lay against the embankment, a veteran of unimaginable endeavors. I thought of all the others who had gone out from this island, such a small island, over the centuries, to every part of the globe, and who had not been as fortunate as I; who had not come back. Then I felt the cold through my oilskin and moved off along the Victoria Embankment.

A group of tramps were standing around a white tea-wagon further down the embankment. I crossed over the road to join them. The tea was cheap enough, only four cents a cup, and, this being a charity organization effort, I was given a bun with my tea. Thus my first meal in Britain in seven years.

One of the tramps, whom I first thought to be about sixty, but turned out to be younger than I—about forty—addressed me: "Just got into the Smoke, mate?" (Smoke being London.)

"Yes, just got in." I sipped my mug of hot, strong tea.

"Where you come in from, then?" He was dressed in an ancient-looking blue suit. The pants were three inches too short. He had a three-day growth on his chin, no socks, and his shoes were badly scuffed and on one the lace had been replaced by string. He had the tortured vowels of a Midlands accent. His hands were soft and smooth.

"The southwest" I offered, so as to keep things simple.

"Cornwall?"

"Out that way."

"Nice country down there," String-lace observed. "Been down there a few times. Deck-chair attendant on the beaches. Good job." He bit into his bun. After a swallow of tea he belched, "What was you doin' down there?" He studied my yellow oilskin. Then he peered at my deckshoes. "You look like you been out fishin'."

"Dead right, mate," I replied.

"How was it . . . good pay?"

"Pretty fair, but . . ." he was eyeing my tatty jeans, "well, you know how it is, easy come, easy go . . ." I moved away, with the half-eaten bun still in my hand.

"Yes, I know," String-lace grinned. "Too bloody true I know . . ."

"Well, got to be off, got a train to catch," I explained.

"All the best then, chum."

So the welcome home was made. I headed for Charing Cross station.

*   *   *

By the time I got to Peggy's house it was mid-forenoon. At noon I was sitting under a tree on Blackheath Common still trying to digest what their neighbor had told me: they were both dead. They had "passed away," as he put it, more than a year ago. Peggy first, then Alec only a few weeks after her. No, he didn't know where Peggy's children lived. Yes, it was a tragedy, for she was a good woman and Alec was one of the best.

"Thank you very much" was all I had been able to blurt to the neighbor. The sycamore trees in the road blurred in a haze as I had stumbled through the garden gate.

I thought of Peggy's struggle over the years for people less fortunate than herself and of hers and Alec's nobility of mind. I first told myself that people like them were rare indeed, but I then realized that this was pitying the living (a futile exercise) and praising the dead (likewise). The dead don't really die. They tell us—or at least their memory does—to get up and shift ourselves. The best way that I could pay tribute to Peggy and Alec was to put my life ahead of their deaths. That sounds self-centered at first sight, but it is because I did this that they live in these words. To light the candle I would need some matches, and I wouldn't find matches sitting on my stern-end.

After sitting under a tree by the duckpond on the common for an hour or so, I decided that the only thing I could do was to get to *Sea Dart*. This decision is a little hard to explain to landsmen or to anyone who does not know what hell *Sea Dart* and I had gone through on the odyssey from Bequia to Montevideo. But she had never let me down, nor I her. She was all I had in the world. If I could get to her, I thought, I'd be *safe*.

With the few pennies I had, I bought some dates at a greengrocer's in Blackheath Village, and set off to walk the sixty-odd miles to Newhaven. Walking sixty miles is not easy. I had to continually force myself to put one foot in front of the other and keep at it. It isn't within the range of activity of the average sailor, but I was under a compulsion, and so it was easier to undertake. It was a bit like being in heavy weather. There seemed to be no end to it, but I somehow kept myself going, reminding myself that each step brought me closer to *Sea Dart* and somewhere to get myself back on an even keel. I was sorry I had not deposited my typewriter at Charing Cross.

The daytime was the best, as I passed out into the more open countryside, out of the heavily built-up areas. It was late summer and already the trees were changing color. I tried to hitchhike, but it was soon obvious that motorists were assuming by my appearance I was one of the "gentlemen of the road." Again I was under my own steam, but to me it was an ingrained habit and I was content enough. Walking alone is like sailing alone —then does a man truly belong to himself.

By midnight I was out of the London suburbs, asleep in a small garden tool-shed, the door of which I had seen ajar from the road. It was a bit cramped, as the tool-shed was only four feet six inches long and I am five feet ten, but eventually, by protruding my feet through the door opening and covering myself with some potato sacks, I was fairly comfortable. I comforted myself further by reflecting that I still had some dates left and I was in my own country again. I fell asleep revelling in all I had seen and passed that day; the English skies, the gardens, the solid, round red letter-boxes, the clean, tidy houses, the well-maintained roads and the bonny, bonny-looking schoolkids at the bus stops.

In the morning I was up a half hour before the sun, and plodding my way south again. Now the wind was an ocean breeze from the west. By the time I got to Tonbridge, about noon, it started to rain, but I kept going, for I had my oilskin, but by evening it was pouring down. I was at a place called Uckfield, and, coming to a bus shelter with a long bench inside it, I decided to spend the night there. I sat down and finished off my pound of dates, then, having wrung my pants out as best I could, I lay me down to sleep.

I woke in a panic. There was a torchlight shining in my face, I was back in the small room in Montevideo. I went frigid, with my hands up above my head.

"Hello, what's all this then?" A booming voice called in English.

I lowered my hands sheepishly. The torch went off and I could see the silver badges and the helmet of a bobby.

"What're you doin' here at this time of night, sir?" he asked. He was burly but polite.

"I'm . . . I'm on my way to Newhaven, officer."

"Bus don't pass 'til six-thirty. It's two o'clock now . . ."

"I don't have enough money for a hotel," I offered.

"You live in Newhaven, sir?" He inspected my clothes up and down.

"My boat's there . . ."

"Boat?"

"Yes, officer, you see . . ." I delved into my backpocket for my passport and produced it. The policeman shone his torch on it. Through what must have been one of the strangest stories he'd heard that year the officer waited silent and patient. When I had finished he said to me softly, "Well, you don't have to stay here. Here, I'll give you a note, go to the police-station back in Uckfield, give it to the sergeant and they'll put you up for the night."

"Thank you very much, officer," I acknowledged. I walked out into the drizzle, in the direction of the town I had left earlier.

"You know," called the officer, "there's a couple of blokes escaped from Lewes Prison, I thought you were one of them at first. But I know you're not. Did five years in the Royal Navy myself . . . I can tell a *matelot* from a mile away." He mounted his mini-scooter. "Now, make sure you go to the station, and good luck, mate!" With a loud popping noise he was off.

I walked back toward Uckfield about a quarter of a mile in

the rain, then I turned round again and started off south for Newhaven. I could not face the thought of more policemen. I was still deathly afraid of them.

I stepped out at a brisk pace along the road leading over the South Downs to the sea. Toward dawn the rain stopped and the wind swung round to the southeast as I reached the crest of the Downs.

I set to thinking about how no part of the whole of Great Britain is more than seventy miles from the sea. The closeness of the sea is felt everywhere; unconsciously by the landsmen, consciously by those who have been to sea. The salt whiff in the wind infiltrates everywhere on the island. It permeates everything; it even tangs up the everyday phrases of conversation.

The salty breeze blows over the hills, the fens, and the downs, it rushes in gusts along the country lanes, it staggers drunkenly along the back alleys, it bowls itself over the village greens, it hesitates and drips with the tired rain from inn signs and Tudor gables, it wafts over the chestnut trees and slithers into palace, cottage, and factory alike. It drives the British to a restless need to wander the oceans that is all but inexplicable to foreigners, who fondly imagine that British windows are kept open through some quirky need to have cold drafts blowing about the house. *"No—it's not the drafts; it's the salt air, that whiff of the ocean,"* I concluded.

I sat for a while on an old milestone at the side of the road and watched the sun break low through the cottony clouds away out over the English Channel, and I could see, from my high vantage point, the port of Newhaven in the distance, about four miles away. I picked out the docks, gray fingers thrust out into the blue Channel, and a cross-Channel steamer leaving them, and my heart quickened. I knew *Sea Dart* was there, waiting for me. The thought of it lifted me to my feet and propelled me forward, downhill now.

I passed an apple orchard on the outskirts of Newhaven, and stole four apples for my breakfast (farmer, forgive me), then, munching them surreptitiously as I entered the town, I headed for the bus station to sleep awhile, until the dock offices would open at nine o'clock. I was jubilant, for soon I would be reunited with my boat. I fell asleep, thinking about how I would refit her (and myself), and by the spring be ready again to voyage, to get out to sea again.

I began to dream of being at sea again . . . I again felt the irresistible fascination of the unknown. I looked, again, on the vast, windswept fields of infinity. Again, I anticipated what might lie between the pulsing, moving waters and the vault of blue above. I heard the wind singing in the zinging shrouds. Rapt, I felt the pull of an unknowable force forward, and felt her deck dropping and lifting up and down to the rhythm of the chasing seas.

Day and night, day and night. By day close hauled, the boat heeling and dancing to my urging as I beat up to the hazy high island ahead; by night I see her ghostly white sails outstretched to catch the night wind, and I glance aft in never-diminishing wonder at the streams of phosphorescent stars shooting out of her sweet wake. Day and night; day and night, I try to catch the uncatchable horizon, I reach for the dreams of the gods. I see the ocean rain clouds as they spawn, the snow flurries, the ice, the far-off mountains, the lure of beauty undefiled, unreachable, always a little further away . . .

I felt again the trembling inside me, as the voyage commences. I thought of the passage ahead, wondering what fresh demands will be made on me; what price will be extorted for all this wonder. And at the same time I knew that the gods could, should they have but the merest whim to do so, drown me anytime at their pleasure.

At sea again; to expose, to offer myself and all I have willingly to all the repulsive dangers and discomforts of a small craft voyage on the open ocean, in exchange for the adventure and the ever-changing novelty, for the pride in hazards overcome and for the experience gained. Willingly, because I answer a call from powers outside the knowledge of man, yet only too well known to him.

Down at Newhaven docks *Sea Dart* also dreamed her dream . . .

*   *   *

I woke as a crowd of shoppers dismounted from a bus, shook myself, and looked at the clock. Nine-thirty A.M. I cursed myself silently for over-sleeping, and headed for the docks, upright now in salty air.

"Morning, sir, what can I do for you?" The shipping officer manager was middle-aged, bland. He could just as well have been a stockbroker or an estate agent. His appearance bore no clue to the rich cargoes he handled from God only knows what exotic parts.

"I see that *Hardwicke Grange* is alongside . . ." I observed.

"Yes, she arrived yesterday from South America."

"I have a boat onboard, being delivered, *Sea Dart*."

"Oh, you're the chappie. Yes, we landed her this morning. She's on dock number one."

"I've come to see if I can put her into the water, maybe find her a berth here in Newhaven . . ."

The shipping manager inspected the bills of lading. He pursed his lips. "Freightage hasn't been paid yet," he murmured.

"No, I arranged with the shippers that I should pay it over the next six months. I arranged it back in Montevideo."

The manager inspected the freightage bill again. "Ah, yes. That's all right, sir. Certainly . . . seems to be in order. Very good, then I suppose as soon as she's cleared Customs you'd better come back here. We can probably help you with the local arrangements, help you find a berth, perhaps . . ."

"Thanks very much, that's very kind of you," I exulted as, my heart pounding, I went to the door, a few steps closer to *Sea Dart*, and stepped out into a newly arrived rain shower.

"Yes, we've inspected her. Everything seems to be in order, sir," confirmed the Customs officer. He looked young and helpful.

"Good, then can I please have a clearance certificate? I want to make arrangements to put her in the water."

"Well, sir, it's not as simple as that. I'm afraid I cannot give you a certificate of clearance until the VAT tax is paid." Now he looked older and adamant.

"The what?"

"The VAT tax. You see, sir, since Britain joined the Common Market we come under their rules for the importation of vehicles and boats . . . let's see . . . it's twenty-five percent of her estimated value, which we've put at three thousand pounds . . . let's see, that's seven hundred and fifty pounds tax to pay."

Seven hundred and fifty pounds? I only had ten pence!

"Well, look, I cannot pay this tax yet. I will have to earn some money . . ."

" 'Fraid we can't let you take her out of bond until the import tax is paid, sir." I could almost see his heels digging in.

"But *Sea Dart*'s a British vessel returning home!"

"Ah, but our information is that she was sold to a U.S. citizen, who owned her for three months before you bought her from him," he said. "Sorry, but that's the law. Technically she's been exported . . . you're re-importing her!"

"Can I go onboard and collect some clothes from her?"

"Sorry, sir, but they're in bond, too. The vessel and all her contents."

"Can I just have a look at her?"

"Certainly, sir, as long as you make no attempt to go inside her."

For two minutes I was reunited with *Sea Dart* as she stood on the Newhaven dock on her three keels.

"She's all right, eh, sir," the Customs officer asserted. She looked abject to me, with the rain dripping from her deck.

"I'll get her out. I'll get her out from under this bloody stupid tax if I have to move heaven and earth to do it," I told him.

The Customs officer, still looking stern, accompanied me back to the shipping office.

There was nothing I could do. Bureaucracy was having a field day. At last it had succeeded where it had failed throughout South America. At last its slimy, sticky fingers were well and truly wrapped around my boat. And in my own country!

I flung my yellow oilskin and typewriter over my shoulder, felt the ten pennies in my pocket, kicked the dirt with a worn-out deckshoe, and set off to walk back sixty miles to London, fuming with frustration and anger.

Up and down the City Road,
In and out the Eagle;
That's the way the money goes,
Pop goes the weasel!

NINETEENTH-CENTURY COCKNEY CHILDREN'S NURSERY RHYME. THE
"EAGLE" IS THE NAME OF A PUB (STILL IN THE CITY ROAD). TO "POP" IS TO
PAWN. "WEASEL" COMES FROM COCKNEY RHYMING SLANG:
WEASEL = WHISTLE AND FLUTE = SUIT.

Shank's Pony

As I tramped out of Newhaven, up across the South Downs by the road I had come only the previous morning, my mind was seething: *"Pay a tax to bring a British vessel back into Britain? Knuckle under to the nefarious plots of bureaucratic troglodytes scheming away behind their flaming filing cabinets in some dank Brussels cellar?"*

I tried to recall the history of the notorious ship-tax that had been imposed on British subjects by someone else who fondly imagined he had a divine right. King Charles I finished up with his head lopped off on his own doorstep in Whitehall. *"None of your American revolution-almost-by-proxy here, mate,"* I told myself, *"with the help of France and at a distance of three thousand miles from London! No; right on his own bloody doorstep!"*

I ranted to myself. *"Common Market? What bloody common market? Highly appropriate name."* I hadn't voted to chuck in my country's lot with Europe. I had not voted to elect a member of Parliament (our parliament) to bind my country to the future fortunes and fate of Sicilian grape farmers or German sausage (and armaments) manufacturers. I did a *volte-face vis-à-vis* the Americans. *"No taxation without representation! Bleeding right!"*

The ghosts of John Hampden and John Bunyan turned in their graves. I bitterly told myself that my country had been sold down the river for a plate of frogs' legs, a bowl of sauerkraut, and, if we were lucky, spaghetti on Sundays.

I looked back over my shoulder as I reached the brow of the Downs, in the direction of France. *"Them and their sodding Code Napoleon (a man is guilty until he is found innocent). Them and their security squads and their numbering and tag-*

ging and labelling from the cradle to the grave! Them and their castrating Académie Française!

"*Pay a tax on a British vessel returning home? I'd rather spoonfeed pineapple juice to whores in a brothel than pay one bleeding penny to those trouserless bastards!*"

I made up my mind, as I sat once again on the old milestone atop the Downs and looked back at the port of Newhaven. Rather than pay the VAT tax, I would either ship *Sea Dart* out again, out of EEC jurisdiction (even if it were only outside the twelve-mile limit—there to set fire to her and scuttle her) or destroy her where she stood, but I'd be damned to hellfire before I would ever pay that iniquitous tax!

I stood up, felt the ten pennies in my pocket, and continued to trudge through the English countryside with the oilskin jacket slung over my shoulders, jauntier now. Toward mid-morning I spied a potato field and managed to "borrow" a half dozen spuds, which were soon bake-burned in a fire I made in a copse convenient to the road, and, wrapped in an old news-paper I had picked up, were eaten *al fresco, en passage.* ("*Impose their taxes,*" I thought, "*I'll steal their bloody words!*")

The day was pleasant, for August is England's driest and warmest month. All around the trees in the orchards were green and heavy with fruit and the hopfields were brown and busy with pickers. But then, as compared to years before, there were snags to walking in the country. The country people seemed to think that anyone walking was either too poor to own a car or had just had a car breakdown and was on his way for succor. In my case it was quite obvious which they thought I was, and the most they gave me was a slight nod of the head if I cared to look them in the eye, and nothing if I didn't. I wished time and again that I was not in southern England, but somewhere north of the legendary line—the Severn to the Wash—where the English are of more Celto-Scandinavian extraction and friendlier to un-fortunates. The British reputation for coldness comes mainly from foreigners' first impressions, and unfortunately these are mainly gained in southeastern England, where the average na-tive is somewhat "toffee-nosed," as they say in Liverpool.

I myself have never subscribed much to the "hearty peasant" ideal. There's an awful lot of crap written about the rosy-cheeked lasses and the barefoot boys dancing together over the hills, and the sturdy, philosophical farmer with his nose into nature. In my experience in quite a few *European* lands the country people are often the least interesting and the least interested. (There are exceptions.) It might be that they are generally deprived of conversational opportunities; but I suspect that it's because of the rigid social structure of small country towns and villages, the petty gossip, the backbiting, the jealousies over property and their inflexible ground-in mistrust of all that is new or strange. Certainly I have usually found it harder to live among them than among sea or city people. No wonder the Nazis found their greatest support among the farm-folk.

Apart from the suspicious glances of passing country motorists, though, my walk was memorable. I loved the fields and the trees and the country air. I felt sorry for the city folk who only experience nature from behind a car-window. In between the noise of cars and trucks passing, the silence was a delight to me, and, as I ambled along, eating my (to me, delicious) stolen potatoes, I made my plans.

I decided that when I reached London I would visit one of the Sunday papers and try to sell them my story. Then I would head for Hampstead. I had some friends and acquaintances there; perhaps I could find them, straighten out my affairs, and get a job. Then I remembered that for twelve years, while I had served in the Royal Navy, I had contributed to the Social Security scheme. I did the sum in my head; say an average of a pound a week for twelve years—over six hundred pounds! In my simplicity I told myself that even if I could recover 5 percent of that money I should be well off—thirty pounds. That would be enough to support me while I found a job. I finished the last potato even as the rain started to patter and I reached the southern fringe of London and got a lift into the city from a truck driver.

It was five o'clock in the morning when I arrived at Charing Cross station, and, because the bobbies were rousing night-sleepers on the station platform benches and in the waiting rooms, I made my way to the arches under the station, which was a well-known sleeping hang-out for impecunious itinerants. There I found several other men and women, mainly elderly, sleeping. I picked some more jettisoned newspapers out of a waste bin, spread them on the concrete floor, and lay down to sleep, first putting my ten pennies in my sock and my passport inside my trousers. I was too weary to dream.

*   *   *

The newspaper office in City Road, about two miles from Charing Cross, opened at nine o'clock. I had washed and brushed myself up in the station lavatory, which had taken five of my precious pennies, and then wended my way a couple of miles to the white tea-wagon on the Embankment for a cup of tea and a bun. I was now down to one penny.

Apart from my deckshoes, which were now falling apart at the toes, I looked fairly presentable, I thought. I wrapped up the yellow oilskin and held it under my arm. The "commisionaire" (uniformed doorman) at the door raised his eyebrows slightly as he made a house-call to the editorial office, but let me pass.

"What can I do you for?" inquired the editor. He was forty-five-ish, heavyset, balding, and had the self-assured, impatient look of a man who did not suffer fools gladly, the kind of man whom ulcers should seek out. I had submitted some writing to him from Bolivia. He knew who I was, all right.

"Well, it's like this . . ." I told him my rambling tale, feeling somewhat ridiculous here in an office in London. I told him of the voyages I had made, of the humor and hazards, of the struggles and the despair I had known, of the arrest of *Sea Dart*. The editor glanced at his watch from time to time. As I trailed off, after about twenty minutes, he said, " 'Course, with you not having been sponsored by us or by anyone else it's a bit difficult. You're not generally known, only by some of the sailing crowd. If you'd been supported, say, like Sir Francis Chichester, you know, by the wool or the brewery people, it would be a different matter, you'd have had the publicity, you see. As it is, we can offer you twenty-five pounds, old chap, but we want your whole life story."

"But I've enough material for a book!"

"Ah, but is it written?"

"Well, I did write one, *Indian Ocean Saga,* back in seventy-three, but the literary agent I sent it to returned it to my friend Peggy Middleton when we lost touch."

"Where's the book now?"

"I don't know, Peggy's dead."

"Ah, pity. Well, as I said, I can offer you twenty-five quid."

"No thanks."

The editor brightened. "What will you do now, old chum, off to sea again?" he asked.

"No—I'm off to see the Social Security people."

"Of course—good idea. Well, toodle-oo. Bear us in mind for the future, eh?"

"Yes. I'll do that. I will bear you in mind. Yes, of course I will." I stepped out again into the dreary City Road, past the brooding Eagle pub.

*   *   *

The walk to Hampstead was, compared to my traipses of the past two days, quick and easy. I was spurred on by the thought of help ahead, and arrived at the Social Security office on Rosslyn Hill about noon. There were about thirty people waiting in the office. I settled down to wait for my turn. I was the only white person in the waiting area, although, with my sunburn, it would have been hard to tell. The others were Indians, Pakistanis, and Africans. There were one or two West Indians and one brown couple stood close to me who conversed in Portuguese. I overheard them talk about Timor, whence they hailed.

The mix of races reminded me of the merchant seaman's recruiting office in Liverpool, where I had been turned down for medical reasons back in 1952. Except for the women, of course. The Pakistani women were a delight to the eyes in their elegant saris and their gold ornaments. There was one Hindu woman there, too, with a Brahmin caste mark on her forehead, and a couple of chubby, jolly Jamaican ladies, who joked about being back in Kingston for Christmas.

As we waited over the office lunch-hour, while the going was slow, three private cars and a taxi pulled up outside. Three more Indian couples joined us, along with one West African in a long, brightly colored gown, which fell to the insteps of his shoes. On his head he wore a small white cap, like the one that Pandit Nehru used to wear. He had four or five gold teeth and on his wrist was a gold watch. Behind him, as the minutes crawled by, another dozen or so Africans and Indians entered before I left. No one seemed downcast; in fact quite the reverse was the case. The women gossiped and the men laughed among themselves. I was interested to notice, however, that there was little or no exchange between the Indians and the Africans, or indeed, between the Africans and the West Indians. Instead, when they looked outside their own groups, it seemed to be with complete indifference, or perhaps even some hostility. To me they showed no sign that they were at all aware I was in the place. I might just as well have been a shadow. This concerned me not, though, for I was very tired and hungry and not in the mood for conversation.

I did notice, however, that as the applicants' turns came up, their demeanor changed. Their faces set in a serious mold, as if life had suddenly confronted them with insufferable pain, insuperable misery. Then, as they came out of the narrow interview cubicles, clutching their envelopes, their faces brightened, the wives joined them and they all—without exception—counted the money before they left. As I watched I was happy for them, especially the ones with children. I had waited with my mother at the Local Assistance Committee office in Dolgellau at the height of the depression. I had seen the dingy halls (no seats in those days) and I had seen my mother's face when she had been handed little pink slips that she could exchange for bread (no money in those days). And I had voted Labour in 1946, so that people who could not work, through illness or for any reason, could at least survive. Now I watched the goodness of Lord Beveridge's intentions come to life before me as these poor strangers' children's future health and happiness was ensured by a system which I, in my small way, had helped bring about. The end to centuries of hunger and soul-destroying anxiety!

At around three-thirty my turn came up. There had been a delay in the process, evidently caused by two Sikh gentlemen not having brought the correct application forms with them. This had meant a wait while a messenger was sent to correct the error. Finally, the Sikhs emerged, counted their money, and left.

I entered the cubicle. Opposite me, sitting at a counter, was a man of about fifty-five. "Take a seat please," he invited. "Smoke if you wish."

"Thanks, I would if I could, but I don't have any cigarettes," I hinted.

"Here, have one of mine." He lit my cigarette with his lighter.

"Now, what can I do for you?" he asked.

"I need some money to find myself some digs," I replied.

"Employment card?" he demanded.

"I don't have one. I've been abroad, see ..." I briefly told him my story. "I'm desperate," I said. "I can't live on my boat. The only friends whose whereabouts I knew are dead ... I want to work, to earn my living and get my boat out of trouble ..."

"Can't you sell your boat?"

"No, the Customs have her in bond."

"Where are you living now?"

"Well, I don't have anywhere yet; that's why I came here, to get some money so I can find a place."

"No fixed abode?"

"Not exactly—my boat is my abode, she's down in New-haven, but the Customs won't allow me onboard."

"Then you'll have to apply at the Newhaven Social Security office."

"But I can't live on my boat until I've paid the import tax."

"Then you'll have to go to Rowton House."

"Rowton House?"

"Yes," he asserted, lighting up another cigarette. "That's the shelter for homeless single men."

"Where is Rowton House?" I enquired.

"Woolwich."

"But that's miles away, on the other side of the river."

"There are buses and trains . . ."

"I don't have more than a penny," I replied. "Look, can't you arrange for my fare over to Rowton House?"

"Sorry, old chap. It's against the regulations. We can only give money to people who live in our area. Single men with no fixed abode must go to Rowton House."

I recalled I had heard the name before, years before. "But that's a doss-house for drunks and tramps."

"Sorry, but I must work to the regulations. After all, if we were to pass money to any Tom, Dick, or Harry who came in . . . well, how long do you think the system would—" He got no further.

"Right. I'm off," I announced.

"You could try the Salvation Army in Brixton," he suggested, as I turned and blindly stumbled through the waiting crowd of exotics and through the front door.

The soles of my deckshoes flapped as I shambled up the hill toward Hampstead Heath. There I found an oak tree to sit under, with a view of the cities of London and Westminster before me.

*   *   *

As the dusk fell across London, until all before me was a carpet of twinkling lights, my anger subsided gradually. I remembered with gratitude that I was in my own country, safe. Then I thought of all the sights I had seen, and the things that had happened around me in the past three days.

I thought about what had transpired at the Social Security office. I recalled that I had been, evidently, the only British-born applicant. *"Then,"* thought I, *"how fortunate are my countrymen."* But I knew that this was not necessarily so, for Hampstead is, on the whole, a fairly wealthy middle-class area. There was probably a bigger percentage of British applicants at other Social Security offices in other parts of London, maybe. Anyway, wasn't it all sort of part of repaying a debt from the days of Empire? But then, I knew that Timor had never been part of the British Empire, and most of the people who I saw in that office were not even alive in the days of Empire.

So what debt and whose? Certainly not mine, nor the forebears of any British worker. All they ever got from Empire was poverty, war, wounds, and widows' pensions. Anyway, if old debts from the past have to be paid, who's going to repay me for all my forebears who slaved away in the mines and at sea from the age of eight to an early death? Who's going to pay for all the Britons who were exiled half a world away as indentured servants and convicts?

As my anger cooled, I reflected that I was beginning to understand what it is that makes otherwise seemingly reasonable human beings turn into Nazis, rabid nationalists, and maniacal racists; it is simply focussing the blame for your personal misfortunes on other people because they are different from you. I reflected that not to become a bigot was a matter of continually being on one's guard against lashing out wildly, of continual effort to rationalize any situation where others are involved.

What had happened to me was not the fault of the other applicants in the Welfare office. It was the fault of the blindly rigid rules and regulations of a top-heavy bureaucracy that had turned away one of the country's own sons while it piled gifts and benedictions (easy to do with other people's money) onto strangers, to most of whom, from what I overheard, the country meant nothing more than a place where money could be gotten easily, without undue effort. And who can blame the strangers for that?

Much later, I saw the funny side of my day. I fell back into the long grass under the tree and laughed. I laughed myself into the night, until I finally stopped, exhausted and hungry, and fell asleep under the English oak.

Last night down our alley came a toff,
A big, fat geezer wiv a 'ackin' cough;
He sees me missus, takes 'is blinkin' topper off—
In a very gentlemanly way . . .
Says 'e . . . I've got some grand news for you to tell—
Your rich uncle dahn in Camberwell
Died . . . just after making out 'is will—
Leavin' you 'is pony an' 'is shay—

"Oh-what cheer," all the neighbours cried,
"Who you goin' ter meet, Bill?
'Ave yer bought the street, Bill?"
Laugh? I thought I should 'a' died—
We knocked 'em in the Old Kent Road!

FROM "THE OLD KENT ROAD," A COCKNEY MUSIC-HALL SONG OF THE TURN
OF THE CENTURY

Down the Old Kent Road

HAMPSTEAD HEATH is the highest point in London. It is exposed to all the weather, regardless of the wind direction. I could have slept in Highgate Cemetery, three miles down the road, but I was far too footsore and tired to traipse all that way, so I made the best of things and pulled my knees up under my chin whenever I was awakened by cold. The rain started at around three in the morning. This is three hours after pub-closing time; consequently the heath and the streets around it were almost deserted, but there was some shelter in the underground station entrance until the rain stopped, just as dawn broke.

Further down Rosslyn Hill there was a bench on either side of the roadway. I made my way to one of them, but then found that iron divisions had been built into the benches, so it was impossible to lie down. I sat there and cursed the Edwardian sadist who had dreamed up this particular form of torture. I wondered what was in his mind when he had designed these intricately twisty iron gurlygews which divided the benches into two-foot-wide sections. Was it to keep lovers apart? Didn't he know that for them the rarest thing in a city is a place to meet, to sit close together, touching? Quite apart from a decent place for a stranded sailor to sleep off the ground. I leaned back, still sitting and closed my eyes.

"Mornin' boyo!" It was a high voice. It lilted at the last syllable. Before I opened my eyes I knew that it was a Welshman calling. He was small, no more than five foot seven, dark and as sunburned as I. On his head he wore a black beret and there were streaks of gray in his hair. His eyebrows were bushy and his nose was the prominent, aggressive Celtic nose of North

Wales. He had a few days' growth of gray beard, below which
an ancient Burberry mackintosh was tightly buttoned under his
chin and tied around his waist with a rope. The mackintosh was
far too big for him, and fell almost to his boots, which were
soccer-footballer's boots with the studs knocked off. His boots
were the most remarkable thing about him, except for his eyes,
which were wise and sad, and yet danced with good humor. He
stood, inspecting my face, my beard, my battered typewriter
case, and my ruined deckshoes. I guessed he was the same age
as myself.

"Morning to you," I greeted him. A bit of civility costs nothing.

"On the road, then? Left the missus? Here, have a fag . . ."
He held out a small tobacco tin. I accepted it gratefully, opened
it, and discovered five rather long cigarette ends and a packet
of Rizla papers. I broke open two of the dog-ends, scrambled
the resulting tobacco with two grubby fingers, then rolled a
cigarette. I lit up and was rewarded with one of the most welcome smokes I've ever had in my life.

"Dai's the name," announced my new-found acquaintance,
as he sat down on the bench beside me. I introduced myself.

"You from around here, then, boyo?" he asked.

I told him my story in spasmodic rushes. Until I hauled my
passport out of my pocket I could see the look of disbelief crossing his weatherworn face, but as soon as he saw the royal crest
on the cover of the document he waved it away. "There's nothing those South American buggers can stamp into your passport
that isn't already on your face, boy-bach." He almost coughed
the hard end consonant.

Dai listened carefully, grunting now and then, as I told him
of what had transpired since my arrival in London, then he was
silent for a minute or two. By now Hampstead was coming to
life. There were milkcarts and postmen making their deliveries.
The manual workers who had streamed past earlier were now
replaced by the lower and middle ranks of office workers, men
and women, the younger ones dressed as fashionably as they

could manage, the older ones already somewhat shabby and resigned in appearance, more set in their ways. None of them glanced at the sky.

"These friends—these Hampstead friends of yours . . . where do they live, Tristan?" asked Dai, after some pensive thought.

"That's the problem, Dai, I don't know. I've never met them here; I only knew them abroad, and their addresses are onboard my boat and I—"

"Can't get onboard the boat," Dai finished for me. "Bloody typical, it is, boyo." He put his hand in his mackintosh pocket and fished around. He came out with a piece of newspaper. He unwrapped it and revealed a ham sandwich, curled at the corners. This he broke in two, and he handed me one half. I had wolfed it down even before he asked his next question. "These friends of yours—what are their names, then?"

"Peter Kinsley is one . . ."

"Oh, God love you, boyo, say no more, say no more . . . why, I've known Peter for years . . . he goes in the Flask pub just up the road here . . . he'll be there at lunchtime . . . a writer . . . isn't he . . . oh, Lord, of course I know him . . . your luck's in, boyo . . . why, I've known Peter . . . always good for a quid is Peter . . . I've fed myself over the weekend and drank many a bottle of plonk on Peter, by Jesus yes I have, boyo . . . isn't that amazing?" He fished again in his other pocket and brought out a bottle. In the bottom was about two inches of wine.

"We ought to celebrate, boyo!" he offered me the bottle. I pulled out the loose cork, took a swig of vinegary liquid, and almost threw up. Dai laughed and swallowed the last of the wine in two gulps. He stood up then, and shuffled over to a wastebasket, where he placed the empty bottle gently on top of the rubbish, like a priest setting down a chalice on an altar, with two incredibly dirt-ingrained hands. Then he ambled over to me again. "The ways of the Lord are wondrous," he intoned.

"Amen to that, Dai," I murmured.

"Now, my lad, it's nine-thirty. It's off to the café we'll go . . . time for morning tea, see, boyo?" he said, as he danced a little

jig. I looked down at my own clothes, then at his. "But . . ." I
patted my yellow oilskin, deeply begrimed. Dai didn't let me
finish.

"God love you, boyo, no need to concern yourself about our
sartorial condition. It's to the back door we're going. Lovely
lady there is there, looks after old Dai-bach like she looks after
her own son she does . . . cuppa tea and a bacon sandwich, no
less. Nothing like keeping the workers well fed, I always tell
her. Comes from Abergele, she does, boyo. Husband used to be
a schoolteacher but he's dead now. Loves a touch of the old
poetry now and then she does, and a bit of singing when I'm in
the mood for it. Takes in Shelley and Byron like a threshing
machine she does . . . and Dylan Thomas, can't get enough of
him, can she? She'll listen, rapt she is, boyo, she'll listen to his
damned ravings 'til the frogs fly and the noon itself turns mazarine."

"Mazarine?" I was puffing now, trying to keep up with Dai.

"Red dye that is, boyo . . . Emily Dickinson used the word
. . . it means a red dye, see?"

"Emily Dickinson?"

"Poet. American," explained Dai. "Woman."

"Oh," I murmured. We were come to the crest of the hill
now.

"Teashop's just around the corner," my friend said. "Yes . . .
interesting woman . . ." He lowered his voice, then he stood
stock still in the middle of the pavement and, throwing his arms
out, he declaimed in a loud bass:

> I found a phrase to every thought
> I ever had, but one;
> And that defies me,
> As a hand did try to chalk the sun.

Dai breathed in deep, beat his chest with one hand and bellowed:

> To races nurtured in the dark;
> How would your own begin?
> Can blaze be done in cochineal,

Here Dai lowered his arms and slowly winked at me, then he finished in an even louder voice: "OR NOON IN MAZARINE?"

Some people passing by while this was going on were trying to ignore Dai. Some, better dressed, were glaring at him. Most of the younger ones, however, stopped a moment and smiled. One or two even clapped in encouragement. Myself, I was almost doubled up, laughing.

A grinning bobby crossed the road and gently told Dai to move along.

"Don't tell *me*, man, tell Emily!" shouted Dai at the bobby.

"All right, old son, you send Emily 'round and I'll tell 'er," joked the bobby, as he placed a hand on Dai's shoulder and delicately started him moving along.

"I knew your dad, boyo," said Dai to the policeman. Someone once remarked that it's a sign of advancing age when the policemen look too young—this one looked, to me, positively puerile.

The policeman said, "I know you did, Dai, I know. Now move along there, mate, at least shove off out of my manor." I had been laughing so much there were tears in my eyes. Or it might have been that I was remembering, in the depths of my mind, other policemen in another world, far away. It was the first time I had even heard of Emily Dickinson.

* * *

"We've distinguished company," exhorted Dai to the teashop lady when she handed out two mugs of tea into the alleyway. "Another Welshman it is, my love."

She, a comfortably chubby soul of around sixty, while doing her best to look suitably stern with these two obvious ne'er-do-wells, almost visibly wilted before Dai's banter.

"Get away with you, Dai-bach," she sang, "you and your palaver . . . why, you'd even make a tree flower in mid-winter, such a terrible flirt it is you are." The teashop bell rang and she fluttered away. I had been choking so much on my bacon sandwich that I stepped into a puddle of rainwater, and, as we both munched on our breakfasts, squished all the way to the Flask pub, with Dai quoting poetry.

"Good bloke, Dai," observed Peter Kinsley, later, over a pint of beer and a steak and kidney pie in the Flask. "He was a journalist, you know, left wing, a bloody good one, had a column of his own 'til the plonk got to him . . . then he couldn't take the bullshit anymore . . . sleeps out on the Heath in summer . . ."

Peter couldn't put me up. I didn't fully understand then, as I do now, that the act of creative writing must be one of the most solitary of all, second only, perhaps, to single-handed ocean sailing. Especially to the writer with a literary conscience, as is Peter. It was impossible for him to put me up. He was working on a book, and in those circumstances he had to maintain his own rhythm, undisturbed. He did, however, introduce me to his friends Barry and Rosie Edgegoose, and that evening I sat with Peter in Rosie's living room and gorged myself on roast lamb and potatoes with green peas. Later Rosie fixed up a bed on the settee. So it was that I spent my first night's sleep in seven years under an English roof, with, at last, a full stomach.

I spent a weekend of wonder in Hampstead. I wondered at the miracle of fresh water coming out of a tap, and a bath with hot water, and books on the shelves; books that were not soggy with mildew or blackened with kerosene soot, and good music on the record player, and good wholesome food and English voices all around me, the clouds scooting over the heath on the south-west wind, and no armed police on the streets.

"How are you going to get your boat out?" Barry asked me, next day. He was about thirty-five, a copy editor for one of the biggest circulation newspapers on earth.

"I'll find a job on Monday. I'll try Harrod's. Then, with luck, I can move down there. I've worked there before . . . I even slept there for three months, back in '68 . . ."

"You can stay here, Tris, there's no rush."

"No, Baz, I don't want to impose any more than I already have done. I want to make it under my own steam," I said. "I got myself into the shit, now it's up to me to get myself out." I paused. "But I'll tell you what you can do, if you like, Baz."

"What's that, chum?"

"Lend me a tenner until I find a job, or get some of my pension . . ."

"Right, Tris, no problem."

"And lend me some writing paper and envelopes . . ."

"They're in the desk," he offered. "There's stamps, too."

"I've a dozen letters to write all over the place, to let people know where I am . . ."

That evening Peter came rushing in. "Get your gear on, Tris," he said. "Rush job. I've seen one of the television blokes I know and he's going to get you on this evening's magazine program—come on, don't worry about what gear you're wearing. They pay about twenty-five quid. I've got a taxi waiting outside. Baz? Rosie? you coming, too?"

Thirty minutes later I was in a commercial television studio, staring wide-eyed at all the fuss, and overhearing exchanges shallower than a bum-boat's keel (the words "God" and "darling" came from them like water from Niagara), and trying to understand why the public—who had been dragged in to watch the show—all looked so awed and overwhelmed. (The last television I had seen was four years before in Djibouti.)

There were several guests who were interviewed before me. Someone had written a book on gardenia-growing, someone had invented a new kind of frying pan (I forget what they'd done, actually), and then it was my turn.

"Go on, mate, give 'em hell!" murmured Peter, as he gently pushed me forward. "Good old Tris," encouraged Baz and Rosie.

I stepped forward. My arm was grabbed firmly by a young woman who would have been more at home, I thought, in the Folies Bergère, and I was led over a wire-strewn floor and thrust into an armchair. Opposite me sat another young lady, who did her best to look even brighter than the glaring lights above already made her. By her side sat a gentleman. At first I thought he was a young gentleman, but then under his thick make-up—almost a rubber mask—it was soon obvious he was at least my own age. Also, he wore a wig. It was like being behind the scenes in some kind of circus.

A microphone was hastily pinned onto my shirt by some anonymous person behind me. I glared. There was a moment's pause, then the young lady interviewer's face changed from sullen boredom to anxious but delighted anticipation. Someone out in the dark floor area signalled. She said, "And now, we have with us one of those intrepid people whom some of us find so difficult to understand as we carry on with our workaday lives. I'm speaking to Tristan Jones . . . the first man ever to *walk* around the world!"

I thought to myself, *"Oh, Christ!"*

"What did you achieve by this extraordinary feat?" asked the Bright Young Thing.

"Just that," said I.

"Just what?" she asked.

I leaned down and hauled up one battered deckshoe. *"Extraordinary feet,"* I said.

The studio audience roared. The interview continued, spasmodically, for another five minutes. I expounded on the difficulties of tramping over the hot sands of the Sahara and the pebbles of the Gobi Desert and how the very worst walking surface was the cobblestones of Belgium. By the time my beamlet of limelight was almost over, both the Bright Young Thing and the Wig were gasping, their faces writhing at the thought of all that walking. The Wig, stumbling over his words with excitement, asked me breathlessly, "Well, it all sounds *terribly* arduous; would you *really, honestly* do it all again?"

"I would," I replied, "but I'd do it differently."

"How would you do it differently, Mr. Jones?" asked the Wig, with one eye on the Teleprompter.

"I'd walk backwards," I exulted.

*   *   *

"You bastard!" laughed Peter as we passed out into the street.

"Still got my twenty-five quid, though, didn't I?—come on, Pete, I owe you a pint!"

Also Time runnin' into years—
A thousand Places left be'ind—
And Men from both two 'emispheres
Discussin' things of every kind;
So much more near than I had known,
So much more great than I 'ad guessed—
An' me, like all the rest alone—
But reachin' out to all the rest!

If England was what England seems,
An' not the England of our dreams,
But only putty, brass an' paint,
'Ow quick we'd chuck 'er! But she ain't!

FROM "THE RETURN," RUDYARD KIPLING

Goodbye, Piccadilly!

SOME of the young hopefuls in Harrod's Department Store personnel office cast what to me appeared to be pitying glances at the old chap waiting to see if there was a job for him, but I was confident enough. I knew the below-streets guts of the biggest department store in Europe better than they knew the latest pop-hits. Far better. I knew every steam and water pipe, every electrical switch down in the basement. So I thought, and it's just as well that I did. It's no good looking dumb and for a job at the same time.

The engineer's office is on Harrod's roof. When I stepped out after the interview I was cock-a-hoop. Mr. Ballcock, the chief engineer, had remembered me from seven years back. "Settling down now, Mr. Jones?" he had asked.

"For a while, sir," I conceded. *Good bloke, Mr. Ballcock.*

"No more running off to sea?"

"No, sir; at least not for a couple of years." *Worse luck.*

"Good, then you can start on tomorrow's afternoon shift—we've new boilers, now, so you can make yourself busy learning the new systems. I'll double you up with Mr. McGinty—you remember him?"

"Of course, sir," I agreed. "Do you mind if I go down there now and have a quick look around?"

"No, by all means; nothing like a bit of enthusiasm, Mr. Jones."

I made my way down to the basement and threaded the maze of busy passages—quite a feat of navigation after seven years' absence—and eventually found myself in the boiler-room, a great cavelike chamber about as big as a five-story apartment house.

All around the noise was ear-shattering. Mack was there,

looking exactly, almost exactly, as I had last seen him seven years before, slight, clean (he always looked as if he'd stepped out of a shower moments before), about thirty-eight, fair, clean-shaven, Irish-green-eyed, he reminded me of an over-alled elf. Mack was from County Cork in the Republic of Ireland. He was the very antithesis of everything that an Irish boiler-tender, in popular legend, is supposed to be. Non-drinking, non-swearing, clean-living, religious almost to a fault.

"Tristan, me old mate, how're ye doin'?" The seven years I'd been away had overlain his Irish brogue with even more London overtones.

"All right, Mack. Back again."

"Been at sea, have yer?"

"Yeah."

"All right was it?"

"Up and down, up and down," I grinned.

Mack laughed. "Sure, everything's changed now. The owld incinerator's gone . . . no more fly-ash in yer face, Tris . . ."

And so it was that I returned to Harrod's boiler-room. I didn't tell Mack that, on one splendidly unusual occasion only four months before, I had dined at the house of one of Harrod's (Buenos Aires) directors . . . I didn't think he would believe me. But when I saw the steel plate still resting against the wall behind the boilers, the steel plate on which I had chalked up the calculations for the *Incredible Voyage,* I thought to myself aloud "Harrod's to Harrod's to Harrod's in sixty thousand million easy steps."

"What's that ye said?" asked Mack.

"Oh, nothing."

". . . and the feed-water line goes over the top of number three boiler now . . ." Mack carried on with the litany.

"Can I still sleep here, Mack, like I used to?" I asked him, when the tour was done.

"Oh, bejasus, no," exclaimed he. "No more, why, the place is shut up tight as a drum by midnight."

"?" I looked at him.

"Sure, it's the IRA scare," he explained. Then he was silent and so was I. There was simply no more to say about it.

＊　　　＊　　　＊

I found a suitable bed in Paddington. It was in an establishment that went by the name of a hotel. Actually it was a genteel doss house, with six beds to a room, but it was of Georgian design, clean, the breakfasts were good and sustaining and it cost only one pound a night. The majority of the clientele were young people from the Dominions and Europe who were touring Britain on the cheap, but there were some "street-people" there, too.

There was also one of the most entertaining people that I have ever met: Jimmy. He was about seventy-nine, with sparse hair. He was a big, lumbering man with a fat face and heavy jowls. He slept in the same room as I, and, unlike some of the younger people, was most meticulous in his appearance. He wore a blue, pin-striped suit and highly polished black shoes. Over his waistcoat he wore a gold watch fob. At first it was his accent that intrigued me. It seemed to be from neither here nor there. Eventually I got to know him and found that he was born in Australia and was a diplomatic courier. This surprised me, for I had always imagined couriers to be James Bond types, the old-school-tie brigade, but Jimmy was anything but that. He had come to Europe with the Australian Army in the First World War and had been badly wounded at Gallipoli, for which reason he walked with a limp.

Ever since the end of the First World War, Jimmy had served with the British Foreign Office as a courier, and he had visited practically every capital city in the world. Not only the capital cities, but every low dive in those cities. To hear him spin a yarn about Istanbul or Shanghai in the thirties, or his Second World War travels and experience, still as a courier, was memorable, and we sat in the kitchen on many an evening, when I was off duty, yarning over innumerable cups of tea. Jimmy told me that couriers were paid by the job, and as he didn't travel much these days (though he went off to Portugal and back while

I was at the hotel), he "wasn't exactly earning a fortune," as he put it, and that was why he was staying in this particular hotel. But I suspect that another reason was that he enjoyed being around youngsters, and there was always someone loafing in the kitchen to whom he could recite his fascinating stories.

The hotel was managed by three young Australians who had been in London for about a year. Here it was that I was first recognized by strangers. The Australians had read some of my stories back home in *Seacraft* magazine, and knew me as soon as I signed in. This was one of the few times when I enjoyed being recognized by strangers. They had bought a catamaran on the south coast, which they intended to sail back to Australia. None of them had ever sailed before, and so I became their sailing mentor. They drove me down to the south coast three times and we sailed out into the English Channel from Chichester. I have never been much attracted to catamarans, or any kind of multihull vessel. Most of them are ugly. I simply do not trust them. I am always too apprehensive that they will flip over. But these were only short runs into the Channel, and the company was excellent. It was a relief to get away from the inside of buildings, too.

The catamaran was thirty-two feet long, built of marine ply, fast as a train and stiff as a London pub. The Aussies, all three in their mid-twenties, knew nothing at all about sailing or navigation, but they made good students and even better hosts and they came from a land (even though some say it is the ultimate suburb) where people have not forgotten that to pick up stakes and move is, sometimes, good for the soul. They were eager to voyage, and, having owned the boat for some weeks without having sailed her, each one of our outings was anticipated by them as if they were knights setting off to chase the Holy Grail. Their enthusiasm entered me like water soaking into a dry sponge, and soon we had the catamaran dancing, leaping, and sitting up on her hind legs, to the dismay of some of the more staid yachtsmen of Chichester.

It was soon clear to me that all three of my young friends had a perception of their little ship as an idea of how man was before the machine age: simpler, perhaps more ignorant, but with infinitely more faith and courage. As we flashed the catamaran's two hulls over the surging, green cross-seas of the Channel, I watched my friends grow along with their learning, and took delight at passing on something even in this small way.

Apart from enjoying the company, simply to be back at sea, even though it was only for hours at a time, even though on two of the three weekends there was rain, squall, and turbulent seas under gray skies, was for me pure pleasure. As soon as we reached the coast in the Aussies' ramshackle Volkswagen, my body and spirit jumped to life like Jack popping out of the box. Between the long, pensive watches in Harrod's boiler-room, I had something to look forward to in my time off, out in the lively Channel with even livelier company.

Having paid Barry back his ten pounds, I now had the invidious task of saving up to rescue *Sea Dart*.

It was soon obvious to me that I would need to work in Harrod's for several years before I could pay off what I owed for the transport of *Sea Dart* home from South America and for the transport of *Sea Dart* out again, beyond the reach of the imposers of an iniquitous tax. I already owed over six hundred pounds for the transport home. Now I would have to pay for her storage on the jetty at Newhaven, and then I would have to somehow find the money to get her shipped abroad again.

For a forty-hour week my pay averaged forty pounds. Out of this was deducted (before I was paid) about eight pounds, for income tax, health insurance, and Social Security(!). This left about thirty-two pounds. The hotel cost nine pounds a week, with breakfast, and other meals cost about seven pounds (I was by no means eating expensively). By the time I had bought a few small comforts, cigarettes and a pint of beer a day, and some clothes and shoes, I was left with seven pounds to put away. My pension, on top of that, brought my total weekly savings to about ten pounds. At the rate I was going, I could look

forward to getting *Sea Dart* out of the grasp of Her Majesty's
Customs at the earliest by mid-1981—six years!

The pubs near the hotel in Paddington or over in the never-
never lands of Kensington and Chelsea were far too touristy for
my taste. They were mostly all jazzed up in fair-ground style or
they were the show-place for itinerant rock-bands. The din they
set up was, to me, about as musical and artistic as two dustbin
lids clanged together, while the frantic antics of the "musi-
cians" put me in mind of the ravings of lunatics. The final straw
was the appearance of five pimply youths and a scrawny female
of indeterminate age who wore safety-pins stuck in her cheeks.
The row they set up was worse than being in a ship's cargo-
hold, full of loose kitchen pans and frightened cats, in a full
gale. I beat a hasty retreat and wended my way on my free
evenings from then on to the Edgeware Road, where there were
still some hostelries whose ideas of hospitality did not include
sending their customers home with a case of raging earache, a
splitting headache, and a sense of alienation.

Most English pubs are owned by the breweries whose beer
and ales they sell. The "landlord" is, unless it is a "free house,"
a manager or rather a tenant of the brewery. There were still
some breweries who had not yet ripped out of their pubs the
beautiful hand-carved Victorian fittings—the bar-shelves and
engraved mirrors, the velvet seats and ornate bar-dividers and
the great chandelier-style lamps of Edwardian days. There
were still some brewers who had not yet jettisoned the wonderful handiwork of the old-time craftsmen who, although they
may have been vastly underpaid, were certainly not under-
endowed with a love of their craft, the like of which we will be
lucky ever to see again. There were still some brewers who had
not replaced the old workmanship with cheap, shoddy plywood
imitations of a huckster's show-room, and it was their pubs that
I sought out for my quiet pint, for there is nothing like them in
all the world outside Britain.

This was not nostalgia on my part—these pubs had been built
a century and more before I was born. It was simply the recog-

nition of something precious and irreplaceable, and the desire to appreciate it.

As I was economizing, I could not stay in the pub long, but in London, in summer, that is no hardship. There was plenty of free entertainment: listening to the soapbox orators at Marble Arch, loafing on the grass by the Serpentine Lake in Hyde Park, or walking down to the River Thames embankment and watching the vessels pass and the seabirds and dreaming of the next voyage, wherever that might be to, and whenever it might start.

On some evenings I took the underground to Hampstead to see my friends, but train fares were expensive, so mainly I contented myself with sitting out in Hyde Park, if it was fine, with a book, until dusk fell. There is no city park anywhere more civilized, and yet at the same time, more sensuous, even sexual, than Hyde Park. For civilization there is no need to search; for sensuality and sexuality, they are everywhere, and yet nowhere, and only those who know how, where and when to look, will ever find them.

The museums and art galleries—mainly free admission—I saved for rainy days and evenings. My favorite museum was the Kensington Science Museum, where I was always on the lookout for ideas or inventions which might be put to good employment onboard a small craft out in mid-ocean. The Tate Gallery was another haunt, until they displayed a bit of wood with nails sticking out of it as a work of art. I concluded that I didn't mind being hoodwinked as long as I knew it, but I was damned if I was going to pretend I didn't know it. If someone wanted to throw a bucket of paint at a canvas awning and call it art, then good luck to him. But if he expected me to call it art then he would wait until I could *walk* across the ocean.

In all my perambulations around London during these weeks, I cannot recall meeting with one working-class Briton who expressed any enthusiasm for Britain's entry into the Common Market. I cannot recall any occasion when the metric system was used for weight or liquids, and I cannot recall hearing anyone approve the decimal coinage, which had recently been put into circulation. The consensus was that it was a trick to cover up rampant inflation and to raise prices on the sly. The general impression I gained was of a people who had become resigned to having lost control of the destiny of the nation.

A couple of times I walked over to the Piccadilly area, but this was all changed since the law banning prostitutes from the street was introduced. All the law did was drive the girls indoors and open up Soho to the pornographers (who, I suppose, pay taxes).

There were many more restaurants with exotic cuisine—Indian, Chinese, Indonesian, Japanese—than there used to be, but Piccadilly itself, which was always exciting and always British, was now a long parade of slot-machine arcades and trashy girlie-shows, and the stamping ground of gangs of Iranian students, all of whom seemed to be well endowed with that prime requirement in Soho—cash. It was now necessary, in order to see the real London, to travel somehow out into the inner suburbs: Camden Town, Aldgate, Battersea, or down the Old Kent Road to the Elephant and Castle. (In the fifteenth century the Cockneys could not pronounce *Infanta de Castilla*.)

The month of August was well advanced when Mack came running back to the boiler-room as he was going off duty.

"Phone call for you, mate, from America!" he gasped. "Up in the passage!" He looked at me as if I was being called by His Holiness himself from Rome. "Nip up and get it—I'll stand in for ye!"

"Hello?"

"Hi, Tristan?"

"Yeah, Tristan Jones here!"

"Cy calling from California. Look, I got your letter—I've got a job for you, skippering a boat . . ."

Cy was an American delivery skipper. He and I sailed together some years before. It was to him that one of my letters had been sent.

"What is she?" (Heart pounding.)

"Fifty-footer—sloop, on Long Island Sound . . . the owner wants a skipper onboard . . . she's to be taken down to the Islands—the West Indies—for the winter."

"How is she?" I squeezed in to let a pushcart go by me.

"Almost brand-new."

"How do I get over there?" I could feel the breeze again.

"They'll lend you your ticket—it's waiting at Pan Am on Piccadilly. It's made out for Labor Day . . ."

"Right, Cy, I'll be out there on Labor Day."

"Great . . . just great. Tristan, how're you doing?"

"Up and down, up and down. How about you?"

"I'm sailing tomorrow for Hawaii."

"Lucky bastard!"

Cy laughed. "Same old Tristan," he said. "Okay, listen—a guy called Tony will meet you at JFK . . ."

"Right, Cy, I'll be there—so long, mate!"

"So long." The phone clicked.

"Good news?" eagerly asked Mack, when I was back in the boiler-room.

"Yes, I'm off to the States."

"No, you're kiddin' me . . ."

"No, I'm off next week."

"Got a job?"

"Seems like it . . . delivering a boat . . ."

"Ye lucky feller, you . . . well, I'm off now, Tris, can't keep the missus waiting."

*   *   *

I paid fifty pounds toward *Sea Dart*'s storage costs and slipped Dai a couple of quid before I took off for America. "Don't forget boyo—mazarine," he said, chuckling, as he shuffled off to buy a bottle.

Richer than when I arrived by a new pair of jeans, a jersey, a pair of shoes, ten dollars, and half the manuscript of *The Incredible Voyage* (written in Harrod's boiler-room), I set out for the airport.

Jimmy the Courier insisted on accompanying me. He was still recounting a yarn about Manchuria in the twenties (or was it Tibet in the thirties?) when my flight was called.

"So long, Jimmy."

"So long, chum, say 'hello' to the Yanks for me," he muttered, then he turned and limped out, looking like an old bloodhound, through the milling scores of colorful Asian, African, and West Indian travellers ambling about in the lounge.

Bag'd

And if you call for a song of the sea,
We'll heave the capstan round,
With a yeo heave-ho, for the wind is free,
Her anchor's a-trip and her helm is free,
Hurrah for the homeward bound!
Yeo—ho, heave—ho,
Hurrah for the homeward bound!

FROM "A WAND'RING MINSTREL I," *The Mikado,*
W. S. GILBERT

A Yankee ship came down the river,
Blow, boys, blow!
A Yankee ship came down the river,
Blow, my bully boys, blow!

What d'ye think they had for dinner?
Blow, boys, blow!
What d'ye think they had for dinner?
Blow, my bully boys, blow!

Ox tail soup and turkey liver,
Blow, boys, blow!
Ox tail soup and turkey liver,
Blow, my bully boys, blow!
                    "Blow, boys, blow!"

THIS IS A HALYARD CHANTY, SUNG AS THE SAILS WERE HOISTED. IT
ORIGINATES IN THE LATE 1840S. AS WITH ALL CHANTIES, THERE ARE A
NUMBER OF VERSIONS. THE NATIONALITY OF THE SHIP AND THE DINNER
MENU CHANGED WITH EACH VERSION, BUT THIS SEEMS TO HAVE BEEN THE
MOST COMMON. IN MOST OF THE WORKING CHANTIES OF THE MID-1800S THE
WORDS WERE VERY SIMPLE. THIS WAS NECESSARILY SO, FOR MANY OF THE
CREW SPOKE LITTLE OR NO ENGLISH.

A Cozy Berth

T HE LINES in the JFK Customs hall were short and swift moving for American passport holders, long and slow for us others. The temptation was to jump from one line to another, which seemed to be shortening, but each time I did this, my new line slowed down while the line I had just left shot ahead. There ought to be a law about this somewhere, like Gresham's Law or Murphy's.

The first change I saw in my six years' absence from the States was how young the Immigration officers were compared with the last time I had been here, and there were women officers, though a couple of them seemed to be young enough to be called girls.

The young man who sat at his kiosk at the head of the line I decided to stay in had thick, double-lensed glasses and hair down to his shoulders. He spoke at length to all the pretty women passing his desk and cursorily dismissed the men with a curt nod of his head after checking their documents. So I knew I was all right. Five men would pass through in two minutes, then a good-looking woman would come up and there would be five or ten minutes of smiles and flirting. Finally, after almost an hour, I was at the desk. I was happy enough, for no one can object to bureaucratic delay when it's for human reasons. The Immigration officer slid my passport over toward him and checked my visa. "Okay," said he, and I was through, in the land of the free and the home of the brave.

Among the crowd of waiting welcomers was Tony. He was dressed in a U.S. Army green waterproof cape. He grinned at me, showing a full set of perfect teeth topped by a black mustache, ruddy cheeks, coal-black eyes, and hair over his ears.

"Tristan?" he said. His voice was very loud, almost raucous.

"The very same," said I. He grabbed my arm and gave me the American focus. He slapped my shoulder and generally behaved as if I were Lindbergh just arriving solo in Paris. It seemed to me as if all the vast hall and crowd of agog welcomers just ceased to exist; as if I were the only person for ten miles around.

The American welcome can be overwhelming. Probably other British people, who had knocked around less than I, would find it embarrassing, for we do not tend to consider that a ten years' parting is really sufficient cause for an emotional display. Usually a handshake is enough for us.

"Hey, Tristan," Tony slapped my shoulder, "Welcome to the States, howyadoin'?"

"Up and down, up and down."

Tony laughed.

All around us the Americans in the crowds acted as if they didn't give a damn about what anyone else thought of them. There was no attempt to make their children "behave." "*Good for them*," thought I, recalling the hundred straitjackets older people had forced me into as a child, which had taken me years of struggle to slough off.

It's difficult for most northern Europeans to realize that New York City is approximately the same latitude as Naples. We tend to think of it as being as north as ourselves. The weather is vastly different, though. In the winter the cold air drives down from the Canadian Arctic, sometimes dumping several feet of snow. In summer the southwesterly prevailing breezes bring moist tropical air up from the Gulf of Mexico. New York is almost always on the receiving end of weather that has crossed a continent, in contrast to Western Europe, which mostly plays host to the Atlantic Ocean winds. The finest time to be in the northeast United States is in the autumn, or "fall." Then the temperature comes down to a pleasant seventy-odd degrees, the humidity, after clamping its suit of armor for six months on everyone who is without an air-conditioner, finally relents; and the smoggy skies give way to a sudden burst of clear blue splendor.

In 1975, fall was late. The temperature outside the airport building was about twenty degrees higher than it had been in London. As Tony and I left through the automatic doors, heading for his car, the air wrapped itself around me like a hot, damp poultice. In a flash I was transported back to Buenos Aires; in seconds I was perspiring like a coal-stoker in the bowels of an ocean liner.

"Nice weather," offered Tony, sniffing the air.

"Yes," I replied, removing my jersey.

"You shoulda been here a month ago, Tristan. Jesus, we had over a hunnerd degrees!" he slid behind the wheel of a long blue Volkswagen landship of a mini-bus with white-wall tires. "Ya know, the Army loves gettin' us guys. They reckoned if we could stand the New York weather, we can fight in any goddam climate!" He switched on the air-conditioner—the cold blast sent me back to the Arctic. I re-donned my jersey hurriedly.

We were passing the main entrance to the airport by now. All along the promenade people were standing, sitting on suitcases, leaning against the wall, all looking bedraggled and exhausted. "Hail, rain, or snow," murmured Tony as he narrowly missed a bus. "Son of a bitch! Yeah, hail, rain, or snow!"

"Hail Mary," I muttered as we swung clear of a yellow cab and swiped the curb.

"Wazzat?"

"Just saying my prayers, Tony."

He laughed and gunned the motor.

"Where're we bound, Tony?" It's always nice to know where you're going.

"City Island, that's where the boat is moored. *Moonglow*— she's on hire to the Villa Club . . . ya take folks out two or three times a week . . ."

"Take folks out? Where to?"

"Well, see the Villa Club is a social organization. They fix folks up for outdoor stuff—backpacking, canoeing, tennis 'n' stuff—city folks who just can't get around to that kinda stuff themselves. So they join the Villa Club and Milt Stougham arranges everything for them."

"What's the pay?"

"Like I told you back at the airport, I don't know about those details. Milt'll be at the boat this evening, he'll take care of all that. I've only worked for him for a week."

"I can't thank him enough, Tony, for the air-fare and all . . ."

"Ahh, that's okay . . . this is where a guy like you should be, Tristan, this is the land of opportunity. Hell, when we heard what you were doing in London, stoking a goddam boiler, hey that's a crocka bull, man! No, this is the place for you . . . anything can happen!"

"Let's hope so."

All around us the traffic—automobiles, trucks, vans, oil-tankers, taxis, long, low buses—drove forward at a steady pace through Queens, a parade of wealth, power, and throbbing vitality, hopefully all going somewhere.

"I'll leave you when we get to the boat—I've gotta be back in New Jersey by seven—my mom'll have dinner ready . . ."

"How far is it . . . ?"

"Oh, 'bout fifty miles . . . I'll be there in an hour if the goddam traffic isn't fouled up on the bridge."

"Fifty miles!" I thought to myself. *"That's twelve hours hard sailing in* Sea Dart."

"If the damned bridge is messed up it'll take me anything up to three hours!" Tony ejaculated.

The Van Wyck Expressway, Kew Gardens, Flushing (looking nothing like its namesake in Holland), then the Whitestone Bridge, and over in the west, over the silver-gleaming East River dark and hazy in the westering sun, the promising, thumbs-up towers of Manhattan, looked to me like a craggy, split Gibraltar, a promise of strength.

We turned off onto the causeway and City Island. Tidy white wooden houses of clapboard and brick, fish restaurants with Italian name signs, a few bars—"Schlitz," "Budweiser"—and several boat chandlers. In the evening sunshine it looked like a typical New England coast resort. There was no indication, apart from the noise of jets in their holding patterns overhead, that we were only twelve miles from the rumbling bowels of

Manhattan, nor that we were surrounded on all sides by the fifteen million people in the Tri-State urban conglomeration.

The gateway to the boatyard was opened by a silent, gray-haired man wearing rimless glasses.

"There she is, Tris," promised Tony.

Moonglow sat alongside a floating jetty slightly bobbing in the short chop set up by the wind coming in from Long Island Sound. We walked past a telephone kiosk, an ice-machine, a Coca-Cola machine, a fresh water outlet valve and an electricity outlet, down onto the jetty.

She was practically all fiberglass. She looked like a machine. She had sleek lines and she was trim and clean, but she had about as much personality as a vacuum cleaner—and inside her that was the first thing I tripped over.

The main cabin was by any standards luxurious. There were two revolving armchairs just inside the companionway, then a divider, forward of which was the galley—a sparkling panorama of stainless steel, a double sink, a plastic-topped work table, and a huge refrigerator. On the starboard side there was a three-sided sofa-seat around a table, also plastic-topped, with the plastic made to look like oak. The sofa was built around the table, which could be lowered, so as to make of the whole grouping a king-size bed.

I walked aft, over the engine housing, which was covered with blue carpeting, wall-to-wall. As Tony watched me, smiling, I was thinking of little *Sea Dart*, inside which I can't even stand up below. The after cabin was like a hotel bedroom. There was a huge bed, and wardrobes, full-length and storage drawers under the bed, a shower, a sink, and, again, blue wall-to-wall carpeting.

"Gotta rush, Tris. Gotta get back to Jersey," called Tony. "You wait here for Milt—he'll be along soon—he's gotta drive in from the city, but he said he'd be here shortly after six." He stooped and leaned into the companionway. "Think she'll suit, eh?" he said.

"She'll do for the time being, Tony," I joked.

As Tony clambered onto the jetty a few drops of rain came

down. I closed the companionway door (it was not a hatch, you walked straight out of the cabin through a six-foot-high door into the cockpit). Then I sat down on one of the very posh velvet-covered revolving chairs and, as I waited for my new employer, Milt, to arrive, I looked around me. The change, the metamorphosis from being a stoker in a London boiler-room to being the sole inhabitant of a luxury yacht in America, all within a matter of twenty hours, was mind-boggling for a second or two, but I took it in my stride, switched the radio on, and listened (overheard) a talk show for a few minutes.

A high nasal voice: "Well, Bob, what about them people over in Crown Heights—why don't they send *their* kids to segregated schools?"

Boom—click, "Whatta you, some kinda anneye-semitic rat-fink?" ". . . Yeah, ladies and gennulmen, you're on the air and the lines are open to the 'Talk In Show' . . ."

I switched the channels. "*Ah luv yu more taday then yestuh-day . . . but dahling naht es mech es tum-ah-ah-ah-row.*" Switch again . . . *Claire de Lune* . . . that's better. I went over to the giant-size fridge in the galley. At first I thought it was empty, but the vegetable drawer in the bottom was full, crammed packed with frosted plastic bags full of . . . I opened one bag, then another, and another . . . asparagus!

I closed the fridge door. The news was on the radio now, I switched back to the talk show.

"Hullo, Bob . . ." A deep man's voice.

"Yes, sir, go ahead, you're on the air."

"Ai've been listening to your chet about getting a teaching job." The tones were unmistakably Oxford English, sepulchary and fruity at the same time.

"Wattaya wanna say? We don't have all night."

"Well, you see, I've got two degrees . . ."

"Wattarethey, Fahrenheit and cennigrade? Ah . . . get off the line . . ."

"Bob?"

"Yesma'am?"

I listened, fascinated, as New York apparently bared its soul for all to hear. I couldn't help grinning as I patiently waited for my new boss to arrive. Controlled free speech . . . talk out of line and they just switch off; pull the plug and consign you to oblivion. *"Not a bad idea,"* I thought, *"except who's pulling the plug?"*

I was roused from my reverie by the noise of someone coming onboard.

I looked up to see Tony, his cape streaming.

"I have your first sailing party here," he said.

"My what?"

"I phoned the club. Mr. Stougham told me to pick up these folks on the corner of Fifty-third and Third and bring 'em on over for a sail."

By now people, mainly men and women in their thirties and forties, all wet through from the rain, were pushing past Tony, all talking, laughing, divesting themselves of raincoats and parkas, then standing around in the cabin.

I looked around me, bewildered, at the twelve expectant, smiling night-sailors. I gestured at the sofa and chairs. "Please have a seat—good evening by the way." I glanced at the clock on the bulkhead: 8:30 P.M. I turned to Tony. "But I've only just arrived," I whispered hoarsely. "I just got into the country only four hours ago . . . I haven't even seen Mr. Stougham yet . . . I don't even know where the charts are. . . ."

Tony seemed not a bit perturbed. "Mr. Stougham said he was sorry he couldn't get over here tonight . . . He'll be over tomorrow, but he said it's okay 'cos you were very experienced . . ."

"You been out on this boat before?" I demanded anxiously.

"I brought a crowd over last week, but the skipper Mr. Stougham hired didn't show up. . . . It was the same crowd, in fact," he said, gesturing at the group of men and women waiting patiently in the cabin.

"You know, Tony, this is a bit much," I expostulated. "I've only a BI visa. That's only good for me to come over here, pick up a boat, and prepare her for delivery to somewhere outside the United States. I had no idea that I was going to be hired to take people on joy rides . . . and especially on a windy rainy night with no charts . . ."

"Mr. Stougham said it would be okay," said Tony, looking abashed. "And I had a flat on the way . . ."

"A what?" I said, mystified.

"A flat tire, on the George Washington Bridge . . ." He gestured with both hands. "Jeez, you shoulda seen the snarl-up . . ." he grinned, "an' these folks had been waiting since seven . . . on Fifty-third and Third . . ."

I looked at our guests, who now were all talking among themselves, the ones who were not staring wide-eyed at me as if I was a creature from Mars. One lady, slightly younger than the others in the company, wearing a jersey, blue jeans, and thick-rimmed glasses smiled at me. "Gee, Captain Jones," she said, "that's a real neat accent you have there!"

"Blimey . . . oh holy Christ," I murmured sotto voce to Tony. "Come on, let's have a bloody go, then. You search all the drawers in the cabins for a chart of Long Island Sound . . ."

Two of the men passengers, obviously friends, came over to me. "Having trouble, Captain?" The smaller one was around forty. Both he and his taller companion wore spectacles and loud-checked jackets.

"Not really." I gave him a bit of the old British understatement. "It's just that I've never taken this craft out before . . ."

"This is my buddy, Al." The smaller man gestured at the other. "We've done some sailing, we'll give you a hand."

"It's not the sailing that bothers me so much . . . it's the engine . . . I don't even know how to start it . . ."

"Jeez," joined in Tony, "I'm real sorry about this . . . can't find no charts."

By this time the rain had stopped. We four men moved out into the cockpit. For a moment or two there was silence. Then Al spoke. "Well," he said, "at least I can go up and get everyone some cawfee out of the machine, and we can sit in the cabin and have a party."

I looked up at the sky. The moon was rising in the east. The clouds were clearing. Out in the Sound the navigation lights

were clear and bright. One by one I picked out the ones I could
see from City Island, one by one I remembered each one, and
the hazards they showed to the mariner, from the last time I
had sailed through these waters six years before.

"Oh, hell," I blurted to Tony. He looked at me mournfully.
"Come on—I'll show you how to unreel the jib and handle the
sheets—there's a nice soft breeze and plenty of moonlight coming up. Come on, we'll disconnect that damned power cable
and sail the bugger out!"

"Right on, Cap'n!" said Tony.

"Yessir," agreed Al's friend.

"Call me Tristan," I murmured to Tony. "Captains know
their ships."

And so it was that four and a half hours after I landed in
America I found myself feeling my way softly under sail into
the Sound, without charts, without a work permit, without a
passenger-carrying skipper's license, with one inexperienced
hand and twelve guests who, I am certain, never had any in-
kling of what was really happening.

But as I steered *Moonglow* past the southern tip of Hart Island, under the moon and the scudding autumn night clouds,
and watched the faces of those city workers as they marvelled
at the eerie wonder of silent night sailing, I knew that it was
worth taking all the risks. The entranced delight on the faces of
some of them as they gazed silently over the moonlight reflecting on the waters of the Sound—that alone made the passage to
America worthwhile. They stared all around them, in silence,
men and women together, and listened to the hiss of the boat as
she slightly heeled over, slid through the almost calm waters.
To them, after the roar of Manhattan, this was perfect silence,
but as jet planes swooshed overhead at intervals and as I heard
the low grumbling of shore-traffic from the land, I wondered to
myself what these people would feel if they could experience
the true silence of the sea: somewhere in mid-ocean, after a
dead flat calm of a few days and nights, when you find yourself
talking aloud to yourself much more than usual, to break the
monotony of the dull thud of the boom, the creak of the boat's

timbers, the mocking slap of tiny wavelets against the hull, and the thought of the inconceivable perfection of the universe, the eternity of silence and sound; and you whistle and bang a spoon in the stewpot, holding it out to the star-filled sky, knowing that the noise will go on and on and on forever, forever, *forever,* clattering through the unimaginable reaches of space. "Whistling for a wind" it's called.

Moonglow came alongside the floating jetty in the otherwise deserted boatyard so gently she wouldn't have cracked an egg. It was midnight and our guests were all chattering happily as they wandered off toward the Volkswagen bus that would take them back to Manhattan. "Thanks a lot, Cap'n," they rejoiced. "Gee, that was great!"

"So long, Tristan, Mr. Stougham will be here tomorrow, I guess," grinned Tony.

"I hope so. It'll be nice to know how everything works. Jesus, I had a look into the engine compartment. I felt like Queequeg looking into the guts of a Sputnik."

I went below, closed the doors of *Moonglow*, extracted a half-dozen sticks of asparagus from the fridge, gnawed and swallowed them, and turned in. So went the first evening in America.

O whisky is the life of man,
Whisk-y Johnny!
O whisky is the life of man,
And it's whisky for my Johnny!

O whisky makes you feel so glad,
Whisk-y Johnny!
O whisky makes you feel so glad,
And it's whisky for my Johnny!

I thought I heard the Old Man say,
Whisk-y Johnny!
I thought I heard the Old Man say,
And it's whisky for my Johnny!

Whisky for the crew today!
Whisk-y Johnny!
Whisky for the crew today!
And it's whisky for my Johnny!

O whisky killed my poor old Dad,
Whisk-y Johnny!
O whisky killed my poor old Dad,
And it's whisky for my Johnny!

It's whisky here and whisky there,
Whisk-y Johnny!
It's whisky here and whisky there,
And it's whisky for my Johnny!

It's whisky makes me wear old
clothes,
Whisk-y Johnny!
It's whisky makes me wear old
clothes,
And it's whisky for my Johnny!

"WHISKEY JOHNNY," A HALYARD CHANTY OF THE 1860S WITH MANY
DIFFERENT VERSES, FOR OR AGAINST WHISKY, DEPENDING ON THE
INCLINATIONS OF THE CHANTY-MAN. THE LAST VERSE, HOWEVER, SEEMS TO
HAVE BEEN INCLUDED IN ALL VERSIONS. "THE OLD MAN" WAS, AND STILL
IS, THE CAPTAIN.

Whisky Johnny!

I WORKED for the Villa Club for the first three weeks in October. It was a strange experience. Parties of members appeared out of the blue at all kinds of odd hours, and I took them out sailing in the Sound in all weathers. I don't know what the U.S. Coast Guard would have said had they known about *Moonglow*. We were breaking just about every regulation in the book. For example, there were only enough lifejackets onboard for three people. But at the time I was unaware of our transgressions; it was only later that I learned about the U.S. government safety rules. Of course, I was very careful, in every other way, never to put anyone's safety in jeopardy. That becomes part of your bone-marrow after sailing for a few years.

The club must have been making plenty of money out of *Moonglow*. I was told that she was on charter from her owner for a very low fee; surely, I figured, less than a tenth of what she was earning. Her running expenses, including my pay and keep, were also low, for I ran the engine only when it was absolutely necessary. Her berth cost about fifty dollars a week. I calculated that my air-fare from Britain to the U.S.A. must have been recovered by the club in the first week.

My working hours were about sixty a week, depending on the length of the sailing trips. For this I was paid twenty dollars per week plus my food and accommodation onboard the boat. However, getting my pay from the club was not easy, in fact it was a bit like trying to extract a Kennedy half-dollar out of a piggy-bank slot. It took almost as much of my time as did the actual maintenance and operation of *Moonglow*.

On one memorable occasion, having spent my cash on food, I had to walk the fourteen miles from City Island to the club headquarters in midtown Manhattan to collect my twenty dollars.

The walk was a varied experience. I was dressed in my blue jeans—now somewhat paint bespattered—my jersey, and sailing cap. This was not affectation; it was all I had. The cap was not to display a jaunty nautical air but to keep the sun off my bald spot.

Walking through Pelham Park, on the mainland side of the City Island causeway, I was closely surveyed three times by different police cars that slowed down and cruised by me slowly, the cops inside eyeing me suspiciously. I just kept plodding along until I was at Westchester, an urban center. From then on I was seemingly in more criminal surroundings, for I was ignored by passing police.

At first the south side of The Bronx wasn't too bad. Long, long avenues surrounded by boxlike factories and apartment buildings. But further on, closer to Manhattan, there were more and more burned-out buildings, more and more potholes in the road, and more and more an air of sleazy hopelessness. By now just about everyone in the area was black. In the street there was a continual procession of gleaming steel behemoths, Fords, Chevys, Cadillacs, green, blue, red, black, streaming along. The sun reflected hostility from their chrome, their riders were hidden behind tinted windows. On the sidewalks, sitting on broken door stoops, ambling around and lounging, was group after group of people, most of them staring sullenly at the passing parade. Many of the younger ones wore dark glasses with chrome frames, from which the sun reflected hostility at the tinted car windows passing by. There was a lot of noise, both from the traffic and the locals. Unlike the poor I had seen in many parts of the world, these people did not seem to be hungry or very ill-clad or sick, especially the younger ones. But I had come from the netherside of the world. I still had with me vivid memories of Massawa and Assab, of Lima and La Paz. I had seen and experienced real poverty; the sort which leaves no time, no energy, for hostility or sullen glares. The look of the buildings, burned-out, huddled on wasteland like witches' covens, brought back memories of the Gorbals slums of Glasgow in the thirties. Compared to those times and those places, though, these people in The Bronx seemed to be living well, I thought, and I trudged on for miles along the sidewalk curb between the two mirrors of life.

I had no more money than the poorest of the poor that I saw.

Row after row of abandoned tenements stood, like old men contemplating a pauper's funeral, wrapped in dreams of their own destruction, surrounded by acres of barren, litter-strewn wasteland.

One bitter effect of poverty is that it deprives you of your own capacity for generosity toward others; another is that, unless you resist caring about it, it humiliates you because it makes you appear incapable and stupid.

On a later occasion I was fobbed off by Mr. Stougham, at his newly bought house in one of Manhattan's most fashionable squares, with the presentation of a bottle of whisky in lieu of cash. I sold the whisky in a downtown bar for ten dollars after wandering about for a pair of hours, and made my way back to City Island in luxury by subway and bus.

Onboard, I was able to slog on, writing some more of *The Incredible Voyage*. I sweated blood over each page.

Working for the club wasn't all low pay and a full day's work every day, though. There was the sailing, which to me, accustomed as I was at sea to days and days with little or no company, was always interesting. I met a lot of friendly people and some not so friendly on those trips out "around the lighthouse."

The club started to run "disco" nights at a hotel in Manhattan. I was to go there and "socialize." On one occasion I agreed to this, against my judgment, but soon got tired of it. One lively woman of about my age offered to "run me back to City Island." Imagining at least a Chevrolet, I jumped at the chance of a free ride back to the boat—and found she had a bicycle made for two! But sure enough, she was serious, and she and I peddled the thing fourteen miles. We parted on the best of terms, bless her!

Toward the end of October it was obvious to me that the

number of our customers was diminishing, the cold weather was on its way, and Stougham had no intention of sending the boat anywhere, much less the West Indies. I figured out my situation. It was nobody's fault but mine that I had landed in a dead-end job. I had been, again, by the standards of the land, too impetuous. Yet there had been *something* directing me, dragging me to New York. It was as if I had been a zombie, guided by some mysterious outer force. There was some reason behind all this, but, rack my mind as I might, I could not find it. All I could do was hope that I could somehow improve my lot, so that I might eventually save *Sea Dart*. This, at the time, was my *raison d'être*, my whole aim in life.

One of the problems of poverty—real poverty, not the Welfare sit-back-and-wait-for-charity kind—is that it tends to blind you to your purpose and aims in life. It stultifies any kind of creative thought; you are too busy wondering where the next meal is coming from. It was an exercise in self-discipline for me to sit down and write a page of *The Incredible Voyage*, and yet somehow, despite all my nagging fear that I would lose *Sea Dart*, that winter was approaching and I would lose my job and be stranded, penniless on a foreign shore with no prospects of a job at fifty-one years of age, somehow I managed to do it. It was as if there was a force inside me which I could not deny, and every time I thought "Hell, what's the use?" a part of me insisted that the day's writing had to be done. The book had to be written, even if no one else ever read it.

Another problem with poverty—and this is much more of a problem in America than in Europe, is that usually it prevents easy movement. The public transport systems in the U.S.A., outside of the centers of a very few big cities, are hopelessly inadequate. A car for the average American is not a luxury, it is an absolute necessity; it is the only means he has of getting from A to B for whatever reasons. It's much more frustrating to be poor in America than it is in Britain, for mainly that reason. The country is so huge compared to tiny Britain, that for someone to pull up stakes and move to another part of the land by public transport is a major undertaking. It would, it seemed, have demanded the organizing resources of an Army General Staff just to ensure that connections could be caught.

If I was going to find a job delivering a boat I would have to be able to cover all the ports on the United States East Coast, from Bar Harbor down to Baltimore. To do it by train or bus would cost a small fortune and would take weeks. The boat world is hardly one in which you can pick up a telephone and convince a complete stranger that you are fit and capable of being entrusted with anything up to $250,000 worth of his property. It is a decidedly face-to-face business, and that meant transport—it meant being able to go and ferret out a job and so defeat poverty.

Destiny, fate, call it what you will, reveals itself in strange forms, as I well knew from previous instances in my life, but rarely had I encountered it in so strange a form as I did on City Island.

It was a dull, cloudy day. I had finished my daily morning chores, preparing the boat for the evening's sail. I turned to walk inside the cabin and saw an Oriental-looking man staring at *Moonglow*. The boatyard was almost empty during weekdays this late in the season. It was a lonely place, made so by the fact that I could see Manhattan's skyscrapers in the distance and always be aware of the millions of people all around me that they represented. At sea, being alone does not necessarily mean being lonely. For one thing, it's a futile exercise because there is no one else around for perhaps a few hundred miles anyway; for another, you are usually too busy to concern yourself about it. But being here, in a generally deserted spot, yet conscious of being surrounded by the throb of a great city, is another thing entirely, and I was happy to chat with someone.

"Nice boat," observed the Korean-American (for that is what he turned out to be).

"Yes, not bad, is she?" I agreed.

"She yours?"

"No . . . I just run her out on trips."

"Looking for a hand?"

"I could do with one, only the club which runs the trips won't pay anyone," I excused myself.

"I would come for nothing if you teach me to sail," he offered.

By this time it was obvious that none of the club drivers would make sailors. It was not their fault. Some of them just did not have the interest or the feel for it. There were so many of them, always changing, that I had given up trying to teach them, and it is difficult to single-hand any sailing craft with a crowd of passengers onboard. The parties always brought their food with them, but it was a real mare's-nest to have to leave the helm to go below and show them how to make coffee, or where to find ice, or the head, especially if there was any amount of wind topside.

"My name's Johnny," he volunteered. I jumped onto the jetty and studied him. He was young. It's difficult for me to tell the age of Oriental people, especially younger ones, but he turned out to be twenty. He had the almost delicate build of people of his race and age. That might be very deceptive, but later, under sail, I found that he was about as tough and strong as many Westerners twice his size. His build didn't deceive me, nor did his strength much surprise me, for on many occasions I had seen how strong the junk-sailors of the East are.

"We sail at about seven," I asserted.

He smiled widely, "I'll be here," he said. "Wanna beer?"

"Okay."

He turned and walked up the jetty. "Be right back."

Soon he was opening the two cans. "You teach me to sail," he said, "and I'll put my car at your disposal anytime you want within reason, when I'm not working. I'll drive you anywhere you want, if you help out with the gas."

I don't usually drink American beer—it's too thin, too "chemical" for my taste—but the beer I drank with Johnny tasted like nectar from the gods. The heavens descended all around me. I had found the one thing vital to any kind of profitable movement in America outside big cities—an *automobile*.

"That'll be nice," I told him, as I coughed in delight, spluttering froth on the ground. All around me, it seemed, the Light Brigade charged, the bagpipes skirled, and the Valkyries rode around the sun now breaking through the October clouds.

Some days later, I gave the Villa Club ten days' notice. Milt made it a week. I had a week to find a boat to deliver outside the U.S.A.

We first drove north, to Groton, Connecticut. On the drive, talking with Johnny, I learned to my surprise that there were many Koreans in the New York area—Johnny thought it was about eighty thousand. Most of them had emigrated from Korea in the last twenty years, as had Johnny's family. They were self-disciplined and determined to get on. If Johnny was an indicator, they surely would. He told me that there were thousands of little fruit and vegetable stands all over New York City that were run by Koreans.

"Long working hours," he sighed, "but you don't need much capital to start one."

Johnny himself was a college graduate and now worked as a hospital laboratory technician. His short-term ambition was to go on a sea voyage for about a month, then return once more to work. Later he would study management and get a position with a big corporation, he hoped.

While Johnny told me all this I thought of the people whom I had passed back in the South Bronx. If these Koreans, who had come from a country that only two decades before was an agricultural wasteland shattered by war, could come to the United States and make their way by their own efforts, why couldn't those whose forebears had been in America for generations? So wondered a simple sailor.

Besides good health and strength, Johnny had the two assets that are most valuable to young people—or to anyone, come to that. He was willing to learn and he kept his word. By now, carefully husbanding my meager pay all the while, I had fifty dollars. With this I could make my contribution to Johnny's gasoline bill.

I had written to Eban Whitcombe, the owner of the newly built schooner *Harvey Gamage*, which, I had been told, was recruiting a company for charter work on the East Coast and in the West Indies. Johnny drove me all the way up to Groton to see Eban. It wasn't my own nor Eban's fault that he could not employ me. He knew of me well, but as soon as I opened my mouth in his living room he interrupted me.

"You still British?" His honest, weatherbeaten face was concerned.

"Sure."

"Sorry, I can't take you on, Tristan. It's against Coast Guard regulations. Besides, you'd have to hold one of their skipper's certificates for passenger-carrying vessels up to ninety tons plying U.S. waters."

"Heck—I never even thought of that, Eban."

"That's the way it is Tristan, probably the same in your country."

"Yes, well, I can't complain. You have to encourage your own seamen."

"I'm real sorry Tristan . . . I'd have loved to have you skipper *Harvey Gamage.*"

"Maybe I can find a delivery job somewhere, Eban?"

"Here," he offered, "I'll give you addresses in Baltimore, Philly, and Boston. But if there's nothing—and you've left it a bit late for boats moving south—I suggest you keep your eye open on the ads in *The New York Times* Sunday sports section."

Johnny's face was downcast as we left Eban's house. Both of us had arrived with high hopes and confidence.

"Cheer up, Johnny," I reassured him. "There's bound to be a job somewhere—there's sixteen million privately owned vessels in the United States. Say a third of them are in the Northeast—that's over five million boats. Surely there's one of them bound south!"

"Yes, but where?" asked Johnny.

"That's where you come in, mate," I replied. "Now, come on, let's head north—there's bound to be something for us up around Boston . . . that's the granddaddy of all sailing ports in the States!"

I believed it myself, and because I believed it, so did Johnny. He was that kind of person.

We found nothing moving in Boston, nothing in New London, nothing in Baltimore, nothing in Annapolis. Johnny and I combed the waterfronts and the yacht clubs in all the Northeast Coast ports, tearing along the highways between cities, sleeping in the car at nights, for almost a week.

I invested in a New York Sunday *Times*—more like a small library than a newspaper—it had about 150 pages, and I hefted it onboard *Moonglow*. I settled down to wade through the piles of paper. I had now only two days' grace before I would have to move off *Moonglow*.

"*Skipper wanted New York West Indies—40 ft. ketch.*" It was there, in the sports section. I ran ashore and telephoned Johnny. "Get the car over fast, Johnny. We've got a delivery job!" Then I phoned the owner, Mr. Grindlay.

*   *   *

Star Rider was a Nova Scotia–built wooden vessel. She was double ended, built of pine on oak, old-fashioned but honest and fitted with the very best of sailing gear for a boat of her size. As soon as I clapped eyes on her I knew she was seakindly, tough as nails, and stiff as the Washington Monument. Topsides, she was as shipshape and comfortable to handle as any forty-footer has ever been. Down below was another story. Like her builders, the Nova Scotians, she was constructed rough and ready, honest and deep, and very complex indeed.

Star Rider's owner, Tom Grindlay, was a New York City schoolteacher. He was about thirty, chubby, warmly dressed, well fed, and married. The boat was to leave her present berth in West Steadyway and I was to sail her down to St. Thomas. The condition for my employment was that I would have to skipper her for charter parties whom Grindlay would send down. He eyed Johnny glumly. Johnny grinned at him.

" 'Course you'll keep the varnish brightwork mirror finish," Grindlay said as I descended the ladder. Straight down. Seven feet.

I looked around me down below. On both sides of the main

cabin there was a berth, the side of which dropped five feet to the cabin sole (floor). There was no table. There was a tiny galley with a stove, all crammed into a space about four feet high and two feet wide. Forward, as I squeezed my way between the mast and the head compartment, a space of about ten inches width, there were two more berths, again built high above the walking level. Concerned, I made my way aft. There was a small door that led through a tunnel alongside the engine, by which, by crouching down almost bent double, I could reach the after "stateroom." This was to be the main "guest bedroom/cabin." I made my way back to the main cabin. It was like crawling through a commando obstacle course.

"What do you think of her, Tristan?" crowed Grindlay.

"Do you want the truth?"

"Sure."

"The only people who will ever be happy chartering this vessel are coal miners or circus acrobats. She was built for eight-foot giants and four-foot dwarfs—she certainly wasn't built for the average human being. Topsides she's a beauty. She's been kept in splendid condition. I can see she's a fine sea boat, but for charter in the West Indies? Forget it. Look, Tom, her ventilation hatches are tiny—she's built for the cold North Atlantic—there'll never be any air down here, and in the island heat . . . she's not built for finicky charterers, Tom; they'll mutiny!"

"You can make a wind scoop," Grindlay persisted.

I was silent for a minute or two. "That galley—how the heck am I supposed to cook for five people on a stove that size?"

"They'll want to go ashore to eat after a couple of days."

"The only way I'll take her on is if I can have a cook onboard. Most manned charter craft of this size carry a hand who does the cooking, and he'll want a return fare to New York guaranteed in case he has to come back by air."

"I can't pay a cook."

"Then I can't take her on. I'll deliver her, but that's all."

"Okay, you find a cook, I'll pay his fare back home from St. Thomas if he comes back before the boat."

"I can try, but he's going to have to be a bloody conjuror to cook on that stove."

"What about the delivery?" Grindlay asked. "I have two people willing to pay for the passage down. Will that be enough?"

"Johnny's coming with me. He's done me a lot of favors; I owe him a sea trip," I said.

Johnny, who was standing at the bottom of the ladder, grinned as Grindlay conceded, "Okay, but only as far as St. Thomas, and I can't pay air-fare."

Johnny's eyes lit up. "Gee, thanks!" he cried as he rushed off to work in his car.

One good turn deserves another. Now Johnny had his ocean trip. I had my delivery and a passage to the West Indies, with perhaps the time to write more of my book and the chance to earn money toward *Sea Dart*'s freedom.

Grindlay looked relieved. "Good," he breathed, "then it's all settled—when do you think she can sail?"

"As soon as we can find a cook," I replied.

"How will you do that?"

"I suppose I'll have to go and look for one."

"Where?" he demanded.

I flung my hand out in the direction of the Manhattan skyscrapers in the misty distance. "Bound to be a few among that lot," I said.

"Maybe. Okay, we'll delay sailing one day, but no longer; I'm behind schedule as it is."

"Right, I'll need a week's pay in advance—I'm a bit short right now."

Grindlay dug into his pocket. "Here, there's fifty bucks," he announced casually. I kept calm as he handed the fortune over. "And I wanna receipt," he added.

So it was that I set off for Manhattan to look for a cook: one willing to exercise his or her skills in a boat's galley about the size of a small washing machine, with a chronically dystrophic alcohol stove and a sink water-pump which did not work, in a clumsily furnished boat which at sea most of the time would be heeled over at thirty degrees and bouncing around; and feed four other people, hungry from the helm and sail tending; willing to do all this for no pay. *"Simple,"* I thought, as I stepped into the subway train. *"I'll drag a cook out of hell if it will get* Sea Dart *out of hock!"*

New occasions teach new duties; time makes ancient good uncouth;
They must upward still and onward, who would keep abreast of truth;
Lo, before us gleam her campfires! We ourselves must Pilgrims be,
Launch our *Mayflower*, and steer boldly through the desperate winter sea,
Nor attempt the Future's portals with the Past's blood-rusted key.

"THE PRESENT CRISIS" (1845), JAMES RUSSELL LOWELL. (THE MOTTO OF
NEW YORK STATE IS "EXCELSIOR!")

Excelsior!

I ALIGHTED from the subway at Union Square. It was an area
of Manhattan with which I was somewhat familiar from my
previous visit back in 1969. Then I had lodged in the Re-
gina Hotel at Third Avenue and Thirteenth Street, but only for
one night; the traffic in the place went twenty-four hours a day
—prossies passing in and out with their johns. It was cheap, but
one night was enough; I had checked out and headed back for
the boat.

The Union Square subway station reminded me of an old-
fashioned gent's toilet back home—and the smell was about the
same. I lit out of there as fast as I could and, leaving the ear-
shattering roar of the subway behind, emerged into the only
just more subdued row of Union Square's traffic, then passed
into Union Square Park to sit down quietly and decide where
and how to look for a cook. This, back in Britain, or anywhere
else, come to that, was a normal thing to do. I soon realized that
I was navigating wrongly.

There was a long line of park-benches curving away along
the path across the park. On all of them sat or lay several gentlemen, elderly, middle-aged, and young, white, bronze, and
black. The older men were generally dressed in old suits or
raincoats and had several day's growth of beard, down which,
in a few cases, dripped saliva. Most had blank eyes and leathery
faces. Some were drinking from cans or bottles hidden inside
brown paper bags. As I strolled by, voices called, a plaintive
chorus, changing in note only with the age of the caller: "Loose
joints . . . Placydill . . . smack . . ." Another bench: "Smack . . .
loose joints . . . Valium." I headed back for Third Avenue.

There's no point in my mixing with drug-users. Apart from
the introverted nature of drug-based relationships, the drug-

dealers have done tremendous harm to the small craft voyager. They have made sailing in some parts of the world downright dangerous with Mafia gunmen and trigger-happy law enforcers tearing around in high-speed vessels, and the suspicion with which the voyager is greeted in many ports, especially around the Caribbean and Florida. A real sailor is "high" already, anyway. Just the memories of the sea and the sky, the stars at night and the wake, are enough to take him well on his road to Nirvana.

As I walked east on Fourteenth Street the scene got lower and lower, from plain plastic sleaze to bawdy decrepitude. But New York is New York and Fourteenth Street is just as surely a part of it as Park Avenue and the Metropolitan Opera. Fourteenth Street has too many memories to be changed in a hurry. Dickens lodged there on his visit to New York. Fourteenth Street and Union Square was, in the old days, the stamping grounds of the American labor leaders and Russian exiles. Trotsky used to hang out there. It was also the birthplace of the film industry, which later burgeoned into Hollywood. D. W. Griffiths had his studio there, as well we Welshmen knew, for he was one of us.

Like many vice-oriented areas in ports the world over, it seemed to be comfortable with itself and accept itself for what it was; Fourteenth Street, nothing more and nothing less. Unlike Times Square, which always seems to me to be apologizing for its present condition, Fourteenth Street realizes that vice and sleaze are just as necessary to a great metropolis as anything else; in fact it is—perhaps unfortunately—generally the amount of those two commodities, among others, that indicate the cultural greatness of a city. Fourteenth Street reminds us that it is impossible to love humanity and to hate vice at the same time. Not even Jesus could do that. If the city had only Times Square and Fourteenth Street, New York would be the greatest metropolis on earth. That's before we even start to take into account all the rest of the island of Manhattan.

Nowhere on earth do people play out their roles so positively and obviously as they do in New York. The pill-pushers on the

corner of Fourteenth and Third, the egregiously tatty prostitutes, including the not-so-obvious-at-first transvestites, the
young pill-purchasers in their long autos with New Jersey
plates, were all so distinctly cut out for their parts that it was
like watching a stage play. There was hardly any subtlety about
it at all. I turned around and walked back toward Fourth Avenue, then south. I had little idea of where I was going to look,
but I vaguely remembered following this route when I had sold
Stougham's bottle of whisky, so I plodded on, reflecting on how
Americans seem to love placing themselves into roles—while
at the same time they vehemently protest stereotyping.

I decided to work my way over to Greenwich Village, in a
southwesterly direction. I remembered seeing tree-lined
streets there, and thought that perhaps there might be somewhere I might find advice in my search.

There's an extravagant variety of bars in New York. Irish bars
and Polish bars, journalists' bars, singles' bars, doubles' bars,
theatrical bars, "gay" bars, topless dancing bars, literary bars,
painters' bars, sculptors' bars—I suppose there must be an un-
dertakers' bar somewhere.

By the time I found the literary bar I was already two sheets
in the wind. Three hours before had been the holy moment of
my first bar-visit in America for seven years. My concern about
the catering arrangements onboard the good ship *Star Rider*
had receded slowly, drink by drink, until the Scottish sunshine
had nudged awake the Celtic dreams, and was sending them,
like stalwart volunteers, striding forward. For the first time in
weeks I did not have to worry about the immediate future, and
everything about me was a rosy glow, becoming rosier by the
hour. It was now well into the late afternoon. By now all the
women were beautiful—all the men interesting and clever.

There were three steps down from street level into the bar.
For once a jukebox was not blaring. The half-dozen patrons
were talking among themselves and bantering with the big, but
for a change friendly looking bartender. Over a whisky my eyes
became adjusted to the gloom. This darkness is, it seems, an
ubiquitous requisite in America to drinking. It must be a relic

—a hangover?—from Prohibition days and shady speakeasys. I raised my glass to the gentleman next to me. He looked seedy in a gray suit that seemed to be coming apart at the stitching, yet his eyes were amused and aware—he nodded at my toast.

I looked around. One wall was covered with book-jackets and literary notices, reviews and publishers' blurbs. Behind the bar were four or five framed photographs of sailing craft. The center of the bar-back was a ship's figurehead in the form of a red lion. I ordered, for the first time that day, a second drink in the same bar. The white-haired man next to me was holding forth. I settled down to listen to the talk.

"Henry James said it," he said. "It's a complex fate, being American. We have to fight against a . . . a . . . what was it . . . something about . . . a . . . valuation of Europe . . . an exaggerated . . ."

"A superstitious valuation," I corrected him, quietly.

White-hair turned and gazed at me, surprised. "What?" he snapped.

I repeated the quote, trying not to sound too pedantic.

The woman next to the white-haired man—small, dark, and birdlike—leaned over. "He's right, Charlie . . . goddam!"

Charlie demanded, "You Briddish?"

"Welsh."

"Yeah . . ." Charlie confided to the woman. "That figures," then he called loudly, "Bartender . . . give this gennulman a drink!"

"Oh, that's not . . ." I started to say.

"My pleasure," insisted Charlie. "Any Briddisher that can tell me what Henry James said . . . well . . . say, you a writer . . . ?" He studied my jersey and jeans. "A poet? . . . hell, I remember seeing . . . what the hell was his . . . yeah . . . Dylan Thomas. Years ago, down in the White Horse on Hudson . . . Chee, could that guy put it out . . ."

"The right-wing rainy-day onanist of the Cardiff semi-detached houses," I burbled.

Charlie clapped a hand the size and weight of an *Encyclopaedia Britannica* volume on my shoulder and roared with laugh-

ter. "Say, Jimmy," he called down the bar, "d'ja hear that one
. . . goddam it . . . here, have another drink!"

"Cheers, Charlie!" Even among the goodwill I could see that
the small dark woman was a little peeved that Charlie had his
back to her now. I shuffled off my seat and stood between them,
so she would not feel excluded from the chat. Charlie started
as I moved. I shook one leg. "Getting cramp," I said, and
moved back onto my seat. Charlie was big. I didn't want him to
think I was moving in on his companion. There was a bulge
in his inside jacket pocket and no way for me to know whether
it was a .32 caliber gat or a volume of Faulkner's definitive
works.

"Waddaya think of Mailer?" shouted Charlie. We were going
through a roll call of American writers.

"Don't know him, much," said I. *"The Naked and the Dead*
. . . that's all I've read of him so far . . . seems realistic enough
. . . I never heard a Yank use the word 'fug' . . . beg your pardon,
ma'am," I leaned over to excuse myself.

"Oh heck, that's okay," butted in Charlie. "Molly doesn't
mind."

Molly smiled.

". . . and a fug is a musty mist . . . an upper-middle-class fog
. . . it's terribly 'U,' as the old maids of Bloomsbury put it—
though I suppose I ought to say Nancies? The rain in Spain,
you know . . ."

Molly burst out laughing. The English joke escaped Charlie,
until Molly explained it to him. "Here, lemme buy you another
drink." He pushed forward some of the money which, in the
American way (I've never seen it anywhere else), he had left
lying on the counter.

"No, Charlie, let me get this one in," I insisted. "I'm sailing
the day after tomorrow . . ."

"Goddam . . . you a seaman?" asked Charlie, in surprise.

"Well, sort of . . ." I admitted, and then fell into a discussion
on recent British literature, which held out for the next four or
five drinks, gradually getting more and more hilarious, until
Charlie suddenly looked at his watch.

"Hey, Molly, come on, chee, we're late . . ." He shook my hand and patted my shoulder. Molly jumped down off her stool, came over and planted a big kiss on my beard, and they left, leaving me with an all right world among a notable set of people.

A short while later, Jimmy came over. He was a big Irish-American, dressed in casual clothes; a pullover, open-neck shirt, slacks, and sandals. Soon we were discussing Irish poets —Yeats, Cavanagh, Clarke. By the time Jimmy and I had knocked back three more whiskies, I could actually see the lake isle of Innisfree; I was planting the nine bean rows there and dismissing the thoughts of the roadside and the pavement gray outside. By the time Jimmy had explained some of the intricacies of Robert Frost's poems, and quoted (as far I knew, accurately) "Birches" all the way through, there was not one vestige of thought left in my mind of boats and sail, or the complex routine of preparing a boat for a winter passage in the Atlantic, or of cooks or galleys or chartering; all those problems had flown. Now there was only poetry and song and memories of the past and a childhood of wonder in Wales. The hard streets of Manhattan were beaten back; they no longer existed. The coming passage through the Devil's Triangle, the witches' weather stewbrew south of heartless Hatteras, were now merely a pleasant outing. The ache for *Sea Dart*'s liberty was now nothing more than a vexing irritation. So the Scottish sunshine did its job.

It must have been a couple of hours later. Jimmy had left and I had talked with several other people and put down at least another six whiskies. Such are a sailor's ways, sometimes, and it is said that the path of wisdom is the path of excess.

"Excuse me, I've been listenin' to you talkin' an' you was sayin' that you was lookin' for a cook."

I looked around and down. He was small, dark, about five foot six.

"Oh, was I? . . . I didn't realize . . . oh, yeah, that's right . . ."

He stuck his hand out. "My name's Jerry," he averred.

"Tristan. . . . Yeah . . . right . . . all aboard for the skylark! . . .

Off to the sunny seas and sparkling skies of the Caribbean we are, mate."

"What's the job?"

I put on the "Shanghai." "Oh, nothing to it. Cook for four people and yourself, see? Got everything there, we have ... ice-box, stove, oven ... three hours' work a day, you can say ... and the rest of the day's your own ... Lay on deck ... sunbathe ... read a book ... see the world ... great life!" I peered at the dim figure alongside me. "What's your trade then, chum?" I asked.

"Well, I ain't doin' anythin' right now. I was in the Air Force, photographer ... I served in Hawaii ... oh man, those beaches ... wow ... swimmin' every day ... I used to spend weekends in a cabin on the beach."

I sobered up. "Did you do any cooking?" I asked.

"Well, I used to cook for myself ... and maybe if a coupla friends came over we used to cook up a clambake on the beach, or somethin' inside in the evening."

"So you're something of a cook, Jerry?" I suggested.

"You might say that ... you might say that. ... Yes, I guess I must be," he laughed, then he was silent for a minute, his face serious.

"There's only one snag to this job," I interrupted his reverie. He looked at me. "There's no pay ... well, at least not for the delivery, but I'm hoping that when we get busy chartering I can squeeze something from the owner for the cook. I'll probably have to squeeze him, he's not exactly the open-handed type, and I don't want to exploit anyone—I've never done it yet—I believe in a fair day's work for a fair day's pay. I can't answer for the owner. He may eventually agree or he may not—it's a chance you'll have to take. ... All I can say is I'll do my best to get some money for you, at least for the time we have actual charterers onboard. ... He can't expect anyone to work that hard for nothing ..."

"Where you goin' to be operatin'?" Jerry asked.

"The Virgin Islands."

"That's U.S. territory, right?"

"Yes . . . at least half of the islands . . . the rest are British."

"But you're goin' to be based in the American half?"

"Yes."

"Then I can just go on drawin' my Welfare checks!"

"Great! . . . what did you say your name was?"

"Jerry."

"Hey, Jerry, have a drink!"

"Right on, man!" he almost sang.

The whisky came up double this time. The cook was lined up to be Shanghied. God was in heaven, all was right with the world.

* * *

I got back to City Island about five in the morning. I made *Moonglow* shipshape after a cup of tea and a cigarette, then called Johnny. By 9:00 A.M., as arranged with Grindlay, we were waiting at the jetty in West Steadyway. Soon the owner, glancing proudly at *Star Rider*, arrived in his car with two other men. One big and tall, one shorter, middle-aged. He introduced the younger man to Johnny and myself.

"This is Al."

"Hi, Al." (*"Jesus, what a hangover!"*)

"Al's a pipefitter from New Jersey. He's payin' crew, understand, and he's handy with tools and stuff," Grindlay said.

"Ever sailed before, Al?" I inquired.

"Just some very small dinghy stuff . . . on the Jersey waterways . . ."

I studied Al. He was about twenty-four and sturdy. There was a calmness about his manner which I liked. He was fair, German-looking. He, in turn, was studying Johnny's Oriental features. Johnny grinned at him, "Hi," he said.

"This is your crew, Cap'n," said Grindlay.

"Call me Tristan, Mr. Grindlay." (*"Captains don't have thick heads."*)

"And this is Hank . . ." Grindlay introduced me to the middle-aged man. "Hank's a pilot . . ." Hank was the image of a suburban American. He wore his hair stylishly at mid-length.

His face was ruddy and obviously well fed. Well groomed and manicured, he wore a loud-check purplish sports coat and gray slacks over Sperry Topsider deckshoes, brand new. He was hail-fellow and seemed anxious both to impress us and to be liked.

"A pilot?"

"Only amateur stuff . . . I'm learning to fly small planes," explained Hank.

Grindlay interjected with a grin, "Hank's also a restaurant-owner. . . . He's coming with you for the trip out, just for the delivery, see. You sure ain't gonna go short of good food on the outward passage . . . you gotta first-class chef onboard!"

"Yeah!" exclaimed Hank. "I'm gonna feed you guys like you never been fed before!"

I looked at Grindlay. "I've arranged a cook for the charters," said I.

"A cook?"

"Yes . . . I lined him up last night. Name's Jerry. Ex–U.S. Air Force. Good bloke he seems, got quite a bit of tropical cooking experience."

"For no pay?"

"That's right, but he wants his air-fare back in case he leaves the boat . . . like I told you yesterday . . ."

"But I said I couldn't do that," he lied.

"Then Jerry won't come—and I can't take the boat," I replied, wondering how I could pay Grindlay back his fifty dollars advance in wages.

"Oh . . . heck . . . well . . . okay . . . I'll guarantee his fare back . . ."

"Air-fare," I insisted.

Grindlay said, "Yeah . . . air-fare . . . but no pay. Where is this Jerry, anyway?"

"He's coming down any minute." I glanced over Grindlay's shoulder. "In fact, here he is coming down the driveway right now."

Everyone turned to look at the approaching figure. There was a dead silence. I hailed, "Hey, Jerry, just in time!" Jerry sang back, "I'm boppin' along, man ... I'm boppin' along ... Where's this boat, Tristan old top?"

"Welcome to H.M.S. *Uno!*" I hailed Jerry.

"Good *mornin'*; *good* mornin' *all*," Jerry greeted the assembled crew.

They stared at him in silence. He was small, neatly dressed, jaunty, and black. "Sure hope you dudes like hominy grits," he said.

I'll sing you one, O!
Green grow the rushes O!
What is your one O?
One is one and all alone and ever
  more shall be so!

I'll sing you two O!
Green grow the rushes O!
What is your two O?
Two, two, the lily white boys, all
  dressed up in green oh ho!
One is one and all alone and ever
  more shall be so!

I'll sing you three O!
Green grow the rushes O!
What is your three O?
Three, three, alive, O!

Four for the gospel makers.

Five for the symbols at your door.

Six for the six proud walkers.

Seven for the sev'n stars in the
  sky.

Eight for the April rainers.

Nine for the nine bright shiners.

Ten for the ten commandments.

Eleven for the elev'n apostles.

Twelve for the twelve disciples.

"GREEN GROW THE RUSHES O!" ANCIENT IN ORIGIN, THIS SONG WAS SUNG
BY UNITED STATES SOLDIERS DURING THE MEXICAN WAR OF 1847. FROM
"GREEN GROWS" SUPPOSEDLY COMES THE EPITHET "GRINGO." IT WAS
POPULAR IN THE ROYAL NAVY, ESPECIALLY AMONG SENIOR RATINGS.

Five for the Symbols at Your Door

EXCEPT for the dull hum of the traffic in the highway, the cries of the seabirds gyrating overhead and the creak of *Star Rider* as she strained against her mooring lines, there were no sounds for a full minute. Johnny, who had been carrying a bag of sail onboard, stopped stock-still. Big Al just stood and grinned, looking from Jerry to Grindlay and back again. Hank stared at the new arrival. Grindlay broke the silence with a fit of coughing.

I said to Jerry, " 'Bout time you bloody well showed up."

Johnny's Oriental features cracked. He dropped his sail-bag and shook Jerry's hand, then the tension dissolved as Al did the same. "Hi," called Hank as, flustered, he climbed onboard.

"Bad cough you got there," I observed to Grindlay, quietly.

He nodded at Jerry and beckoned me to one side, to walk along the boatyard driveway with him. When we were out of earshot Grindlay demanded, "Who's this guy? . . . Is he the cook you were telling me about?"

"That's your man, the very same," I confirmed.

"But . . . do you know him . . . where did you meet him . . . ? I mean you gotta be damn careful who you take sailing with you."

"I met him last night. I was introduced to him at a party. He seems to have all the necessary credentials for the job."

"Yeah . . . but . . ."

"And I know him better than I know the two blokes you've already signed on."

"Yeah, but Hank's a property owner . . . He owns a business . . . and Al's an employee of a buddy of mine . . ."

"Well, I doubt if the sea will much take that into consideration, do you, Tom?" said I. "Anyway, Jerry seems willing enough and for sure he's not bad company . . . and where else we going to get a cook willing to do the job for almost nothing?"

Grindlay thought for a moment. Then he warned, "Well, it's your responsibility . . ."

Jerry looked over and grinned at me. "How's your head *to*day, man?"

"Which one?" I asked him. He gave a short laugh, then climbed onboard.

"What age is he?" Grindlay asked, nervously.

"Thirty-two, he told me," I said.

"Oh . . . well . . . he seems okay," allowed Grindlay.

Star Rider was in absolutely A-one condition and almost ready to shove off. One thing I'll say for Grindlay, he cared for his boat.

While Jerry was ashore with Hank and the owner, shopping at the nearby supermarket, Johnny and I went over the rigging and sails. Al, who had been appointed mechanic for the trip, studied the engine maintenance manual and later checked the engine installation over with me.

Soon the stores for six days, until we should arrive at More-head, in North Carolina, were onboard and stowed away. Due to the lack of sufficient storage lockers in the galley, most of the food was crammed into clothes lockers all over the craft. Diesel fuel was taken onboard, then, last of all, fresh water, and, after words of admonition from Grindlay about "responsibility" "taking care" and "economy," we were ready to make our departure.

As I usually do before a sea voyage, I went for a short stroll, alone, along the driveway and out into the highway. I took in the neon signs, just lit for the evening, the garish supermarket across the way, and the streams of traffic roaring and honking by, and tried to convince myself that I was tired of all this and that I wanted to set out and get to know the sea again, and leave the winter to claim its own.

I turned away from the noise, the lights, the people passing, and made my way back into the boatyard. I thought of how every setting out in a small boat to challenge the forces of the ocean is supposed, in fiction, to impart its own feeling of high endeavor. But if there were any thoughts of glory, or courage, or heroism among my crew, they did not show it. Johnny was eager to let go the mooring lines. Al was having a last word with a pretty lass on the jetty, Hank was busy filling little pastry hors d'oeuvres in the cockpit, and Jerry was trying to light the oven, cursing every time the stove blew back at him and flared up.

"Weeel . . . goddam muthafuckah . . ."

I poked my head through the companionway and peered through the fumes below. Soon I picked out Jerry's glowing eyes in the smoky gloom.

"Having trouble, mate?"

"Naw . . . nothin' 'cept this muthahfuckah just about burned half my goddam Afro off . . ." Jerry's eyes gleamed.

"Hang on . . ." I clambered down the vertical ladder and made a paper taper, then I showed Jerry how to light the alcohol stove.

"You never used alcohol before?" I asked him when I'd got the oven lit.

"Only in the bars . . ." he replied, grinning, "and sometimes on the stoop." I ascended Jacob's ladder again. It was time to go. There was no fuss and palaver. I switched on the navigation lights. The green starboard light suddenly cast an eerie glow on the rigging and deck on that side of the doghouse. Blocks creaked. Johnny called from the foredeck, "All right, Skip?"

"Right . . . cast off, Johnny" was what I said for *Star Rider*, and she and I became as one, for I was her skipper. Johnny heaved in the lines that earlier had been doubled around the mooring posts, I pushed the engine control-lever forward at slow revs, and we moved into the twilit channel leading to the ocean between the ghostly mud flats. Again I felt the momentary chill I always feel at the start of a voyage, until I glanced over the side, in the red glow of the portside navigation light, and heard the sleepy murmur of waters pushed aside. One minute *Star Rider* was tied up to the mooring posts; the next minute she was moving out into the channel. We were off to sea.

Hank had carried on making his little pastries, in the dark on the fantail, as we moved down the channel. Johnny and Al had remembered my request and had moved aft of the helm, so as to give me a clear view along the channel. The engine purred in the windless evening as the mud-banks on one side, and house after suburban house on the other, slid by.

As we reached the two-mile mark, about halfway out to sea, Hank carried the pastries down below and placed them in the oven. Jerry came to the companionway and stuck his head out into the cool night air.

"When we movin' out?" he asked me.

"Come up here and have a look," I replied. He climbed out into the cockpit. Then, after his eyes had become accustomed to the dark, he watched the land slipping by. He looked up, at the slightly shaking mast, the white glow of the masthead light shimmering from the truck, and the truck itself, as the boat rose and fell now to the rising sea-swell, moving its admonishing finger among the scatter-dust, shining galaxies of the Milky Way.

"Oh, man!" he shouted at the stars. "What them dudes in the city are *missin'!*" He looked ahead at the floodlit bridge and beyond it, the edge of the darkness of the sea.

"Wow ... that's sump'n, man ... wow ... oh, wow ..." he murmured. Then he turned to me, his face glowing with excitement and pleasure. "Hey, it ain't like this all the way?"

"Let's hope not, Jerry," I murmured, as he lit my cigarette.

"Why? This is great," he said.

Johnny said for me, softly, "We need a wind outside, so as to get into Norfolk tomorrow evening."

"Weel ..." observed Jerry, "it's just fine by me if we just keep boppin' along like we're doin' now, man ... that rough stuff, that's for the birds, man, for the birds!"

"Dead right," I told him, as we passed under the bridge. "Just a nice little breeze will do us fine, as long as it's westerly off the land, so the sea stays nice and smooth."

Jerry climbed down below again to get supper ready. "Nice and smooth ... that's what I mean ... yeah ... nice and *smooooth!*"

Johnny murmured to me, "He's puttin' that stuff on, you know, Tristan."

"What stuff's that, mate?" I asked him.

"All that jive . . . they do that when they're not sure . . ."

"Who does what, Johnny?"

"Black people . . ."

"He's one of the crew and he's the cook, Johnny." I said so the others in the cockpit would overhear.

"Yeah . . ."

"Yes."

"Guess you're right, Tristan," conceded Johnny, sounding abashed.

I leaned forward from the wheel. I yelled for Jerry to come up, above the noise of the engine—I had just increased the revs. Jerry poked his head through the companionway. I checked that Hank and Al could hear me.

"I think we ought to agree on the number one golden rule in a crewed small craft," I said. I knew it might sound as if I were pontificating. "The most important rule of all"—I had to lay this on the line—"no one ever criticizes anyone else's appearance, traits, habits or mannerisms, or way of work, outside of that person's hearing." I waited a moment, then I turned round and looked straight at each man in turn.

"Agreed?" I asked each in turn.

"Okay," responded Al, quietly.

"Got it," acknowledged Johnny. Hank nodded.

"Jerry?"

"Yeah?"

"Agreed—what I just said?"

"Right on—you're the man . . . gotta do what the man says . . ." He disappeared back below again.

"Johnny," I explained, "sorry, mate . . . there's no first amendment out here . . ."

He laughed. "No, I guess not . . . I know what you mean . . ." He went to climb down below. "I'll go and help Jerry, looks like he needs me to get the hang of that goddam antique stove . . ."

"This is going to be a good sail, Tristan," said Al.

"No one but the wary ever think of snares until they're tripped up," I said as I handled the wheel.

"But how do you tell that someone is wary before you sail with him?" he asked.

"You probably can't," I replied, softly. "Few people are the same ashore as they are afloat."

"And afloat you're a hard son of a bitch," joked Hank, laughing.

"I'm a hard bastard," I admitted, "for my boat—now, Al, let's see how you make out getting that number two jib hoisted, then you can give me and Hank a hand to hoist the main." I turned to Hank. "You take the helm, Hank. Put her into the wind until the sails are up, then take her off the wind and steer southeast until I check the course . . ."

Soon all our sails were spread to catch the northwest land-breeze and pass around Sandy Hook. We winged our ghostly way under the rising moon out, out, clear at last of the trammels of the land. It was a gentle breeze, so that by the time I changed course southward, *Star Rider* hardly heeled more than a few degrees. Now and then she bobbed a gentle curtsey to the sea gods, to let them know that she acknowledged their dominion over the moving moonlit waters. Most of the time though, even after we had set the fisherman stays'l to close the wasteful gap 'twixt mainsail luff and mizzen leach, she barely leaned over more than five degrees, so stiff was she, as stiff as a Nova Scotian's leg breeches in a January blizzard. Comfortable she was, too, as sea-kindly as a hammock, and she pushed the waves aside like a child's nurse chiding her charges. There was one word for her in easy breezes—*stately*. We had one thought for her as the wind increased and she started to show her paces—*kind*.

By the first pink peep of the dawn on the eastern ocean-edge, there was a full-scale love affair raging between the five men on the one hand and a bewitching duchess on the other. *Star Rider* sailed as if she knew it. On this leg, down to Cape Henry, even the breeze itself seemed to contest us for *Star Rider's* favor. It stayed in the northwest quadrant, gently increased to twenty knots, and eased her, not too gently nor too lively, ever south. The sea abetted the wind and lulled all except one onboard. That one, having balanced on the razor's edge of the ocean's enchantment for a long, long time, kept one eye over his shoulder, one to leeward, and his inner eye on the chart spread out on the berth down below. That one worked up his sights twice in the forenoon, twice at noon, and twice in the afternoon, just in case the year and more without taking sights had rusted his craft.

Star Rider was well out into the Atlantic Ocean offing—about fifty miles. Close to the low shores of New Jersey is no place to be in a sailing craft making passage. The wind can always change onshore—only a tyro or a fool counts on the wind direction remaining stable near any coast.

All four of my companions were up and agog to see the sunrise. Sunrise over the ocean is like no sunrise seen on land. Sunrise on the high seas is like a rousing chorus of color. It is a sight that we seem to hear, as well as see. First there is a low bass hum as a shy, trembling ever-lightening purple breaks the blackness of the night on the eastern horizon. Then, gradually, the sky over the edge of the nickel-colored sea changes, from dark, hueless gray to opaque pearl as the celestial tenors and sopranos raise their voices. Soon, across the eastern quadrant of the sky glow-blades of fire stab through the diffused, pale light of promised day from behind the now-revealed low, horizon-hugging clouds of the Trades. Then, with magnificent dignity, Sol reveals his majesty to the world. At first blood red and terrible, a perfect sphere of fire, he allows us to gaze on his imperious face. Then he casts off mercy before the shamed, defeated stars in the retreating dark in the west, and he mounts his blazing car to take command of his infantry, the pacing ocean seas, his cavalry, the charging winds; and his artillery, his own children, begot by him 'twixt wind and water, the lumbering clouds.

Over breakfast, which we took in the cockpit, so fine and dry was *Star Rider,* I told the crew about an even more wondrous sight—the "green flash." That I have only seen in the deep ocean—a thousand miles and more from land, at dusk. Then, just a split second after the sun's upper tip sinks below the horizon, and the sun shines through the sea, the whole sky shimmers in a pulsing deep-emerald glow, a green so green as to shame the fields of Ireland. I have seen the "green flash" three times in my life. It was as if I were on another planet. The colors all about—the sea, the clouds, the boat itself, my skin— all glowed brilliant green.

By the time *Star Rider* passed the laid-up ships of the U.S. Navy Reserve in Norfolk and through hundreds of miles of inland waterway, and finally sailed into Morehead, we five onboard were no longer five individuals of two different nationalities and three different races. We were a crew. We knew where all the gear onboard was, the tools, the engine parts, the different sails, the spare running rigging—the thousand and one different components which make a sailing craft. We also knew her handling characteristics in calm, in a medium blow and under power, and we had a good idea of our own assets and limitations, at least as far as these could be observed in eight days.

Al was steady, reserved, always quietly observing and learning. He was to leave *Star Rider* in Puerto Rico, en route to join his brother, who was running a holiday camp in Jamaica, where he was to be employed as maintenance foreman.

"Tristan," he asked one day as we were chugging quietly down the waterway into Carolina, "when you get a craft ready for sea, what's the most important thing to take into consideration?"

"The same thing that's the most important in any vessel at any time."

"What d'ya mean . . . the hull?"

"No, Al, the most important thing is the people involved . . . everything else follows from that. The most important consideration at sea is the life and safety of the people, first in your own vessel and then the people in any other vessels."

"What about if you're alone?" Johnny had been overhearing us.

"Same applies."

Johnny was also eager to learn. He was somewhat impetuous —though that was an attribute of his age more than of his nature.

Hank was a few years younger than myself. He had sailed a couple of times before in seagoing vessels. I suspected, at first, that the fascination of seafaring, which he had in great measure, was that for brief spells it gave him relief from a separation from natural things and people. I had the impression when we first met that he seemed to hunt life, to track it down, rather than being part of it. As we came to know each other, I learned that he was anxious, that he felt trapped by property and things— *unnatural* things, like his cars, his domestic machinery—that he had found himself chest-deep in the mire of perhaps unnecessary responsibility, and yet at the same time he could not, he told me, think of giving up some of the comforts and safeguards with which he had beseiged himself, while he unreasonably admired those who had done.

Hank seemed to think that the events of the past decade had ruined all he stood for—all America stood for. He reflected that once in Vietnam the United States "should have gone all the way."

"So you suffered your first defeat," I told him.

"That's serious!" he declared.

"We've lost more wars than you've had hamburgers," I observed. "The Boer War was our Vietnam . . . Cyprus, Palestine, Kenya . . ."

Then, for the first time ever in my life, I had an argument with an American about not who had won the more battles and victories, but about which of our two nations had suffered more setbacks and defeats. This was a turn-up for the books, and I began to realize how much America had changed since I was thrown out of a Brooklyn bar in 1948 for daring to say that some of the Soviet sailors I had met were decent fellows.

"Goddam kids," Hank sniffed, as he steered. He peered

around in the night gloom to make sure that Al and the others were turned in below. "Hollering and screaming and causing goddam riots here at home while our boys were getting their balls shot off in Vietnam . . . This goddam generation is no goddam good," he said, nodding toward the companionway.

"Well, they are about the same generation as the ones who got their balls shot off . . ." I averred. "Let's face it, Hank, there's nothing really new under the sun as far as human needs and reactions are concerned . . . All they did was the same as the French Army did in 1916, the same as our lads did in the Calais Bullring in 1917."

"The what?"

"The Army mutinies in the First World War. They just asked themselves why people should get blown to bits because of some bloody stupid politician or some doddering general sitting on his fat ass behind the lines . . ."

"Ah, you're as bad as they are . . ." retorted Hank.

"I wish to Christ I was half as good," I said. "I was involved in five different bloody wars, and three of them were . . . well, lost, you could say, and only one of those was necessary—and not even that one if the politicians and generals had done their job in the first place."

"Hold the wheel for me, Tris, I'm goin' below to make some goddam cawffee," Hank said, and disappeared, leaving me alone with a steady star around which the forestay staggered.

When Hank came up with the coffee I told him about the Grenadier Guards officer during World War I who had come direct from the slaughter in the trenches home on leave to London. The club-members had asked him to tell them exactly what the war was like. "Simply awful," the officer had replied. "The noise! And the *people!*"

Hank stood frowning for a moment, then when the joke dawned on him he roared with laughter until there were tears in his blue eyes and we never again discussed Vietnam. But ever after on the trip to San Juan, whenever one of the little crises to which sailing-craft are prone occurred, Hank caught my eye, pursed his lips, and said, "The noise! . . . and the *peo-*

ple!" My stock reply was, "Simply awful, old chap!" and the tension dissolved.

Hank would never share my tea, of which Jerry had brought a small stock onboard. "Only sissies drink that goddam crap," he said.

Finally I retorted, "In America, maybe—it tastes like gnat's piss."

Hank grinned. "Yeah, simply awful, old chap," he said.

The others liked my strong brew, though. Earl Grey—just about muddy enough to stand a spoon upright in the mug.

We all helped with the food preparation chores—the ones not on the helm, and also the dishwashing. That left Jerry with time to take the helm himself for spells, to relieve the others of the monotony of steering—the tyranny of the tiller.

Jerry, unlike the other Americans onboard, had the ability to cut himself off. In a small cabin, with four other men all talking, one minute he would be there, involved, and the next minute he was not. He seemed to retire within himself. It was as if a blind had dropped. His eyelids lowered, he leaned back, and he was gone into his own company. This, to a small-boat sailor in crewed boats, is a priceless gift, not only to himself, but to all the others around him.

On our arrival at Morehead we made ready for an ocean passage of approximately eight hundred miles. We did not, as sailors are supposed to in popular legend, paint the town red. Seafarers mostly tend to do that when they're "on the beach," not while they're on passage.

It's a good idea, in a crewed boat, for all the company to take a meal ashore together before setting off on a longish passage. This gives them time to communicate outside the cramped quarters of the vessel and to relax in each others' company. So far, we had spent only twenty-four hours at sea and six days on the long slog, mostly under power, down through the Intracoastal Waterway stretch from Norfolk to Morehead.

On the waterfront in Morehead is one of the finest seafood restaurants I've ever eaten in, the Hygienic. It isn't a fancy place, in fact the tourist souvenir counters at the main entrance, piled with useless junk, almost put us off going inside, but once at the tables what a treat it was! Succulent clams, oysters, lobsters, crabs. I've tasted seafood on six continents, and chosen fish in some of the most renowned seafood eateries on earth, including those in Paris and La Rochelle, Lisbon, and San Francisco, and ate at none of them such a memorable repast as we were served in the Hygienic.

"We go direct from here to the Virgins?" asked Al. Jerry and Johnny paused over their lobsters and beer.

"No, San Juan, Puerto Rico, first. It's a direct straightforward deep-water sail passage all the way. We'll avoid having to wend our way around all the gubbins in the entrance to the Virgins after a long sea voyage that might be a little bit rough at times . . ."

"Rough?" demanded Jerry.

"Yes, just a bit . . . We're heading right down the gut of the Bermuda Triangle . . ."

"What do you think of all these tales about mysterious disappearances?" asked Hank. Al and Jerry were all ears.

"Let's go and find out," I offered.

"Right on," whooped Jerry. He wagged his head from side to side. "Let's bop right on down through the Devil's own yard!"

Ye rambling boys of Ireland, ye rambling boys beware,
When you go onboard a merchant ship, blue dungaree jumpers wear.
Lay aside your working jackets, keep them at your command,
And beware of the cold nor'westers on the Banks of Newfoundland.

I had a dream the other night; I dreamt I was at home,
I dreamt that me and my true love were in old Marylebone,
That we were on old England's shore with a jug of ale in hand,
But when I woke my heart was broke on the Banks of Newfoundland.

We had onboard two Irish lads, Mike Murphy and Pat Moore,
In the year of 1844 those sailors suffered sore,
They pawned their clothes in Liverpool and sold their notes to hand,
Not thinkin' of the cold nor'westers on the Banks of Newfoundland.

It's now we're passing Sandy Hook and the cold winds they still blow,
With a tug-boat right ahead of us into New York we will go,
We'll fill our glasses brimming with a jug of rum in hand,
For while we're here we can't be there on the Banks of Newfoundland!

"THE BANKS OF NEWFOUNDLAND." THIS SEEMS TO HAVE BEEN AN IRISH
EMIGRANT SONG WHICH HAS BEEN ADOPTED BY SAILORS, ESPECIALLY THOSE
FROM NOVA SCOTIA. IT ORIGINATED IN NEW YORK, AROUND THE 1850S.
MARYLEBONE IS AN INNER SUBURB OF LONDON.

Through the Devil's Triangle

Star Rider started from Morehead bound for San Juan in the early dawn, even as Jerry, by some alchemy of his own, had breakfast for five sizzling on the tiny stove-top. Pancakes—a score, bacon—two pounds, eggs—twenty-four, *and* hominy grits!

The rest of us—Hank, Al, Johnny, and myself—all bundled up in *Star Rider*'s yellow and red oilskin suits—unlashed the main and hanked on the jib. The scene all around, the waterfront buildings, the shipshape harbor vessels and fishing craft, the town in the distance, looked like a woodcut, all pale and colorless in contrast with the bright hues of the previous afternoon.

There was not a capful of wind. In the distance, through the harbor entrance, the sea seemed a leaden sheet, its far edge blotched by the scarlet gashes of the dawn under lowering clouds.

I nodded to Johnny, who seemed to love casting off our tenuous links with the land. Smartly he hauled the doubled tow mooring line aboard, all dripping with dew. I glanced over my shoulder. Al had dropped the afterline end in the harbor. I paused for him to recover the end of his line, then gently shoved the gear-lever into forward. There was a splashing of disturbed water astern, then *Star Rider* moved forward slowly, wheel hard over, and we were off.

"Shall I hoist the mainsail?" asked Hank.

"Not much point," I replied "no wind at all, yet . . . There's no point in frapping it under power, and it looks to me like we'll have to head well out into the offing before we get much breeze. We may as well have breakfast as we chunder off out into the wild blue yonder."

"Don't look too blue to me," said Johnny, passing aft with the now coiled forward mooring line wrapped around one shoulder. He was right. The day was all gray. The air was rank with the bitter iodine smell of seaweed, a pretty sure indication of the promise of fog.

"As soon as we're out of the harbor I'll press on southeast as fast as we can go without pausing too hard, then we'll be clear of any coastal fog," I reflected to Hank. "There's a dampness around that I don't like the smell of." I sniffed the air again. "Bloody fog—I'd rather spend a month in gales than an hour in fog. The most dangerous hazard of all."

"Like flying in a cloud—gives me the heeby-jeebys," he shuddered.

We headed out into the open sea, into a snot-nosed red-eyed day which for the rest of the morning couldn't make up its mind whether to grin or cry. It just sat on its marbled-smoked ass snivelling, while *Star Rider*, with the engine pushing along at a steady chug, rose up and down, gradually increasing her movement until we were pounding in a sloppy gray sea under a sloppy gray sky ten miles offshore. Soon a fog-bank, as creamy-white as the leeside of a dowager's writing pad, was hiding whatever we might have been able to see of the low Carolina shore astern of us.

By the early afternoon, everyone onboard except Jerry was queasy to varying degrees, myself included.

"Feeling rough, Skipper," moaned Johnny.

"Stick it out, mate."

There's no point in displaying too much sympathy with seasick victims, not even yourself. It's simply a matter of patience, at least for the first forty-eight hours. If the symptoms of heavy vomiting and loss of morale had persisted in any one person, then I would have put into port and landed him.

The only one who did not seem to suffer was Jerry, who stayed down below and carried on performing chores in the galley. This is unusual, because it's generally the galley crew who is affected first.

Hank suffered the worst. By evening he was miserable. We were still under power in the undulating seas, crashing up and down. Still the wind taunted us, sending slight flurrys over the sea-hills. Three times we hoisted sail in joy, three times the wind dropped, and disgruntled we pressed on under power.

"Why don't we heave to and maybe the movement will be better?" suggested Al.

"Anything will be better than this bouncing," moaned Hank.

"Look—we can do three things," I replied. "One, we can turn back and you can spend another miserable night approaching the coast and possibly a fog at dawn. Two, we can heave to in the full strength of the Gulf Stream and be carried north all night, in the direction of Cape Hatteras and all its hazards. Or three, we can press on under power until we are beyond the full flow of the current, and wait there for a wind which will lay her over and make her movements much easier." It's not easy to be sympathetic when you are feeling the weather yourself. Self-pity never yet helped to complete a successful passage. Reluctantly, Hank yielded to my explanations of the alternatives, and we pushed *Star Rider* out into a dark, cloudy night, as black as a grenadier's boot and as cheerful as a waiting hearse.

By the time Johnny relieved me at the wheel at midnight, he was more his old self again. The sea had eased off and the sky far to the east seemed to repent the previous day's hysterical teetering.

"Keep her heading southwest," I told him. "If you think that there's a wind, slow her down so you can feel it and give me a shout."

"Right on, Skipper!" Johnny grabbed his mug of cocoa as *Star Rider*'s bow dropped violently into yet another watery hole.

I'd had a long day, because with three of the crew down ill, Jerry and I had shared the steering between us, me doing most of it, him relieving me at odd intervals for short spells. It's not easy to go to sleep on the first night out in a heavily pounding boat, but I seemed to have managed it without too much delay. No sooner was I asleep, though, when I was shaken awake again. It was Johnny.

"Wazzup, mate?"

"There's a wind . . ." He got no further. I was out of my bunk like a sprung hare and rose up Jacob's ladder by, it seemed, levitation. I felt the breeze on my face. I glanced down at the red-lighted compass rose, then up at the tell-tale ribbon on the mizzen shroud. Southeast. I grabbed the saloon-roof as *Star Rider* lurched heavily on a sea, and ducked my head into the companionway. Johnny was still below.

"Yoiks, tally-ho . . . come on, me lucky lads, hands off cocks and onto socks . . ."

Everyone who had been turned in was out in a second, fully dressed. Hank's red-shot eyes in the dull glare of the cabin night-light reminded me to speak, if I could, American. "Okay, you guys, haul up the stars 'n' bars, the golden eagle's gonna shit any minute . . . Get your goddam asses topsides . . ."

Everyone was laughing. Johnny was up at his sail station, unlashing the mizzen as Hank climbed up with Al close behind him, whooping.

Soon we had all working sail hoisted and the sheets hauled in. *Star Rider* thrust herself at the weather like a wanton wench warming a weary warrior. This was the first time we had close hauled her, that is, sailed her into the wind. Until now we had been more or less sailing away from it; but now she was headed and she showed her brave Nova Scotian colors like a thorough-bred at Ascot. She tasted the wind, gobbled it up between her taut sails, and spat it out over her quarter so that it caused the sea in her wake to corrugate and tremble and the men on her deck to laugh with excitement, until, one by one, their eyes were transfixed by the wonder of the star-laden sky above and ahead and the diamond-scatter of her rushing wake below and astern. I watched the others, all four of them, as they gazed at eternal miracles, then as, one by one, their eyes turned back onboard. They all looked like people who have just come out of church.

"Great," exulted Hank. "Feel a million times better, can I take the helm?"

Al again stared at the shining sky and sea. "Fantastic . . . gee."

"Pretty, ain't it?" I agreed, quietly. "Best time in the world, in fine weather, well clear of the land at sea in the small wee hours. . . . look . . ." I pulled the boat's rough logbook out of its stowage inside the companionway. "Look, you can read out here, the starlight is so bright."

Al and Jerry bent their heads, as if in prayer, to read what I had written for the previous evening. ". . . wind nil, working heavily under power . . . course southwest, looking for breeze . . . expect light southeast wind at approx. 2:00 A.M. . . ." They both looked at me mystified.

"How did you know the wind would come up? It was . . ." Al turned to Johnny, "What time did the wind come up, Johnny?" he asked.

"Two oh five."

Al turned to me again, "How did you know?"

"I didn't know . . . I just expected it."

"How?" Al insisted.

"Well, when I saw how bloody miserable you buggers were last night I rattled the old ju-ju beads . . . They always do the trick . . ."

Jerry grinned widely "He's got his mo-jo workin'," he murmured.

*   *   *

We had fine weather for the following three days. I warned the lads to watch out for squalls once we were clear of the warm Gulf Stream and into the immense whirlpool of water that, on the ocean side of the current, drags into its mighty maw colder water from the north.

At first my four American friends did not seem quite as adaptable to the discomfort of life onboard a cramped sailing boat as other crews I had sailed with in the past. It was difficult for them, after the seasickness had passed, to sit quietly doing nothing. The melting of the last slivers of ice in the food-box was met with much moaning. There was, for the first couple of days, regret at the inability to communicate easily with people ashore. This was especially so with Hank and Al. Johnny and Jerry did not seem to mind the isolation much at all.

All this passed by the fourth day out, and we had melded into a crew of separate, distinct individuals, yet each one now forever related by shared experience to the others.

Their conversations seemed to be of a much more serious tone than among a British crew, but that might be because of the difference in the sense of humor. There was much less play on words, much more on ideas and situations among the Americans, and yet when something funny was said, it seemed much, much funnier. Between themselves it was as if these four Americans communicated more by the *sound* of words than by their content.

Of the four onboard *Star Rider,* Jerry, the ex–U.S. Air Force photographer, had by far the most sensitive humor. He caught every one of my-sometimes (hopefully) subtle cracks, and often broke up laughing.

Al was the most active of the four. He looked after the engine religiously and always, when he was not on watch or sleeping, he had the tools out, tinkering with something from either the engine or the electrical system. He was a wizard with tools.

Hank was still a bit queasy unfortunately, and could not stay anywhere near the galley stove while the boat was moving, so he had to content himself with sitting in the cockpit, in the open air, leaning down to shout instructions on the cooking to Jerry—who, most of the time, did it his own way anyhow.

Johnny studied ropework and fancy stuff, as we sailors call macramé. He had a good feel for ropework and once I had shown him a knot or a hitch he never forgot it.

While Hank was sitting in the cockpit, which was most of the time, I spun yarns about some of the voyages I had made. Here again destiny was at work. I did not know of the change in my life that these chats would make, nor by what fantastic coincidence.

Probably the only thing they learned from me, apart from

some nautical tips, was how to be content with less than they were used to, though I was not, at the time, conscious of it.

I was sleeping the afternoon off, resting after my morning watch. All was steady. *Star Rider* was still headed by the wind, still forcing her way into it, still leaping from sea to sea like a lively stag, with her sails hauled in taut. By now we had all become accustomed to the jerky movement of a sailing boat, as she leaned over at a regular twenty degrees and pounded from one sea to the next. Suddenly, for no apparent reason which I can fathom, I sat up bolt upright, wide awake. I listened to the sounds of the boat for a second or two. She was trying to tell me something. I scrambled off my berth and up the Jacob's ladder, eyes half closed still with heavy sleep.

The sun was shining with a tropical warmth. There was not a cloud in the steely blue sky overhead. The sky looked so brittle that I felt it could be smashed into fragments with a hammer. I peered ahead.

There was a line of clouds right across the horizon all ahead of us. The white, fluffy-cotton clouds of the Trades. And there, right ahead of us, like a wolf among a sheep flock, was a great big squall, as black as a Bible.

I didn't wait to see how big it was. I had seen enough. "Come about!" I hollered. "Come about—get her on the other tack NOW!" I roughly shook Al and Hank from their sunbathing doze on the lee deck. They were up and ready to bring the sheets over in a flash. I grabbed the wheel from Johnny.

I could have brought her about myself, but I wanted to strike their memories.

"Ready about!"

"Ready!" came the acknowledgment.

"Hard a lee!" I rammed the wheel over. With a snapping crack the jib shot over in the swiftly strengthening wind. The mainsail followed with a *thunk* and *Star Rider* was over, now heading south instead of west.

Once *Star Rider* was steady on the new tack, I looked over at the glowering squall we had avoided sailing into. I estimated that it was about three miles away. It was all of seven miles long. Its leading edge, which would likely have passed over us if we had maintained the old tack, was brilliant white in the sunshine, while its trailing edge was gray with rain. It was moving like a funeral train.

"Line squall?" Al suggested, when we had all regained our breath.

"No . . . that's a full-blown anti-cyclonic mini-storm," I told him. "A regular, plain, old-fashioned tropical squall. The wind on the leading edge of that bastard is blowing at about sixty-five knots. Look," I pointed, "the sea ahead of that leading edge is white. The wind is blowing the top off it. The wind is so hard it's actually flattening the sea."

"Something like a big tornado," suggested Hank, standing high, holding the mizzen mast.

"That's it. There's an area of flat calm in the middle of it all."

Jerry spoke up. "That what causes the boats to go missin'?" He had broached a subject that everyone had avoided since we had left Morehead. "That why they call this here lot the Devil's Triangle?"

"That's it—you hit the nail on the head, Jerry. Only it's not only the squalls that do it—it's human negligence and ignorance."

"How so?"

"Well, what we have here is simply a huge mass of hot tropical air impinging on cooler air from the temperate continent and streams of comparatively cold seawater, making a real brew-up, causing these squalls. As we get further to the southwest, so they will increase."

"All these tales about mysterious forces and monsters and beings from out of space—what about them?" asked Al.

"Load of old codswallop, mate. Dreamed up to put the living fear of the sea into little kids and make a lot of money. There ain't no little green men and things that go bump in the night. There's just a lot of people who come out here, in this area of the sea, who have never experienced semi-tropical weather before. They are more accustomed to the steadier, more predictable patterns of the temperate zones. Here this area, this so-

called 'triangle,' is right next to one of the most heavily populated land masses on earth. There's a tremendous amount of
traffic through and over it, though it may not appear so to us,
but remember our horizon is only about six miles right across."

Now that the squall had slouched itself away to the northwest, we resumed our original tack, heading west again.

"So what makes these craft come to grief?" Al demanded.

"Dozy navigation," said I. "People come out here. They get
away from the coldish autumn, the graying skies of the coast,
and they pass through the Gulf Stream. When they reach the
other side of it, there is brilliant, warm sunshine and steady
Trade winds. Out come the sunbathing togs and the li-los. Then
sail is piled on and off they go. Suddenly, with all sail standing
and a bored helmsman (if they don't have an automatic pilot
steering the boat) and everyone else sleeping and relaxing in
the sun, along comes old Harry there"—I gestured with my
thumb at the now disappearing squall—"and before you know
it the boat is sitting upright with her sails flapping in a dead
calm. Everyone shakes their heads and says, 'oh dear what a
nuisance' . . . and then . . . as fast as greased lightning, like the
hammers of hell, the squall wind is upon them and knocks the
boat over flat on its side in the sea so violently that she fills
before you can say 'Jack Robinson' and poor old Jim and Doris
and little Willy and the cat are floundering around in a raging
sea with no lifejackets four hundred miles from land."

"So what's the answer, then? I mean, what about if there are
a lot of these squalls about?" insisted Al.

"The answer is to keep your eyes open all the time. If you
can't avoid a squall on your present tack then for Crissake
change it, and change it while you're still well clear. If you can
aim for the trailing edge of the squall then do so, by all means,
for there's generally a good breeze there, not too strong."

Jerry asked, "What about all these planes that go missing
around here?"

"Hank should know more about that than I," I replied.

"Let's hear your version," offered Hank.

"It seems to be only small planes that go missing. I haven't heard of any commercial aircraft that have gone down around here, at least not lately—in the past good few years. No, it's usually small craft, private and military training planes. Here again you've a lot of people who are accustomed to flying conditions over the continent, with steadier weather in the main. Then they come out here . . . now look. A plane's altimeter . . . what is it? A barometrical instrument, right? It works on air pressure. So there's Charlie Lindbergh flying his Piper Cub away to the islands. Suddenly he's in clouds. He looks at his altimeter and sees that his altitude is rising. He's got no horizon to relate to . . . and he's in the middle of one of those squalls, where the air pressure is low . . . so what does he do? He pushed his joy-stick down and down he goes . . . straight into the North Atlantic . . ."

"But why are there so many ships and planes that went missing with no trace . . . no sign of any wreckage or . . . what's it called . . . floating garbage?" Johnny asked.

"Flotsam. Now look around you, Johnny. Look at the ocean; look at the immensity of it. Imagine trying to see someone who's fallen overboard, for example. Even if they only fell over five minutes ago. Imagine trying to see something the size of a human head and shoulders among those moving hills . . . and then try to imagine searching all the vastness of the ocean for bits of floating wreckage that the currents and wind can carry miles away and disperse like dandelion seeds in a high wind."

"Like looking for a needle in a haystack," suggested Al.

I turned to him, "More like in a cornfield. Look, what it all boils down to is this . . . there are other sea areas like this . . . with evil names that seem to automatically make the landsman shudder: there's the 'Devil Sea,' south of Japan—again, where warm winds blow over cold water near a temperate or cold land mass, again near a highly populated country, again heavily trafficked; there's the Bay of Biscay, though there the notoriety came from the days of square riggers, which, unable to sail into the wind, got themselves trapped in the huge bay, with the wind blowing onshore most of the time and hardly any ports safe for them to enter. But when it comes to another area very similar in weather conditions, such as the Mozambique Channel, for example, off Southeast Africa . . . exactly, almost, the same conditions . . . but who the hell's ever even heard of the Mozambique Channel here where these fairy tales about the triangle are written and read? But the main difference, in fact the only difference between the Mozambique Channel and the so-called Devil's Triangle is that the triangle is slap-bang next to a highly populated country, and so more people venture into it."

"Then you think it's all simply accidents?" asked Hank.

"We can formulate a law, Hank. Call it the Devil's Triangle Law if we like . . . or Jones's Law . . . it's this: 'In any given area, the more humans present in that area, the more the number of accidents likely to occur.' "

Hank laughed and repeated it to himself, "I like that."

"There's an adjunct to the law, Hank," I said, as we made ready to come about again, to avoid another squall ahead.

"Wazzat?"

" 'The more accidents that occur in any given area, the more paranoia-mongers will attempt to bestow supernatural explanations for those accidents on an ever-increasingly gullible section of the population, preferably in the country geographically closest to the given area.' Like I said, it's a load of old codswallop."

"I thought you guys were supposed to be superstitious," queried Johnny.

"Only in the mating season," I told him. "Ever since Voltaire explained that Admiral Byng was not shot for cowardice, but to encourage the other admirals not to be cowards!"

"*Pour encourager les autres,*" Johnny quoted. Bright lad. College.

"I didn't know you spoke French, Johnny," I observed.

"Only in the mating season," he replied, sliding down below.

I leaned forward. "*Touché!*" I shouted.

The rest of the passage to San Juan was in moderate to fresh winds, mostly in sunshine, dodging heavy squalls, tacking east and south the whole time. We spoke with a Greek freighter, but to no one else until we were a hundred miles from San Juan. A radio broadcast from the U.S. Coast Guard reported that another cruising yacht was making distress signals from eighty miles north of the port. She was not really in distress. The navigator had lost his position. We kept a look out for her, sighted her bright strobe light flashing above the heavy seas, radioed a helicopter to her, and then made our way into the dramatic entrance of San Juan harbor, as shipshape if not more so, than when we had left Morehead ten days before. Which is no more nor less than a delivery crew is supposed to do, and I had earned another hundred dollars toward *Sea Dart's* freedom.

Sally Brown had a daughter, Nellie,
Way, hay, roll and go!
Sally Brown had a daughter, Nellie,
Spent my money on Sally Brown!

Sally Brown is a black mulatto,
Way, hay, roll and go!
Sally Brown is a black mulatto,
Spent my money on Sally Brown!

Sally Brown she loves me dearly,
Way, hay, roll and go!
Sally Brown she loves me dearly,
Spent my money on Sally Brown!

No-one knows how I love Sally,
Way, hay, roll and go!
No-one knows how I love Sally,
Spent my money on Sally Brown!

I'll be back to see my Sally,
Way, hay, roll and go!
I'll be back to see my Sally,
Spent my money on Sally Brown!

Sally Brown is waiting for me,
Way, hay, roll and go!
Sally Brown is waiting for me,
Spent my money on Sally Brown!

"SALLY BROWN." THIS IS AN EARLY VERSION OF A CAPSTAN AND WINDLASS
CHANTY, SUNG WHEN HAULING UP THE ANCHOR. LATER VERSES WERE
CHANGED FOR SHORESIDE PUBLICATIONS. THE SECOND VERSE WAS
CHANGED TO "SALLY BROWN WAS A WHITE MAN'S DAUGHTER." THIS IS THE
VERSION MY FIRST SKIPPER, TANSY LEE, BORN IN 1866, USED TO SING. IT'S
PROBABLY THE ORIGINAL ONE. "SALLY BROWN" APPEARS IN A NUMBER OF
CHANTIES INCLUDING "SANTAYANA" AND "JIMMY BOWLINE."

Beautiful People

ANK left us as soon as I'd entered *Star Rider* through Customs into San Juan. He was in a hurry to get back to his business. Al was also anxious to fly on to Jamaica. He left, too, just as quietly as he had come, a silent technician, a quiet American.

Johnny, Jerry, and I remained in San Juan overnight. We wandered through the marina and listened to tales of stirring derring-do from yachtsmen who had also recently arrived, and inspected the damage caused by the weather in the Devil's Triangle—broken bowsprits, broken arms, and broken booms. We rolled our shoulders smugly back to *Star Rider*. She sat as neat and prim as an English nanny. Her high bow made her seem as if she had her nose in the air and was sniffing in disdain at the other boats, as if they were bedraggled female relatives who had somehow strayed into the stables with the groom.

"It's a wonderful feeling to be self-righteous and smug," said I to my two companions, "when you've every reason to be. They tried to avoid the 'triangle' by sailing way out to the east and then down—and they hit the tail end of a weak hurricane. If they'd come straight through the gut of the triangle and did what we did, avoided the squalls, they would have arrived here in good nick."

"Yeah, those dudes shoulda boogied right on down the middle, man," Jerry said. "Man . . . it's hot here!"

"Okay, we'll fuel up, take some water in, and look around town," I replied.

I've always liked San Juan, especially the Old Town. It's lively day and night, it's picturesque, and the locals are friendly. With Johnny and Jerry in tow they were even friendlier. During the early evening we rambled around looking at the old Spanish fortifications around the harbor, and it was all I could do not to bore my crew with accounts of how the fortresses were built to guard South American treasure awaiting the galleon convoys to Europe in the colonial days. I had no need to worry, though. They were both deeply interested.

"Them dudes sure got the loot—they sure knew where to look for *change*, man," concluded Jerry as we headed for a beer. "That's what it's all been about—all that history shit—lookin' for *change*."

I was puzzled. "Change?"

"He means money," said Johnny.

"Bread," added Jerry as we got to the bar. "Tooty-frooty booty-loot pleasuh and treasuh ... yeah!" He bounced his small frame up and down.

"That's dead right," I said, lifting my glass. "Here's to it—and sail!"

"Sail," toasted Johnny.

"I dig it," Jerry said. "Yeah ... I really dig it."

*　　　*　　　*

The harbor entrance of San Juan after dawn was like a backdrop for a scene from *Treasure Island*. The land in the south was misty green hills overhung with dramatic dark gray rainclouds that rolled over the peaks so that the hills looked like they were erupting volcanoes. Nearer, the white houses of the city gleamed almost silver in the morning sun. The ships in the harbor stood out like painted models as their colors reflected the light. On the eastern side of the entrance is the old Spanish fortress of El Morro, huge and shadowy. It was overhung with palm trees bent to the prevailing easterlies, their leaves glistening emerald over the pinky-gray stones of the fortress rooted in black rocks washed by blue, blue water.

As *Star Rider* sailed out of the harbor slowly in the light breeze, Jerry, taking a break from his breakfast cooking, peered fascinated at the scene.

"El Morro—what's that mean, Tristan?" he said.

"The Moor—it's what they used to call Moroccans—or anyone who came from Africa, come to that," I replied.

"Wow . . . cool . . . I gotta goddam castle named after me," Jerry shouted as he descended Jacob's ladder into the depths of the boat. A conch shell sounded from an inward-bound fishing craft. I waved and we were out at sea again, heading north to clear the coast of Puerto Rico, before starting our long beat to windward and St. Thomas.

Star Rider, once out of the shelter of El Morro, started to lift and lower in the scend of the sea. There is nothing else like it. It doesn't matter if a boat has been gathering barnacles in port for a year or has only stayed overnight, as *Star Rider* had done. The feeling of freedom and exhilaration is there as soon as the ship salutes the ocean with her first long resistless heave, as soon as her decks are aslant after the lifeless equilibrium of the harbor; as soon as she shivers and trembles and rolls her hull to the far-echoing tremor of all the limitless miles of moving, restless, rolling ocean.

Now that we were only three onboard, the boat was much less crowded. Johnny had taken on the topside chores, while I had the engine maintenance and running to look after. But now that we were in the Trade wind area, with almost always a breeze of one kind or another, the engine was run only long enough to charge the electric batteries, a mere hour a day.

I mistrust boat engines. The only boats I ever sailed where the engines did not fail were the boats that had no engine. For that reason I always consciously try to sail any boat as if she had no engine. In tropical waters the noise, the heat, and the smell of any engine, diesel or gasoline, is enough to make any sailor swallow the hook. I know that for many people engines are necessary. I know that they increase the efficiency and safety of the average coastal cruising craft by a good 25 percent. I know that they provide electricity for domestic comfort onboard, but I still mistrust those damned iron Judases. It's the only way you can be reasonably sure that they won't let you down at some crucial moment.

I don't mistrust engines, like some sailors, because they don't understand them—I do; at least as well as any average skipper. I can maintain an engine in running order for years and still

mistrust it. They are demanding of time, energy, and sweat;
noisy, smelly, and downright treacherous. The only advantage
to them, apart from perhaps getting a small craft in and out of
port on a windless day, is that they are probably the cause of
practically every new curse word in the English language in
the past one hundred years, especially at sea.

Sails, those outdated (according to many landsmen) "engines" that use God's own wind, are everything that the average
boat engine is not. They are accessible, they are silent, and they
are easily reparable without having to lock oneself into a system
which involves the activities of thousands of other people, most
of whom are no more aware of your needs and existence than
they are of each others'.

"What kind of an engine should I take on a world voyage?"
asked Johnny, as he took over the helm. We had been beating
steadily east, ten miles north of Puerto Rico; all day *Star Rider*
had bounced and spit off the seas from her thrusting bow. It is
a tiring thing, to beat.

"One that's easy to get out of the boat," I said, "and heavy
enough so that when you're on a lee shore in some remote
God-forsaken spot, you can tie it up to a big chain and heave it
over the side as a deadman. It should hold you off the rocks all
right."

Later, when I'd rested, I discussed different types with him,
but I still warned him against putting too much faith in them.

*   *   *

Considering the size of the food allowance from Grindlay, we
ate well enough in *Star Rider*. For lunch Jerry cooked up
chicken and french fries. He had learned well from Hank. In
San Juan he had bought a large live chicken, cheap. As we
fetched up with Vilques Island that late afternoon, he sat on the
poop deck and plucked it, then he stuffed it with broken crack-
ers, onion chopped fine, sage, a handful of rice and a curry paste
which I mixed for him. That night at supper we ate like lords,
as the boat lay hove to, waiting to enter St. Thomas in the
morning. There was no hurry. The wind dropped during the
night. We entered abjectly, under power, so that when Johnny

looked at me I felt like swallowing my unkind words about boats' engines. He grinned at me. I grinned at him.

Soon the litany of a sailing-craft's arrival—the tying of sails, the lagging of sail covers, the coiling and flaking of halyards and sheets, the topping up with fresh water at the jetty, the inflation of the rubber dinghy and the shipping of its outboard motor, the motoring out again to anchor among the hundred other cruising and chartering craft—was done. After the boat was settled at anchor, I ran Johnny over to the airport in the dinghy and said farewell to a good steady lad. One day he will be renowned.

On the way to the airport I had dropped Jerry ashore on the town waterfront to go to the post office to collect any mail that might be waiting for us. "Anything for us?" I hollered as the dinghy bobbed alongside.

"This is for you," he said, handing me a package of letters. "An' I gotta telegram."

"Not bad news, I hope?"

"Yeah, I gotta go home—my mom's sick in the hospital."

I collected enough money for the air-fare back home from Grindlay's credit account at the marina office and handed it to Jerry.

We went back to *Star Rider* in silence. Jerry collected his gear, then I ran him back to the waterfront again. "You'd better leave that telegram with me," I said. "Grindlay's going to be pissed off at paying your air-fare as soon as you get here."

He gave me the telegram. I placed it safely in my pocket.

"Hey, thanks for a real groovy trip, Tristan . . ." he said.

"Thanks for all the good cooking," I said. Then he was gone.

The telegram was genuine enough. So was Jerry's return. He was the only son of a widowed mother in the South Bronx.

Now I was alone again. I settled down to keep *Star Rider* in good order, write some more of *The Incredible Voyage*, and wait for charterers to arrive.

So goes a sailor's life of hellos and goodbyes.

*   *   *

All November and most of December I waited for charterers to turn up. I filled in my days. I cleaned surfaces already spotless, rubbed down and varnished brightwork already so mirror-perfect that it would have taken a brigade of Spartans to drag Narcissus away from any one of them, washed down decks, and scrubbed sails. In the evenings I read or wrote letters and parts of my manuscript. Each week a payment for running expenses, food, and wages arrived from Grindlay and each week I sent most of my pay on to the shippers at home, toward the money I owed them.

To many ocean sailors there are few experiences more frustrating than performing useless chores, expending energy to no apparent purpose. The amount of work that goes on in charter craft simply to tart up the boats is a wonder. I spent hours, days, delicately rubbing down varnished deck-boxes that would have been just as well decorated and a hundred times better protected with two or three good honest coats of paint and a thousand times less work. This is a small example of practicality sacrificed to superficial gloss. When the vessel is at sea, the salt-water that splashes on the deck-boxes leaves a white-brine powder behind that makes the boxes look tatty and immediately attacks the varnish. The most telling disadvantage to this particular practice of varnishing everything is that the sunshine strikes it and sends reflections out strong enough to blind the helmsman or lookout. It's mostly bullshit, to impress the arriving innocents who turn up to pay to be carried around the islands. Varnish freaks say they like to see the wood, but it could be that they like, more, to see themselves.

There were, and I have no doubt still are, many good, honest, capable seamen among the yacht-charter fleet—and especially among the smaller-craft owners. People who genuinely give a good return to the charterers for the fees charged. Some of the smaller-vessel owners were ocean voyagers taking time off from long passages to make some money for the next voyage. There were others, not many, but some, with whom I for one would not cross a water reservoir. These were the ones who are usually to be found with the latest yachting gear, the "in" magazine under their arms, and their caps at a jaunty angle, on the lookout for some unlucky soul to exploit. They're called "jetty-sharks." If they were not looking for someone to give short measure to on charter, they were looking around for some wandering kid to do their skivvy work for a pittance. Some youngster with a dream of sail, sun, wind, and stars who will wind up slaving away in conditions that would make a hotel scullery-hand go pale. An Edwardian household kitchen skivvy would feel absolutely at home in some of the more notorious ships. They were slave-ships of the late twentieth century. And these jetty-sharks have the nerve, the effrontery, to call the kids they exploit "boat-bums"!

There were many good honest folks in well-run vessels in the West Indies charter fleet. There were some who, a century or two ago, would have been hanged, drawn, and quartered. These hell-ships were only few, but they *were* and no amount of bad cess aimed at me from advertising circles will change the fact. The local governments of the West Indies islands, if their concern for human rights is genuine, would do well to look closely at the conditions of employment in the charter-boat industry.

It is not only in the West Indies that this racket goes on. I have known dozens of cases in many areas where these kids work for weeks—really heavy, hard labor—helping to prepare a vessel for sea, for no more payment than perhaps their food and the hope of sailing with her. Then time after time I have seen them callously shoved aside. The days when sailing a boat was thought to be sufficient payment for physically arduous manual jobs of preparing and maintaining a seagoing boat in good order ought to be over. Nobody can live on just fresh air and sunshine. Anyone who gets a job refitting a vessel on the understanding that he or she will sail with the boat should make sure he or she gets a signed contract. Local laws vary, but they all contain provisions for preventing a vessel's departure in case of a civil action.

Real idling is having the freedom to do what you want to do. Enforced idling is damned hard work. After weeks of enforced

idling I was more than fed up. When word arrived from Grindlay that I could pick up people for short charters locally, I was
relieved. Without a local license it was against the regulations,
but once out of American waters, who cared? Anyway, we were
already operating outside the letter of the law, for I myself was
not American and had no American license to carry passengers.
There had been no attempt on my part to obscure this fact—
Grindlay knew it full well.

My first (and only) charterers arrived at Christmas. They were
a newly wed young couple from Chicago who had flown to the
Virgin Islands on speculation of finding a boat to sail them
around for a week. Several other people had looked the boat
over, but they had found her so awkward and uncomfortable
down below that they had turned her down. I couldn't blame
them.

Mr. and Mrs. Newlywed were delighted at their find. The fee
was, they thought, reasonable and they evidently found my
company suitable. I had luckily found a young woman to do the
cooking at a fair wage, and off we went, early on Christmas
morning, scooting off under all sail for the British Virgins. It
was glorious to be under way again, and with such friendly folk.
"Mainsheet Annie," the cook, was a little blond lass from one
of the Dakotas. She was a marvel, not only in the galley, either.
She was a natural born sailor, as quick and light on her feet and
strong in her arms as any tar-bucketed salt I ever clapped my
eyes on.

Annie was twenty and what the Americans call "cute." She
was also very intelligent. Her face went into rapture when *Star
Rider* was under sail, that aware rapture, when as well as shar-
ing the dream of sail you feel everything, every little nuance of
movement onboard the boat. Annie was also good company.
She had knocked around on quite a few charter craft and was
full of stories of the people she had met.

Annie was more than eager to go ocean sailing. Later, when
she took off on a "pier-head" jump with a couple of shifty-
looking characters, I begged her not to go. I pleaded with her,
but the pull of the long trail was too strong for such an indepen-

dent-willed descendent of pioneers and she sailed off to Panama with two wily-looking sprucers. Ever since, I have wondered what became of her; if she managed, as she maintained she would, to "hold her own" with those two birds of passage.

"I hope so, Annie, I hope so, or if not, I hope that I meet up with these blokes. The world of sailing is small. Our bows may yet cross," I told her.

Annie promised to write me, but I have not since had word from her.

When we took off from St. Thomas on that day in December, *Star Rider* seemed to know that she had blithe spirits onboard. She fairly leapt through the almost flat seas of the Drake Passage, and, after weeks of morbid immobility, she lived again, and joyfully curved her wake from one calm anchorage to another, until it was time for our return on New Year's Eve.

Star Rider was at anchor in Jost Van Dyke, one of the tiniest and friendliest of the British Virgins (and that is saying something). A hundred and more other boats, cruisers, and charterers had arrived for New Year's celebrations. All around us there was the noise of cheery celebration and jollity and merrymakers heading for Foxy's Bar on the beach. I've never been much of a one for crowds and noise, but as I made my way forward to haul up the anchor I turned around to see the Newlyweds watching everything with sadness in their eyes.

I reflected to myself, "*The hell with it—what a way to end a honeymoon—sleeping ashore in crowded St. Thomas.*" I went over to Mr. Newlywed.

"We're not sailing today," I said.

Mr. Newlywed's face lit up. "Why not?" Mrs. Newlywed's eyes danced.

"It's bad luck to sail on New Year's Eve," I lied. "I'll run you over to *Maria* for supper—my mate Mike McMineman invited us over—if we don't sail—we'll head back for St. Thomas tomorrow."

Mr. and Mrs. Newlywed were so overjoyed they both hugged me. I knew that *Star Rider* was grinning to herself beneath my feet, just as Mainsheet Annie was doing in the galley, where she was busy fixing up a cocktail.

When we got back to St. Thomas we were all so reluctant to go back to anchor that we sailed her for a couple of hours inside the harbor, whizzing around the anchored boats under full sail, making her weave and dance the sail ballet on all points of the wind, to the music of the southeaster in her shrouds, because I loved her and Mainsheet Annie loved her and the Newlyweds loved her and we all loved each other and she knew it and we knew it and the wind itself knew it.

* * *

A New York publisher's editor—let's call him Mr. Geelunker —sought me out in early January. He knew of me through some of my stories published in *Sail* magazine. When I told him I was halfway through writing a book and showed him some of the pages, he seemed more than interested. He gave me his card. "I can't take the manuscript with me—I'm on my way to catch a plane right now, but you make sure when you get back to New York you come see me," he said.

"Right, I'll do that, Mr. Geelunker," I said.

As he walked away with his friends along the jetty, I watched him, and there was music in my ears as the heavens opened up with the grand march from *Aïda*. *"Thus are authors—book authors—brought to life,"* I thought. Now the road to *Sea Dart*'s freedom was delineated.

* * *

Grindlay showed up a month later.

"I'm not in the goddam charity business," he fulminated as we walked along the marina jetty. "That's twenny-four extra hours these people had, and not a goddam cent to show for it . . ."

He ranted on and on. I let him, until he quieted down. Then I said to him, "Do you still want me to skipper *Star Rider* or not?"

"Sure I do . . . she's in beautiful order . . . not a scratch on her . . . sure I do." He was quiet for a minute as two charter-boat crew passed us in the hot sunshine. They were drinking beer from a can. Then he said, "That's one thing I never want to see or hear of you doing, Captain."

I was puzzled. "What's that?" I said.

"Drinking beer out in public, in front of the other boats, walking along the jetty," he replied.

That did it.

"Mr. Grindlay," I said, "I like . . . I love *Star Rider* . . . almost as much as I love my own boat . . . but you can stick your job. . . . You don't need a skipper, what you need is a bloody chauffeur!"

Grindlay must have been fishing for a showdown and a parting of the ways; at least he was prepared for it. As I moved my gear off *Star Rider* an hour later, a very young couple were waiting to move onboard. They looked pleasant enough. I didn't speak to them, because I thought that in the circumstances it would be best to hold my peace, but I silently wished them luck.

They piled *Star Rider* onto the shore off Cape Henry a few months later. She was pounded and became a total loss.

But each New Year I receive a card from Chicago, and so *Star Rider* still lives.

*   *   *

I looked for another boat to skipper, but it was far too early to deliver any back to the States, and all the charter vessels already had skippers. The only vacancy was onboard a large schooner wearing the Panama flag. Her owner, a balding, sunbronzed man of about fifty, was looking for a skipper. I went onboard to apply. The owner turned out to be Colombian. The vessel was immaculately rigged with every modern device, especially radar, of which she had two sets, and two eight-hundred-horsepower diesels. This, with the appearance of the crew, five very canny-looking Colombians and three silent Americans, and the strange feeling of the boat, was enough for me. If you eat with the devil you sup with a long spoon, and I wanted nothing to do with running what they were probably running.

"But the pay is five hundred a week," said the Señor.

"Sorry."

"But why not? You are just right, you speak Spanish . . ."

"I just don't like schooners, Señor."

"That's ridiculous, just because you don't like the sails," he protested, "and we have very good, strong engines . . ."

"I don't like schooners . . . They always remind me of biscuit-boxes and tea-caddys." (Not true, but better to be considered crazy than suspicious.)

"You crazy!" the Señor shouted as I headed over his gangway.

When I had walked off *Star Rider* I had just sent some more money to the shippers in England, to pay for *Sea Dart*'s passage home from South America. When I flew back to New York I was much richer than when I had arrived there last time. Now I had a hundred dollars.

*   *   *

At JFK airport I excitedly phoned the publisher's office. A female voice said "Mr. Geelunker? . . . Sorry, he left the company last week. This is his assistant, Mzz Spielhummer. Look, he told me about you . . . bring the typescript around on Monday."

Shaq'd

To lay aloft in a howling breeze
May tickle a landsman's taste,
But the happiest hour a sailor sees
Is when he's down at an inland town,
With his Nancy on his knees, yeo-ho!
And his arm around her waist!
Then man the capstan—off we go,
As the fiddler swings us round,
With a yeo heave—ho,
And a rum below,
Hurrah for the homeward bound!

FROM "A WAND'RING MINSTREL I," *The Mikado*,
W. S. GILBERT

O Stormalong is dead and gone;
To my way, you Stormalong!
O Stormy was a good old man,
Ay, ay, ay, Mister Stormalong!

We'll dig his grave with a silver spade,
To my way, you Stormalong!
And lower him down with a silver
chain,
Ay, ay, ay, Mister Stormalong!

O Stormy's dead and gone to rest,
To my way, you Stormalong!
Of all the sailors he was best,
Ay, ay, ay, Mister Stormalong!

"STORMALONG." A LEGENDARY CHARACTER, LIKE THE FLYING DUTCHMAN
AND REUBEN RANZO, STORMALONG APPEARS IN A HALF-DOZEN CHANTIES.
HE SEEMS TO HAVE BEEN A TOUGH, GAME OLD BIRD IN HIS DAY. THIS
WINDLASS CHANTY COMES FROM THE 1840S.

Adrift

As I replaced the phone on its hook I stared around me at the JFK airport lounge for a minute, trying to get my bearings. Then I slung the duffel bag and yellow oilskin over my shoulder, headed for the airport cafeteria, and thought things out over a cup of tea and a hot dog.

There are six vital necessities for survival ashore. At sea there is a seventh, which takes precedence over all the others, because life itself depends on it. This is to keep the boat afloat.

If sailors at times seem a little casual about all the other six basic necessities for shoreside survival, it is mainly because they have the habit of not considering them to be the most vital of all considerations. When sailors are ashore, free for a spell of the continual responsibility for the well-being of their vessel, they may take on an air of irresponsibility, but that is because at sea their sense of values is arranged differently than the landsmen's. It takes time to fall into the ways of the land. Some mariners never do.

The average sailor is a man of a seemingly blunt directness. He has a way of getting "down to brass tacks" that is missing among the majority of landsmen. The seaman's ways are not the ways of the landsmen, who are, whatever their circumstances, far more sheltered than he. The landsmen's morals are not necessarily his, nor are their beliefs. To the sailor the greatest crime is disloyalty, whether to his vessel or to his mates. But if the sheltered landsmen's ideas on politics or religion sound a mite weak and watery to him out at sea, and their litanies and catechisms, manifestos and *pronunciamientos* read a little hollow, he is at rock-bottom no less a religious man, no less socially conscious, and probably no worse a man either.

The mariner's overriding essential, in my case, simply meant paying *Sea Dart*'s debts and getting her away from Britain. If I could sell my half-finished book, this might do the trick. It was a long shot, but what's one more long shot in a life full of them?

To take care of the prime essential, I would have to look after the six basic needs of shoreside survival in their order of priority.

The first three vitals ashore are food in your belly, clothes on your back, and a roof over your head. In some climates the latter two don't matter all that much, but in New York City in February they matter a great deal.

Food is crucial no matter where you are, and when the survival chips are down ashore it must always be your first consideration. I knew that I could keep my food bill well down by eating at cheap places or buying a loaf of bread and feeding myself. It was possible, I knew from the previous year's experience, to sustain myself for a dollar a day. It wouldn't be Olympics training diet, but it would keep me alive, and it would be no worse than the fare I had survived on, sometimes for months, in the past.

As I munched my hot dog I reflected on how food is all things to all men. Like everything else that is vital to survival, there is no definitive authority on food. No matter whether you're rich or poor, food is a problem that you have to solve in your own way. The only conclusion that I ever came to about right and wrong foods was that hunger for food is the best appetizer and the worst aphrodisiac. The only conclusion that I ever came to about the *supply* of food is that it is as vital to us as is the supply of air and water. Food should not be a commodity to be bought and sold like things that are not basic to human survival. Anything that causes an obstruction to the flow of enough food to anyone on earth should be eliminated . . . phased out.

There's nothing like the prospect of the living death of hunger to bring out the real "anarcho-Socialist-Conservative" in a man. If you want to meet an irreconcilable human being meet a hungry one. If you want to see and hear and read poets, feed them roast beef and lodge them in Bloomsbury, Hampstead, or the Village.

I scoffed down the remains of the hot dog and thought about the other necessities for shoreside life.

Clothes—I was not badly off. I had a spare pair of patched jeans, two pairs of socks, and three T shirts, which, if the cold got to me, I could pile one on top of the other under my jersey and so keep reasonably warm. My footwear, thin canvas deck-shoes, was my only real concern in this area, but it would have to do for the time being.

The roof I would have to look for. A cheap hotel to start off with, down in Greenwich Village, where my paint-bespattered jeans would, I thought, not stick out like a collar-bone fracture.

The fourth essential, money, was tied up with the first, and meant trying to earn it by writing. With my visa I could do nothing else.

The fifth essential, social intercourse, would, if my past sojourns ashore were anything to go by, look after itself.

The sixth, the reciprocation of love, was, at my age, more of a luxury. It would not be essential, but if it came along it might help. This is the one great advantage that age has over youth when it comes down to survival—the need for recognition at fifty is not, or should not be, as strong as at twenty. But perhaps for landsmen it is different. Perhaps I had found one of the rare advantages that sailors have over them.

I headed for the bus to the subway and Manhattan.

*   *   *

The Duke Hotel on Jefferson Place had three things going for it. It was reasonably priced—seven dollars a night—it was close by to several inexpensive eateries, and it was in Greenwich Village. That it was fixed up like a prison mattered little to me—at least once I was past the bullet-proofed windowed doors that were remotely controlled by the guard-receptionist.

The daytime guard was small and thin and nasty. He almost always had a grin on his face, but this was deceptive. He was a mean little bastard with a high piping voice.

"Yapaifuhduhnite?"

"What?" I had checked in with him only an hour before.

"Wazzamatta—you on a trip or sump'n?"

"Sorry." I bent down so I could hear him clearly through the grill.

"I said yapaidfuhdanite?!" Nasty's blue eyes glared at me.

"Oh . . . yes . . . I'm paid up for three days."

Nasty glared at me. *Zzzzzz!* The electric door-lock opened and I was out again in the street. Nasty's attitude was not surprising, considering his attitude to the people he had to deal with much of the time: prostitutes just arrived in town and looking for a pad or "resting" (the Duke did not allow them to work there); drug-dealers and pushers, black, bronze, and white, usually well dressed, in their teens and twenties; and middle-aged white men in worn suits who went out the picture of quiet sobriety and returned a few hours later muttering and staggering. There were also two or three elderly couples who seemed to live in the Duke, but they kept themselves very much to themselves, coming and going silently like ghosts from the past. They had a European look about them. They reminded me of refugees I had seen decades before, in London and Tangier. Their faces and their clothes had the same look about them, as those others long ago; clean, tidy, of good fabrication, worn, and infinitely sad. I did overhear one pair talking to each other in the soft-sounding German of Austria. Nasty treated them all the same way.

In Nasty's case his meanness with all and sundry, for no obvious reason, was likely caused, I thought, by his being in a situation that was either beyond or insufficient for his own sense of power. If he had been less arrogant, I would have put the former as the case, but as he was not, then here was a typical frustrated *fuehrer*. "*So to hell with him,*" I thought to myself. "*Anyone who has not the wit nor the will to live his own real life, and yet is not impaired in some way from doing so, deserves to feel frustrated.*"

The night porter-guard-receptionist, Joe, was the opposite of Nasty; he was big, ugly, tough, and one of the most politely concerned people I ever met in Manhattan.

" 'Evenin'. Yuh seein' the publisher, Cap'n?"

"No—just been out for a hamburger. He's away—I have to see one of his staff tomorrow."

"There y'are—key number sixty-nine . . . Well, goodnight, Cap'n . . . an' good luck tomorrow!"

In New York, I was later to find great common courtesy in the most surprising surroundings, from some of the most surprising people. Some of it was the kind of courtesy that would be recognized in the finest mansions in England—a "please" or a "thank you" from some of the roughest, most decrepit human beings I have ever met. But there was another kind of courtesy, more by action than by words—and this was the most striking of all. An offer of a drink from a paper-bagged bottle . . . a cigarette, the last in a pack . . . half a sandwich . . . even a hail "Hey, howyadoin'?" Many of the American drifters I met—they came from all over the States—were, in these ways, more courteous than their affluent brothers. It must be as the Turks say, that "the courteous learns his courtesy from the discourteous." Hollywood, with its portrayal of American drifters, is perhaps where they learned their courtesy. The films I'd watched had been the most discourteous of all to them.

Once inside the Duke and safely inside the double-locked door of my ten-foot-by-eight-foot room, I was comfortable, compared to the accommodation I have had for long stretches of my life. There were no windows—it was an inside room—but there was a television set. The TV sound didn't work, but to someone like me, who had lived without TV for so long and who enjoyed the silent films of my childhood so much, that was no great loss. Besides, it was amusing to put my own dialogue into the mouths of the actors. I sat on the bed and for hours did this, sometimes aloud, sometimes laughing fit to split my sides.

The other advantages to my room were that the ceiling was all of fourteen feet above the floor and the room didn't heel over, nor did it bash up and down. It took a couple of nights to become accustomed to not listening for changes in the wind strength or the slap of water on the hull, and I found great difficulty in sleeping more than a couple of hours at a stretch.

Then I would hide my money in my sock and go out for a walk around the block.

"A spokesman for the FBI said there would be no charges in connection with his disappearance ..." the radio informed us.

"Now you take care, Cap'n," Joe said, looking up from the novel he was reading.

"Where shall I take it?"

"Some mean folks out there. Stick to the lighted streets an' don' go in the park ... Where yuh goin' Cap'n?"

"Out for a cup of tea."

"Hey, bring me back a cawfee, huh?"

"Anything else I can get you?"

"Yeah ... ahehmnrienmayo."

"What? I'm sorry ... you'll have to tell me slowly."

Joe grinned. "Yeah, I forgot, you're one o' them Briddishers —I wanna sandwich—you use that word, sandwich, yeah?"

I told Joe about Lord Sandwich stuffing himself on three inches of sliced sirloin stuck in a cottage loaf and having the Hawaiian Islands named after him.

"Yeah, right, well get me a ham sandwich on rye ... yuh know what rye is ... you use rye over there?"

There was a flash in my mind of how the towns of Rye and Sandwich, only forty miles from each other, are so similar. Both are on the southeast coast of England, both are Cinque Ports, both ports are now almost isolated from the sea by the build-up of silt and mud over the centuries. I mentioned this to Joe and then said "and rye, the Americans make whisky out of it."

Joe found this hilarious. He laughed and spluttered for a good five minutes.

"Naw, man, this is bread ... a sandwich, see. Right ..." He frowned, remembering. "Now, what the hell wazzit? Oh yeah, ham 'n' rye 'n' mayo."

"Mayo?"

"Yeah ... mayonnaise."

"Oh, of course ... mayonnaise, right."

"That's Briddish dressin' ain't it ... or is it French?" Joe read a lot during the long night watches.

"Spanish, actually."

"I thought it was from France . . . They got a place . . . Mayenne?"

"No, it's from Port Mahón, in Minorca."

"How the hell it get over here?"

"We were in Minorca for two hundred years. Probably our sailors brought it over."

"Gee, you guys sure get around, huh?"

"Oh, we do a bit. Now, what was it again, Joe?"

"Ahehmnrynmayo."

"Right, got it. Ahehmnrynmayo."

"Yagotit . . . great," said Joe.

I left the hotel pleased. I was making headway with yet another shoreside necessity. I was learning the *language*.

In the three days and nights I was at the Duke Hotel I learned a lot about the American language from Joe.

I can never understand the attitude of people who contend that words don't count—that they are remote from reality, when it is in the words themselves that reality is reflected. To me, Joe's words made the reality of Joe.

As regards my appearance, poorly dressed as I was, I soon found that this was, on the street, a great advantage. I was rarely bothered by pan-handlers or hucksters. Indeed, they seemed to look upon me and treat me as one of their own. I rarely met up with one who was at all threatening or hostile. Most of the others were just disinterested.

It was very cold when I headed at last for the publisher on Monday. On Sixth Avenue a low voice accosted me.

"Hey, Mac . . . gotta cigarette? . . . Thanks . . . Say, ya gotta quarter fer a cawfee? . . . okay . . . hey, you're okay, man . . ."

He was about thirty-five, but with a three-day growth and the effects of several weeks' living rough, he looked sixty.

"Okay . . . see yaround." I tried to sound native, unconcerned.

"Hey . . . wait a minute . . . say, you're *all right*, . . . you're good people. You havin' a hard time?"

"I'm a bit short, my . . ." I grinned at him as I tailed off.

"Naw . . ." He dove into his jacket pocket. "You goin' some-place?"

"Uptown . . . er . . . I'm walking."

He brought out a half-dozen subway tokens. "Here, take a coupla these . . ." he said.

I took them. When you're impoverished you don't even bother about a gift-horse's mouth. Thus it was that I thought I had yet one more necessity for survival in a big city. I thought I blended into the scene. I imagined that, to all appearances, I was one of them. As long as I kept my mouth shut they would not know otherwise.

He looked at the manuscript package under my arm. "You a messenger?" he said.

If in doubt, tell the truth. "No, I'm a writer," I said. "I'm taking this up to a publisher."

"You been published? . . . Hey, that's *all right!*"

"No, not yet, but I'm sort of living in hopes. . . ."

He glanced across the avenue. "Hey, gotta go, bloke," (he had me figured out now—only Americans use the word "bloke" so) "now you take care, yahearme?" He strolled off, leaving me fingering the subway tokens in my pocket. I decided to walk uptown, anyway, but the cold got to my feet through the deck-shoes. I boarded the Independent Subway at Twenty-third Street and arrived in midtown with my toes cozy and warm.

Every person in the world who refuses to believe that the quality of human life on some parts of this planet has not diminished in the past hundred years should ride at least once on the Manhattan subway system. Like many other phenomena in America, only the superlative can be used to try to convey any sense of the noisiest, dirtiest, most crowded, most dangerous (to the more affluent than I), and . . . the most lively and interesting transport system on the face of the earth. Never a dull moment. It is the only place, it seems, where the faces of New Yorkers relax and you have the opportunity to study them as they really are: in all their scared vulnerability, the lone travellers, and, in their paradoxical open-closeness, the groups. That's in the comparatively "safe" hours, the daytime and evening. In the deep night the privilege of being on the Manhattan subway should be reserved for child molesters, wife beaters, necrophiliacs, shrews, and Nazi war criminals. They should be locked in with supplies of junk food and water fed to them at intervals, and be made to travel up and down the IRT for the remainder of their natural lives. The BMT line should be reserved for traitors.

But everything comes to an end, even the purgatory of a New York subway ride, and I washed up, eventually, with a human tide on the fantasy-shores of Rockefeller Plaza, all stone and chrome. It was to me, like walking ashore out of the reeking foc'sle of H.M.S. *Bounty* onto the beach at Tahiti, despite the cold rain and the ice-skaters.

A quick sprint from Rockefeller Center across town a few blocks and I was inside the publisher's building. Acres of glass seemed more to be suspended from the sky than rising up to it. The smooth, silent elevator worked like God's own bosun's chair. The corridors, fifty stories up in the building—seemed to run on and on forever. The reception office, all pastel shades and concealed lights, reminded me of the fabulous Black Cat whorehouse in Tangier.

"Mzz Spielhummer will see you now, Mr. Jones," said the receptionist. She was nothing like the sirens who guarded Cary Grant's office in the movies. She was at least my age and thrice my weight. I picked up my package and, like a man not sure if he was going to execution or to a palace reception, I followed a plaid-skirted, red-haired lass who looked as if she would have been more at home in a Hebridean crofter's cottage. Another half-mile hike and we were in Mzz Spielhummer's own domain. She was small, dark, and looked at me through thick spectacles. At first her stare was daunting, but she flashed a wide smile and bade me sit down.

"Mr. Geelunker has left us, as you know," she said in a monotone. "But we'd like to look over your work and we're hoping you can leave it with us until one of our editors gets around to reading it . . ."

"How long will that take?" I asked her. My spirits hovered.

"Oh . . . I'd say about a month to six weeks. Not too long . . ."

My spirits plunged. I mentally counted my seventy dollars.

". . . actually you're lucky. Usually, if an author doesn't have an agent it takes much, much longer—that is if we decide even to read the book at all . . ."

"Yes . . . but I just haven't had the time to find an agent, and it takes ages for an unpublished author to find one . . . Yes, I suppose I am lucky . . ."

Mzz Spielhummer started to write on a notepad. "Now," she asked, "do you have . . . you *are* staying in New York, Mr. Jones?"

"Yes, at least for a while."

"Do you have an address where we can reach you?"

I gave her the address of the Duke Hotel.

"That's down in Greenwich Village," she commented. "That's a nice area of the city, quite a few of our authors live down there."

I told Mzz Spielhummer to write me care of Joe and, as the croft-lass showed me out, wondered what to do next.

I had a month to six weeks to wait for an answer from the publisher, and seventy dollars to do it with. Then I remembered that I also had some of my Naval pension due . . . twenty-five dollars. I felt better as I walked back downtown. I'd save the subway tokens for more urgent occasions.

I was not too disappointed at the offhanded welcome at the publisher's. I knew instinctively that a great clamor of welcome does not necessarily aid success. It's a bit like when a small-boat voyage starts with masses of people and bands playing Godspeed. It doesn't mean the voyage is going to get any farther than the nearest safe haven, beaten, with the boat in a bloody shambles. That's why I've always made quiet departures and arrivals, at least until then.

My first venture into the book-publishing world, it seemed, would be a slow business. I decided to write something for magazines, when I had found a place to stay, and try to earn some money that way.

When I returned to the hotel there was an official looking letter waiting for me with "O.H.M.S."—On Her Majesty's Ser-

vice—on the envelope. I ripped it open. The British Internal
Revenue Service had levied my pension for taxes due on two
stories sold to magazines in London the previous year.

* * *

"How'dit go?" said Joe that night.

I had already checked out of the Duke before I went to the
publishers.

"A bit rough, Joe. I've got to wait a month or so for a reply."

"So?" he said. "So ya wait a month . . . that's no big deal."

"It is for me. I don't have a lot of money."

"Oh Jeez, right . . . you're Briddish . . . no Welfare checks,
huh?" Joe thought for a moment then he said, "What ya gotta
do, my friend, is head over to the East Side . . . go to the Men's
Shelter . . . Here, I'll write the address for ya . . . They'll tell ya
where ya can find a cheaper hotel . . ."

"Thanks, Joe. I wrote to a couple of friends . . . gave this as a
forwarding address."

"That's okay . . ." A wide, gold-toothed grin cracked his black
face. "G 'luck man . . . have fun, yahearme?"

Outside with my duffel bag, I read the piece of paper which
Joe had given me. "Bowery Mission, 227 Broadway." I'd forgotten to ask Joe for the directions. I stopped a passer-by.

"Excuse me, please, which way is the Bowery?"

He was big, stout, about forty, well wrapped up in a parka, a
black mustache on a pinched face. He passed by without an-
swering.

"Excuse me, please." This time louder, in case he was deaf.

He turned around, momentarily. He scowled. "Ahh . . . get
lahst . . ." he growled and left me with the cloud-covered night
sky, looking up at it stupidly, trying to remember if Gemini was
rising in the east—or the Crab? Leo? Virgo? Leo?—Taurus,
that was it, Taurus with Aldebaran and the Pleiades trailing old
Al in the northeast. Joe had said it was the *East* Side. There
was no glow in the sky, no sign of a star. I walked to a street
sign and got my bearings, then I turned around in the freezing
rain and started to trudge eastward, with my pilgrim's load on
my shoulder, to *get lahst.*

When, in disgrace with fortune and men's eyes,
I all alone beweep my outcast state,
And trouble deaf heaven with my bootless cries,
And look upon myself and curse my fate,
Wishing me like to one more rich in hope,
Featured like him, like him with friends possess'd,
Desiring this man's art and that man's scope,
With what I most enjoy contented least;
Yet in these thoughts myself almost despising,
Haply I think on thee, and then my state,
Like to the lark at break of day arising
From sullen earth, sings hymns at heaven's gate;
    For thy sweet love remember'd such wealth brings,
    That then I scorn to change my state with kings.

SONNET 29, WILLIAM SHAKESPEARE

Heaven's Gate

I LEARNED long ago that when things are at their rock bottom, when there doesn't seem to be much hope or relief, there's always one thing that we can do—go to sleep. I found that this was not as easy ashore, on a cold February night, as it might have been at sea. I had found one advantage that mariners have over landsmen when the chips are down. At sea I could just heave to, as long as the boat was not drifting ashore, and turn in. Here I must walk two miles in the freezing rain.

As I trudged along I thought about suffering. I tried to rationalize it. I came to the conclusion that I wasn't really suffering with the cold, lack of money, food, work, and sleep, but because I had brought this plight onto myself. I had done this because I rebelled against my *real* suffering, which was being parted from *Sea Dart*. So what it boiled down to was that suffering was either having what you didn't want, or not having what you did want. Simplistic, but it's best to be simplistic in the cold rain at 2:00 A.M. Perhaps there was something in all of us which can only be brought out by suffering? It seemed to me, then, that the more I thought about things that are worthwhile, the more I seemed to be looking at one kind of suffering or another. It seemed that all the good promises, all the resolutions, we made about trying to reform ourselves so we would become better people were in the main so much chaff in the wind. It seemed that perhaps only suffering could make us really change deep down, and make us love our neighbors.

I decided, as I always have done when I'm in real trouble, to blow my nose, cough, and take the short-term view of things. Simple—find a warm place to sleep and earn some money. I looked around me, at a thousand windows, some lit, some blank, in a hundred buildings, and I felt better. With all that shelter around there simply had to be somewhere for me.

I thought about what Joe had told me, about taking great care and hiding any money I had, and remembered an old sailor's trick.

There are several reasons for bandaging your hand. The first is because your hand has something wrong with it. The second is if you are alone ashore and looking for company. In Paris, especially. There's nothing like a bandage for arousing Parisian interest and curiosity. In Paris a bloody head-bandage is preferable—it must be a throwback to the days of the guillotine. The third reason is to have somewhere reasonably secure about your person to hide your money on the New York Lower East Side, and it's a lot more comfortable than a Papillon-type rectal suppository, especially if you have a great deal of walking about to do, that is, unless you're accustomed to trotting along with your knees touching.

I had noticed that the attitude of New Yorkers to the walking wounded was quite the reverse of that of the Parisians. New Yorkers tend to shy away from invalids.

Besides being an almost sacrosanct reliquary for the sacred dollar, a bandaged hand has other advantages on the street. It makes you look like a desperado. Street people are wary about a bandaged hand, not knowing if it was caused by accident or by violence, not knowing whether the violence was self-inflicted or directed against someone or something else.

In an all-night drugstore on Eighth Street I bought a bandage. In a convenient dark doorway I tightly wound it around my left hand, with sixty-five dollars tucked safely inside the palm of my hand. I then tucked my remaining three dollars into one of my socks, as petty cash.

Eighth Street is a sort of bridge between the more affluent West Village and the poverty-poxed East Village. It is a main. shopping street and almost always crowded with as mingled an ethnic mix as can be found anywhere in Manhattan—which is to say anywhere on earth. That night, at 3:30 A.M., despite the cold sleet, it was still as busy as many an English High Street at high noon, with people heading in and out of the all-night movie theater and the all-night junk-food joints and the monstrous neon deceptions flashing on and off overhead. There were also quite a few dope-pushers hanging about at the western end; pot, coke, heroin, Quaaludes, Valium—you wanted it, they had it. There was quite a trade going on around the corner of Fifth Avenue, and the pushers looked reasonably content, patient, and prosperous. At the St. Marks end, though, the rain started to really pour down. I made for an all-night greasy spoon. As I approached the welcoming light streaming from the window, a couple—a blond kid and his girl friend—stopped me.

The Kid said, "Hey, man, like this chick is feeling rough . . . ya have fifty cents?"

In the light I saw that the blond kid had a black eye. His hair was long, well over the collar of his denim jacket, which was studded on the chest with small silver stars. He was tall and lanky and I guessed his age at around twenty. There was a pinched look about his face and his eyes were somewhat dreamy. It looked to me like he was suffering from severe lack of sleep.

My glance turned to his girl friend. She was tiny—no more than four foot ten. At first I had thought she was a child of about twelve, but I saw her face peeping out from her damp, long black hair, and realized that she was about the same age as he.

"I'm just going inside for a coffee," I told them. "Join me, if you want. I'm a bit short myself, but it's okay . . ."

The café was almost empty, only two or three customers, and two Greeks behind the counter. I ordered three coffees and we sat down at a side table. I placed my duffel bag securely between my feet.

"Hey, this is cool, man," said the Kid. The woman smiled. The Kid studied my face, sunbronzed, and my gray beard. "You some kinda seaman?" he asked me.

"Used to be . . ." I replied, as one of the Greeks brought the coffees to our table. He was surprisingly friendly and courteous. ". . . I'm hanging around now, looking for a job . . ." I trailed off.

There was silence for a minute. "Ya smoke?" asked the Kid.

"Only cigarettes . . . I'm a drinker," I excused myself. "Whisky . . . when I can get it." This was no place for angels, not at 3:30 A.M.

The Kid smirked. "That's cool," he said. The woman smiled.

"What happened to your eye?" I asked him. "You walk into a door?"

Out of nowhere the woman spoke for the first time. "We're junkies," she said.

"I know," I replied. I didn't—at least I wasn't sure, but I thought it would make them more at ease as if I told them I knew.

"We got into a pushin' match with some Spanish guys down in the Fourth Street subway entrance . . ." the Kid said. "Jeez, this has been a rough night, huh?"

"The pits," murmured the woman. "Sonuvabitch!"

"Rough?" I asked them.

"Yeah," said the woman. "We're on methadone treatment at the meth center on Second Avenue and Twelfth Street. Jeff . . ." she turned a glance at the Kid, "he told them we was goin' back home to Kansas to see my folks. So they gave us ten days' supply of bottles . . ."

"Yeah . . ." the Kid broke in, "but we wasn't goin' to no Kansas, we was goin' to Fourth Street to sell that shit and buy more smack and that's where the Spanish guys were, see. Them crazy dumb bastards! They was drinkin' an' shit on the stairs, see, an' that's where the fuckin' around happened . . . an' the meth bottles fell down the goddam stairs an' all the shit got out—goddam sonuvabitch!" The Kid slapped one fist into the other. "What a bitch! . . . Them crazy spic cocksuckers!"

"Well," I said to the Kid, "you were lucky, they could have used a knife."

The Kid's eyes, light blue, stared at me. "Lookit this," he said. He put his hand inside his open jacket and, holding one flap of the coat open, pulled out a switchblade. "Any goddam motherfucker fucks with me or my chick gets"—he flicked the knife open with an ominous click—*"this!"*

"So what are you going to do now?" I asked them, to defuse the tense air around the table. Through the café window I could see the gray haze of dawn hovering.

"We're goin' back to the goddam meth center. We're gonna tell 'em we got ripped off, see, an' then we're goin' to sell the shit . . . but this time it's gonna be Fourteenth Street!"

"Yeah, Fourteenth and Third," said the woman. "It's rough around there, too, but nobody fucks with Jeff an' stuff on Fourteenth Street."

"You goin' uptown? We'll walk up with you," offered Jeff, standing up. He was, I noticed, wearing good-quality leather boots with a design carved or stamped into them.

"Thanks all the same, but I'm heading down to the Bowery," I said.

"Hell, like that, huh?" said Jeff.

"Yes, like that." I picked up my duffel bag.

"Well so long man . . . thanks for the coffees . . . stay cool!"

They turned right. I watched them walk off arm in arm along the soggy litter-strewn sidewalk. Then I turned left to head down the Bowery just as the rain started to spatter again. Anywhere else it patters—on the Lower East Side it *spatters.* For a moment I was tempted to go back into the café, but one of the Greek counter hands was sweeping the floor. It's depressing to sit in a café void of customers, while the staff are sweeping the floor, so I moved on.

It's a strange thing about danger. You almost never fully comprehend it until after it has passed by, or until it has been overcome. I shivered at the memory of the switchblade knife clicking open and two fanatical light blue eyes, half closed, staring straight at me. I was still, even now, on my own, poker faced. Then I remembered that we only truly fear in other people what we know is inside ourselves, and I felt better. At least the Kid did not attempt to deceive me—and that's a far worse crime, to me, than scaring someone. I dreaded deceit, and yet that in itself is foolish, for the very dread of deceit is deceiving. It tends to make us miss out on experiences and things that can be useful or rewarding to us in the long run.

I had seen both ends and the middle of the scum-infested drug-trade. I had seen the Colombian, Bolivian, and Paraguayan end and the pot-bellied bastards who pay peanuts for the stuff to half-starved Indian cultivators. I had seen the middlemen poncing around in the posh hotels of Bogotá and Cartegena, Lima, and La Paz; I had been onboard the poxy whore-schooner in St. Thomas. Now I had met two of the end products of this chain of mental mutilation. I thought of all the kids—not just those two—all the kids who were born into a world more beautiful than ever they imagine, even under the most beatific influence of the stuff their dreams and nightmares were made of. Kids who should be the inheritors of all the poetry and beauty that man has brought into this already wonderful piece of mechanism that we call Earth. The pedestrian crossing sign flashed across the almost deserted, wet Bowery. The green sign was defective and flashed white. "*Walk . . . Don't walk. Walk . . . Don't walk. White, red. White, red. Flesh, blood. Bone, meat. Bread, wine, left right, left, right. Walk, Don't walk.*"

I walked.

I reflected that I hadn't been forced to spend fifty of my precious cents on the Kid and the woman for the privilege of seeing the end of this vicious process. The woman had been shaking and cold. It was more shrift than those sons of bitches, the whole slew of them, from the poppy fields to the street corner, would ever get from me. If the murder of bodies is cause for life imprisonment, why not murder of the mind? I trudged on—but I no longer felt like a piece of driftwood.

         *   *   *

They were offhandedly helpful at the Men's Shelter. The reception clerk, a thin, wiry man of about thirty, told me that they did not provide accommodations—only food. Breakfast was at 7:00 A.M., I must wait outside the office. "Where can I find a bed?" I asked.

"The best place you can go for a bed," he said, "is the Uncle Sam or the Clover. They had another joint ready, the Majestic, but it's closed down now . . . Here, I'll write the addresses down for you."

"How much do they charge?" I asked, anxiously.

He looked up and replied mechanically. "Two bucks."

"Oh, right, thanks a lot."

The clerk nodded at my duffel bag. "Wouldn't take that there," he said.

"Can I leave it here?"

"We can't take responsibility for it. Against the rules."

"Anywhere else you know where I can leave it . . . perhaps rent a locker?"

The clerk thought for a moment. "Well, there's Grand Central or the Port Authority Bus Terminal . . ."

"Where's that?"

"Forty-second and Eighth."

"How much is a locker there?" I persisted.

The clerk gave a deep sigh and stood up. He opened the door behind him and poked his head through. "Hey, Charlie!" There was a muffled reply.

"There's a guy outhere wantsta know how much is a locker at the Path Terminal!" Again a muffled reply. The clerk turned around and shuffled again into his chair. He was silent for a moment, looking at his counter. Then he looked up at me. "Fifty cents a day," he said, quietly.

I decided right away to see if Joe back at the Duke would guard my typewriter and clothes. It was a two-mile walk in the rain, and two miles back to the doss house, but at least my typewriter would be safe. Such are the soul-consuming concerns of the impoverished.

*   *   *

The Men's Mission dining room was bare of any refinement, but clean. Breakfast was surprisingly good. There was corn-flakes, two eggs, and ham. The dining room was crowded by 7:00 A.M. with about a hundred and fifty men of all ages, but mostly over forty. There were as many whites as blacks and

Hispanics and some of them were, at least to my eyes, quite well dressed and obviously looked after themselves. The majority, however, were rigged out in old clothes. Except from the serving, there was no loud racket. The men, those not silent, spoke among each other in muted tones. Being among the first in the door that day, I soon finished my breakfast, my duffel bag clutched between my knees, and was out into the street again with the traffic, in lights-regulated phalanxes, ripping black bandages from the smoking bedrock roaring past. It was cold, but fortified as I was, I stepped out briskly for the Duke Hotel, to get there before Joe went off duty at 9:00 A.M.

"Hey . . . Cap'n . . . howdja makeout?"

"Okay, Joe . . . Look, I've got a couple of hostel addresses here to go to . . . but I can't leave my duffel bag safely there . . ."

"Ya wamme ta . . . ?"

"I was wondering . . ."

"Naw . . . not here. It'll get ripped off. Look, go roundda Julius's bar on West Tenth. Tell Mickey I sencha. He'll look after it for ya; it'll be safe there."

I turned to leave.

"Hey, Cap'n," Joe said. I turned to see him grinning. "Don't forget, man, the old stiff upper lip, huh?"

*　　　*　　　*

The Uncle Sam turned out to be a big Victorian brick building not far from the Men's Mission. It had, in its hey-day, been a medium-class full-blown hotel. Now it had the air of being—not just condemned—damned. It was a doss house and it did not pretend to be anything else. Inside the seedy reception hall about twenty men sat or stood around aimlessly. The elevator was broken down, "under repare," according to the cardboard sign hung over the door. The carpet on the stairway was so worn that it was like walking over hemp. Upstairs, many of the walls that had once separated rooms had been removed; now there were several big dormitories, each crowded with single beds so that there was only eighteen inches of walkway between them. The man who showed me the dormitory was short,

bald, fat, and friendly. He wore overalls over his shirt, and
sneakers. He was about forty-five.

"Ya'll be okay here, mister, only ya can't come in ta sleep
until eight o'clock—say, where ya from . . . you a seaman or
sump'n?" Without waiting for me to reply he glanced at my
bandaged hand. "Ya had an accident or sump'n?"

"Muscle strain," I said.

"No kidding? Whaddaya do?"

"Typing," I said. I told the Cleaner about the articles and
short stories I had written. He looked at me doubtfully. I pulled
out one of the stories from *Sail* magazine which was in my back
jeans pocket. It was dirty and frayed, but it did the trick. The
Cleaner's eyes brightened.

He invited me to the janitor's room for "cawfee."

"I'm the cleaner here," he said, as we sat down at a plastic-
topped table. He switched off the radio.

"As you can see by this li'l six-pointed star around my neck"
—he pulled out a little silver pendant from his shirt—"I'm Jewish."

I told the Cleaner that I had been in Israel. He was excited
and I spent half an hour telling him of the places I'd seen and
the people I had met. When I paused the Cleaner was silent for
a while, then he said, "I suppose you're wondering what a guy
like me is doin' in here?"

"Well, I thought you were working here."

"Yeah, butcha know how it is with people over here . . . I
mean with me bein' Jewish . . . Hell, I should be the owner of
the place, they think. I know they think that right away . . ."

"I didn't think that," I said.

"Hey, that's interestin' . . . Why not . . . why didn't ya think I
was the owner?"

"Because you didn't show the slightest embarrassment when
you showed me that bloody barrack-room upstairs."

The Cleaner burst out laughing. Then he confided in me. "I
only been here a coupla months. I was on—*are ya ready for
this?*—Welfare before . . . me on Welfare, oh Jesus."

"What's wrong with that? There's millions on Welfare all over the place," I observed.

"Yeah, but I'm a Jew for Crissake! I gotta family, three kids and a wife."

"So?"

"So look, the stereotype Jew in this country—he's supposed to be goddam successful, see? Not only socially, but financially, see?"

"But if it's a matter of survival . . ." I said.

"Survival nothin', my friend. There's not a Jew in this country who'll settle for that. Sure, during the Holocaust, in Nazi Germany, then it made sense, all this stuff about survival, but here, in *this* country? A Jew talks about survival here an' he's either gotta be kiddin' or he's just plain goddam *poor*. American Jews are supposed to have all that survival crap behind them, right?"

"If you say so." I was getting lost.

"I mean, we're supposed to be in the center of every goddam thing—the news, the theater, the arts, right?"

"I suppose so."

"The way we made it over here," the Cleaner said, frowning, "was by competition, see. If it was brains, we gave 'em brains. If it was money we ran 'em around in circles, if it was muscle" —The Cleaner flexed a chubby arm—"we gave 'em muscle, right?"

"Okay." I was bone-weary after a sleepless night. I wondered to myself if I could remain awake.

"But we ain't supposed to compete for cleanin' jobs, see? I'm not supposed to be cleaning up in this flea-pit. The whole Welfare scene, unemployment, old, sick people, that just ain't a Jewish scene, see? Look at all the guys here—ya look at 'em tonight. Blacks, Puerto Ricans, Greeks, Italians, WASPs, even Japanese, French Canadians . . . Indians . . . and ya won't see one Jew, 'cept me. And all those Jewish big-shots up there, out in Scarsdale, an' Connecticut, it's like they're shoutin' down at me 'Hey what the hell are you doin' cleaning that dump? You're supposed to be out here, wid us!' "

I asked him, "Are you happy? I mean at least you're working."

"Me? . . . I should be happy!"

"I wish I'd known you were here, I've got a typewriter . . ." I told him the morning's story. His eyes lit up.

"Ya gotta book half written, huh?" he said. "Ya bring that typewriter back here, and your paper, and ya write here in the goddam cleanin' room. I can lock your typewriter up in the broom closet at night . . ."

"I can really do that?" I was delighted.

"Sure . . . ain't no goddam *schmuck* ever goin' to say that us Jews didn't encourage the arts!" He stood up to return to his sweeping. "And ya watch some of those bums out there, huh?" he said, as I headed for the door.

"Oh, I expect they're all right," I said.

"All right . . . nothing," the Cleaner retorted. "They're the pits . . . some of 'em. Cut me in for five percent."

I stared at him.

"Ahh, get the hell out and bring that typewriter." His brown eyes gleamed with humor. "I was just kidding ya! Goddam limeys . . . no sensa humor!"

In the best humor for days, I paced the four miles to the West Tenth Street bar and back. I hardly noticed the cold. I had a place to keep my typewriter and a place to write and a place to sleep. America the beautiful; in four hours from homeless wandering around to having a full belly, a bed, and a base to work from. When you're on the bottom, there's only one way—*up.* If I could hang on in the Uncle Sam, I could perhaps earn a few dollars writing for magazines, and if the publisher wanted my book I'd have *Sea Dart* out of trouble in no time at all.

"Only one snag," I thought, as the Cleaner cleared the table back in the Uncle Sam cleaning room. *"Now I'll have to unbandage my hand so I can type."* I went to the men's room and bandaged up my left elbow instead.

"Ya hand better now?" asked the Cleaner.

"Yes, it's a muscle pain—arthritis, it moves about a lot," I told him.

"Yeah? . . . Who's kidding who around here?" he said jocosely.

"You never told me your name . . ." I said to the Cleaner, "or perhaps I forgot it."

He peered at me: "Didn't I tell ya? Hell . . . it's Peter." He paused then he said, "For you, I should be the gatekeeper, huh?"

And not by eastern windows only,
When daylight comes, comes in the light;
In front the sun climbs slow, how slowly!
But westward, look, the land is bright!

FROM *Say Not the Struggle Nought Availeth*, ARTHUR HUGH CLOUGH

Daylight

SLEEPING at the Uncle Sam was not exactly restful. Although we were all frisked at the door each night for bottles, some still got through. All night there was muttering in different corners, coughing, spluttering, wheezing, moaning, a continual going to and from the men's room, the rustle of brown paper bags, the gurgle of "Irish Rose" and the cries of those who even asleep found no peace, no comfort of the spirit.

There were a half-dozen night-ramblers, mostly very old men who found it impossible to sleep. They spent the night creeping around and around the dormitory. They made no noise at all. They put their overcoats over their underclothes and, in the dim light shining from the stair landing, they looked like meditating monks as they silently paced the cloisters of some dim nightmare monastery. One or two, who softly muttered to themselves, seemed to be telling their rosaries, though I knew they were most probably cursing someone or something. I lay awake, wary of them at first, until it was obvious that there was nothing they wanted from me. Still, I made sure my bandaged arm was under my body before I closed my eyes. I felt sorry for the poor souls in the city around me who had no bed that night, who shivered on the streets. The first night I was exhausted, but I slept only in snatches.

There were bed-creaks and moans.

Most people, those who ever give it any thought, must think that men who sleep along the East River, in doorways, on the Bowery have no sex life. It's not quite true. Some of them do, but it is a sex life that would be more common to a boarding school or a reformatory than, perhaps, the bedrooms of the middle classes. Perhaps some of the ten thousand men on the Bowery in 1976 were there because there was no expectation from anyone of love, of affection, of reciprocity from them. Perhaps they had none to give. For most of the street people, though, it was a sexless life—and where sex did exist there was no status-jockeying about it, as there usually is with sex among the more affluent. There were many buddy-partnerships, but they seemed to be matters of mutual respect or protection rather than sex.

"Sonuvabitch, shaddap furcrissake!" A high-pitched voice.

"Who let that bum in here?" A gruff bass. "Fuckin' asshole!"

"Havdrink."

"Ahh, get your goddam ass outta here!"

That there were violent criminals among the men in the dormitory I had, and still have, no doubt. There were probably burglars, muggers, rapists, and possibly a murderer or two. But the need for sleep overcame bodings, fore or after, and fear never yet solved any problem or eased a troubled mind, so I closed one eye, as sailors do, and dozed. I thought it curious that even here there was segregation of sorts, with most of the whites sleeping in one part of the room, and the blacks and Hispanics in the others.

I made up my mind to get a bed on the side of the room, even if it meant bribery. It did—a whole dollar, the next day, to the "room supervisor." This was another name for the "chucker out," a huge bruiser whose earlier function in life was betrayed by two cauliflower ears, a broken nose, and blank eyes. Presumably his present role in the scheme of things was to prevent fights and any other disturbances in the dormitory. This he did by dozing in a chair. I only once saw him give a humanlike reaction—when he took my dollar bill. "Ugg," he said. Thus the origins of privilege and taxation.

* * *

At the shelter the previous morning, I had wondered that all these men had shown up so early for breakfast. I had imagined that one of the attractions of an idle life ashore was lying in bed late. I had noticed that some of them seemed a little unsteady on their feet and many seemed to be groggy. I had put this down to overindulgence. Now I discovered that it was I who had overindulged—in ignorance. The fact of the matter was that many of these people simply did not sleep, unless it was in a drunken stupor. They were caught in a vicious circle. If they made an attempt to resist their craving for liquor, they were kept awake all night by those who didn't. The only way to rest, at all, was to drink themselves into oblivion. At breakfast on the second day I looked at the other men with different eyes. One man—he looked ancient—wore a bicycle inner tube around his neck, like a tie. The valve stuck out in front of him, like a symbol of defiance or, as the Freudians would have it, a tiny phallus.

"Excuse me, please." I almost dropped my plate of scrambled eggs in shock. I hadn't heard those words since I left St. Thomas. I turned my gaze away from the tire bearer. I looked behind me. He was medium height. In one hand he had a battered fedora and a mug of steaming coffee. I had noticed that most of those wearing headgear didn't bother to remove it indoors even at meals. In his other hand was his plate of scrambled eggs and dry bread. Both hands shook violently. He had graying hair, streaked, and steel-rimmed glasses. His overcoat, opened for lack of buttons, was shabby but clean.

He continued, "Would you like my egg? . . . I'm allergic . . . cholesterol, you know."

This could only happen in America. As we sat down at a long table by the wall, he introduced himself in a clear, sonorous voice. ". . . but among my friends here I'm known as the Colonel. They like a bit of rank, you know." He laid his hat down on the bench beside him, and took the two slices of bread off his plate. That done, he reached into his pocket, pulled out a not-too-clean checkered blue and gray—or was it white?—handkerchief and spread it before him on the plastic table top. On the handkerchief he shakily placed his bread. "The Supah back at the Uncle Sam told me that you're some kind of a writah," he said. I guessed his age at about sixty. Later I found he was forty-seven.

"Well, I've written a few short stories and quite a lot of articles."

"What's your field?" the Colonel asked. "I trust you write about life?"

"Oh, mainly sailing and seafaring . . . I was a sailor."

"Ah . . . yes, extraordinary chaps . . . Melville . . . he was a New York Customs Inspector, you know, for many years . . . Conrad . . . imagine, being Polish and writing English so precisely, so deeply . . ." The Colonel, his hands still trembling violently, broke off a chunk of bread and brought it to his mouth.

"I'm curious about your accent, Colonel," I said. "There are so many different ones over here, and I have the British habit of trying to place a person by the sound of his voice. . . . Perhaps it's a mistake . . ."

"Boston, old chap, Boston." He sounded as if it were unimportant. Then he said, "Ah . . . yes, life . . . that's the subject . . . but then I suppose that writing about the sea *is* writing about life, too."

"A lot of landsmen look upon it as escapist writing."

"Ahh my boy, that's because those who have not fully lived tend to denigrate those who have tried to, or who do, live their life to the full. Human natchah." The Colonel managed, somehow, to lift his coffee mug and spill about as much as he sipped. "Dog in the mangah," he said.

My curiosity was roused. "What do you mean, life to the full, Colonel?"

"*Faux pas,* old chap. No such thing. What I really mean is what we think of as life to the full. Life may be wide, high, and handsome, but it is nevah absolutely full . . . nevah quite full. Theah's always something else, energies, activities, deeds . . . all hopefully creative . . . and emotions . . . I suppose they're the mirror of the rest . . ."

"Do you consider your life to be 'what we think of as full'?"

"Of course it is, old chap, of course it is."

"Of what is it full?"

The Colonel pronounced his words slowly and distinctly. "Inertiah my friend . . . Goddamned inertiah."

At that moment we were interrupted by a very hairy, evidently youngish man. On the Bowery, age is the ratio of any specified number of years to the total magnitude of the number of years of those present in any given group counted as one lifetime of 70 years. I did a quick calculation. In the Mission dining hall, I estimated the total number of years lived among the men was something in the region of 6,700, so, though he was 25 anywhere else, here on the Bowery, Hairy was only two weeks old.

"Hey, Coinul, what's doin', man?"

"Ah, Jimmyjo . . . and how are *you* this fine morning?" said the Colonel.

Jimmyjo looked like a U.S. Army sergeant's jacket that had sprouted brownish-red hair. It didn't appear to come down off his head but to have thrust its undeniable growth up through the collar of the khaki jacket and released itself. His beard had never, it seemed, been trimmed or combed or brushed. It rambled all over his face, so that all that you could see of the real Jimmyjo were two bloodshot blue eyes from behind a mass of hair. It was like looking at a debauched Scottie peeping from behind a heaped-up pile of rough string. As he spoke he weaved from side to side like a small sailing craft at anchor in a high wind.

"Hey all right, man, cool," said Jimmyjo as he looked me over. "Who's your buddy, Coinul?"

"Ah . . . this is a British acquaintance of mine, Captain Jones, he's . . ." The Colonel looked at me sideways, grinned, and said in a proprietory voice, "He's staying with us, for a while . . . He's . . . accommodated in the Uncle Sam."

"He workin' Howston wid us?" asked Jimmyjo as he waved at me with a mitt the size of a young porker.

"Ah . . . no," said the Colonel. "I'm afraid my friend . . ." He looked at me sideways again through his steel-rimmed spectacles. Again I was reminded of a schoolteacher ". . . is othahwise engaged."

"He doin' somp'n else . . . What's he doin'?" demanded Jimmyjo.

"The Captain is pursuing a literary endeavah . . . in the Supah's office at the Hostel Uncle Sam," said the Colonel.

"Huh?"

"Ah . . . he's writing a book."

"Aww . . . gee . . . shit . . . well . . . seeya, Coinul, I'm headin' fer Howston . . . Gonna get me some change. Seeya, buddy!" Jimmyjo again waved brusquely at me, made for the crowded doorway, where he pushed his way through a mob of ill-clad men who stood around as if they were waiting for a train that would never arrive.

I said to the Colonel, "Howston?—I always thought it was pronounced Hooston . . . Texas, isn't it? That must be a tremendous journey . . ."

The Colonel burst out in a tittering half-cough half-laugh. "Ah . . . no, my friend . . ." he said eventually, when he had coughed up and spat out half the bread he had eaten only moments earlier. "It's the name of a street—quite neah here, actually. The boys go down theah cleaning the windows of cahs and cabs which stop at the lights, you know. They do quite well, in four or five hours they make . . . oh . . . enough for a bed, a bottle of wine, and perhaps a few cigarettes." The Colonel stood up, or rather he tremblingly pulled himself to his feet. "Actually, I'm off down theah myself . . ." he said. "If you'd like to come along, you'll be welcome. Of course you won't be able to work . . . we're a tight group . . . quite tight, you see, but at least it will be an outing for you?" As he said this his eyes were fixed longingly on someone drinking from a brown paper bag.

"Thanks, Colonel, of course I can't stay down there long . . . I'm trying to write nine thousand words for magazines . . ."

"Ah . . . really?" The Colonel's eyebrows shot up. Then he stared at me for a moment and glowered. "You *do* have a contract, I hope?"

"Not yet. I'm going to write it first, then take it uptown and do the rounds . . ." I said as we ourselves shuffled through the door-throng.

I had never heard anyone ever actually say it before, or at

least never heard anyone pronounce it as it is written, but the Colonel did. "Tut-tut," he said. "My boy—in this country always get something in writing before you put the *featherest* stroke of your pen to papah!" It was the first literary advice I had ever received anywhere.

It was fairly cold out, but much milder than the previous days. The sun shone benignly on the figures of men. They shambled along the Bowery sidewalks and possessively sat on stone doorsteps, or aimlessly wandered through mountainous piles of rubbish on muddy, rain-puddled vacant lots. The Colonel explained, as we passed, the function of each coterie of figures, and how the likely pickings were apportioned off. At the very bottom of the scale were the idle indigent. These were the cripples—the "paraplegics," the Colonel called them, as if a softer sound would soften their sufferings—and those so old and worn out as to be hardly able to move around. They, unless they were military veterans or in receipt of some kind of pension, were looked after, more or less, in varying degrees by the higher orders.

A man in boots, old and filthy, passed us wearing a ragged woman's dress, hat, and coat, singing softly to himself.

The garbage-pickers were fairly well up on the scale, as were the car-window washers, but the *crème de la crème* were the car-park attendants. They could earn extra money letting "street ladies and theah clients" use parked cars for their tricks ("conduct their negotiations," the Colonel called it). "Some of those car attendants earn up to twenty . . . twenty-five dollahs a day," explained the Colonel, then, with a regretful tone in his voice he said, "but, unfortunately, our West Indian friends have rathah sewn up that particular market." Then he looked on the bright side. "That's one advantage that our large American-made cars have—plenty of room inside." We waited for a pedestrian light to change. I watched the Colonel's face, silhouetted, serious, between streets. "I don't know how they'll manage when the foreign-made compacts become even more populah than they already are."

A woman, quite young, black, passed. She seemed to have

elephantiasis. As we passed by each bar, the Colonel told me the hours when they gave away free food, so that for the cost of a beer I would be able to eat, too, and keep my supper cost down to sixty-five cents.

At the corner of Bowery and Houston there was a regular scheme of business activity in progress. On one side of the road was a small flea market where the more presentable of the garbage-pickers' findings—old clothes, small tables, chairs, mirrors, mostly battered and worn beyond belief—were displayed to attract possible customers from among the traffic halted at the lights. As the cars, trucks, and cabs stopped, the Colonel's team all swung into action as the Colonel told me who was who: Jimmyjo; Big Bluey—his name was a mystery to the Colonel, Bluey was ebony black; Hot Shot—he was from Haiti; the Denver Kid—who was cadaver thin and at least sixty-five; and Maximum, barrel-chested, crew-cut. Over the road, empty windows stared like grief-stricken widows.

"Maximum?" I queried the Colonel.

"Ah . . . that's because if one asks him how things are, it's his standahd reply, my boy . . . but don't dare to call him Max . . . He hates that."

On the sidewalk, twenty yards away, a youngish man lay on the curb, moaning.

As I watched this display of American business enterprise and organization in action, the Colonel explained the system. "Ah . . . notice that they never approach the cab-passengehs for . . . funds. It would nevah do, of course, to alienate the cab-drivahs, now would it?"

"S'pose not."

The Colonel's team of window washers seemed to be able to gauge the attitude of drivers right away. If the driver joked, they joked; if he smiled, they smiled; if he was silent, so were they. The operation was like a stage performance: there was music and rhythm to it. The team stood back as the traffic roared past with the lights at green. Then the lights changed to red and the traffic halted. The troupe took command and danced into action, one to each vehicle if there was only a driver and one passenger, but sometimes if there was an out-of-town car with four or more people in it, then two of the team sprang at it, as if to devour it, wiping windows fore and aft. There was an air of circus clowning, yet it was also like watching a surrealistic ballet. Indeed I have seen less graceful movement on stage, less perfectly synchronized, and certainly much less alive. The Colonel stood on the sidewalk, like the ringmaster or choregrapher, and all the while the paper litter on the garbage heap across the road fluttered in the wind like flags and banners, or an audience clapping. All the team members were dressed in rags and dreamed only, probably—though who knows?—of bottles and bottles of plonk, but their performance was not impaired or less eager for that. In between their performances, there was a sort of piety about their patience.

The Colonel commented: "Some of the drivahs can be quite nasty, you know. Theah have been one or two cases where guns have been pulled . . ."

"Guns?" Great monstrous, leviathan-like trucks, spouting oil fumes, roared past us, grinding their gears as if they were cursing.

"Off-duty police officahs," the Colonel shouted over the din, as he pulled a bottle out of his coat pocket.

"Oh."

"The out-of-town tourists are the best prospects, you see, Captain. They pass through heah to the Williamsburg Bridge . . . I suppose they imagine it's some kind of colonial relic . . ."

A middle-aged woman, dirty, loaded down with paper and plastic shopping bags, moved slowly along the sidewalk, singing or moaning to herself. The Colonel took a swig as she went out of earshot.

"How do these people get here, Colonel, I mean all the people at the Shelter . . . how do they travel here? There seem to be men from all over the United States . . ."

"Ah . . . not just the United States, all oveh North Americah," said the Colonel, almost proudly. "Our friends from north *and* south of the border come to visit us quite frequently." He took another swig from his bag.

"How do they do it, do they ride the rails, like they used to?"

The Colonel looked at me as if I were a child. "Ah . . . no, my friend, not at all. Well, I correct myself, very few. No . . . busfares are so very reasonable these days that they—I should say we, for I travel quite an annual distance myself—we ride in style on Greyhound buses along smooth intahstate highways." He thought for a moment. "The intahstate highways were one of the finest things that evah happened for us. For a mere sixty dollahs or so we can cross the whole continent!"

Maximum ambled over onto the sidewalk. "Goddam!" he said.

The Colonel greeted him with, "I trust all is well, Maximum?"

"That mothahfuckin' sonuvabitch . . . goddam Joisey prick!" bellowed Maximum, a pained look on his face. He was big as a bosun's mate, big and tough. Standing by the Colonel, he reminded me of a battleship with a grubtender berthed alongside.

"To whom are you referring?" the Colonel asked him.

"Lousy asshole inut goddam cab wid Joisey plates!" Maximum trained his turrets at a faraway automobile now slowing down for the next set of lights at Houston and First.

"Something amiss, my friend?" said the Colonel. "Not Maximum today?"

"Yeah . . . Maximum pissed." Maximum's voice dropped an octave, "Fuckin' asshole creep let me clean his goddam window 'n' took off 'fore I could get a lousy mothafuckin' dime!"

"Ah . . . well," said the Colonel, "every profession has its hazards."

"Waddafuck you talkin' 'bout, man?" said Maximum. He took a swig from the brown bag that the Colonel was holding out for him. Maximum leaned his crew-cut head back to gargle the wine in his throat. Then he said, quietly, "I hope that Joisey wop mothafuckah's spaghetti breakfast turns into goddam fishhooks an' drags his cocksuckin' guts out next time he shits!"

"You have a point there, Maximum . . . you do have a point," said the Colonel quietly, as if to himself.

"I hope that goddam spic-wop bastard drives off'n the goddam bridge."

"That, too," said the Colonel as he gazed vacantly at the roof of a burned-out building in the distance. After a moment of only screeching, grinding traffic noise, he turned to me.

"Ah . . . Captain, I'd like you to meet my good friend, Maximum."

"Pleased to meet you," I said, as the traffic lights turned to red.

"Yeah," said Maximum. "That fuckin' asshole . . ." He turned and rolled his shoulders over the street, back to work.

I watched the activity on the street for an hour or so, as I listened to the Colonel. He was an erudite man who could, after his first two or three swigs of Irish Rose, quote Shakespeare, Milton, Blake, and Dostoevski by the ream. I had work to do, though, so I reluctantly made my way to the Uncle Sam and the Super's room, passing car after heedless car.

It was much later that I learned from Maximum that the Colonel had been a university professor until 1970, when he had taken to the bottle and the Bowery.

* * *

Writers must have peace and quiet in order to be able to concentrate so they can put their thoughts and remembrances down on paper in a neat, orderly fashion, and bring grammatical order out of the chaos of vaguely related events which are used to relate real life. A writer should be read and not seen. Only ambitious nonentities and mediocrities exhibit their work in the rough. Writers must be secretive and gloomy and doubtful about their work in progress and not discuss it with anyone. Writers must have isolation and a view that will not disturb the creative process as it bubbles up in their minds, preferably a featureless brick wall. Writing is a solitary occupation. Anyone who disturbs the writer is his natural enemy. Writers must be completely alone and uninterrupted and somewhat ferocious with interlopers if they are to do their job properly and get it finished.

Fortunately, at the Uncle Sam hostel, I was unaware of all

this, simply because no one had told me. In a week I had written two drafts of my nine thousand words—three serial articles about some experiences of *The Incredible Voyage.* Most of the time someone was looking over my shoulder and chatting, except when Peter the Super came into the cleaning room, clanging and banging his buckets. Then he took command. "Hey, you guys, for Crissake leave the Capt'n write—can't you see he's tryin' to do some goddam work? Gedda hell outta here . . ." The miscreants fled. Peter came over and picked up the latest typed sheet, full of pencilled corrections and additions.

"Yeah . . . ain't that sump'n?"

"Pressing on," I said, blocking his presence out of my mind.

"An' all wid two fingers, too!"

I stopped rattling away.

Peter said, "Hey, look, I gotta clean up in here . . . Why'nt ya go to the desk for a while . . . Charlie won't mind . . . I told him about ya."

Hardly thinking about it, I automatically picked up my typewriter, my paper, and pencil and moved, like a sleepwalker, into the hall desk space, a cubicle separated from the hallway by a counter. There was no room on the desk, so I put my typewriter on one chair, and, sitting on the other chair, carried on writing. It was still more comfortable than writing in *Sea Dart*'s tiny cabin.

"Wanna bed," a voice whined.

"Okay, write ya name down here," Charlie replied in a monotone.

"Cain't write," said the voice.

Charlie murmured, "What's ya name, mac? I'll write it for you." All the while the radio blared music and song about love and heart and together, and I pecked away at the typewriter keys.

*   *   *

I still had a gift subway token left the next week when I went uptown with my precious brown envelope and logbooks. I alighted at Thirty-fourth Street. It was now early March. I went to the offices of a yachting periodical that aims itself at the affluent and the would-be. The journal had already turned my work down twice—the first time it was a story I had sent them from the Indian Ocean, back in '71, the second, in '74, after *Sea Dart* had worked her way against the Humboldt current off South America for over three thousand miles from Panama to Callao, the smallest recorded vessel ever to do so. The magazine "didn't think their readers would be interested in such far-fetched material" and "didn't find the story suitable for their readership." I thought that if I actually turned up myself with the stuff in hand they might find "close-fetched" material "suitable."

It was soon obvious from the attitude of the gentleman and his two lady assistants who received me that again my story was not thought "quite suitable" for their readership. The gentleman, who looked to me as if he would have been more at home in a duchess's pantry, peered over my precious pages, turning them gingerly, as if he were inspecting lamb chops to see if they were suitable for her ladyship, sighed, and shook his head slowly, half-smiling. The two young women inspected me, became bored, and floated off. It was obvious that again my work was "not suitable"—there was a coffee stain on page fourteen —the result of one of Peter's slaps on the back.

I offered to show the gentleman editor my logbooks. The covers were grubby. His nose wrinkled.

No, it seemed I simply was not up to their standards, social, material, aesthetic, literary, sartorial, and probably moral.

I headed for the street and made for the offices of *Rudder* magazine. I had met the editor, Martin Luray, in the West Indies some weeks before.

"Hi, Tristan." Martin was a short, slight, laconic, decent man. "What can I do for you . . . Say, why don't we go out and have lunch?" He could have done worse offering me the keys to the city.

On the way down in the elevator I told Martin what I was about. In the building foyer, Martin took my envelope, glanced through the typescript for a few minutes, then replaced the sheets of paper in the brown cover.

I waited. I was now down to eighteen dollars, fifteen cents.

Martin said, "We can use those three stories." We started to walk to a nearby café. Above the noise of the traffic in the street, which now, to me, sounded like the Halleluja Chorus and "Land of My Fathers" sung by a Welsh rugby crowd, I heard him say, "I can offer you nine for the whole lot. Three apiece."

"*I must have misheard him,*" I thought. "Ninety dollars?" I cried hopefully.

Martin grinned at me. "No, you dummy—nine *hundred* for the whole series, three hundred apiece! I'll take them now." I gave him the envelope in a daze.

As the music in my head drowned out the traffic roar about my ears I said, "When can I be paid?"

"I'll put a check into the works for you this afternoon—it should be outta the pipeline in about a week. You can come and collect it next Monday."

At lunch in a crowded café I talked with Martin about some of my sea-times, but my mind was only on one thing—getting out of the Uncle Sam to somewhere I could really work to rescue *Sea Dart*.

When I left Martin I was practically singing. So much so that I forgot to ask him for a ten-dollar cash advance. It was now too late to return to *Rudder*. I made the second phone call since I had arrived in New York. Ten cents.

"Mr. Luray?"

"Here . . . that you, Tristan?"

"Yes, I'm wondering if you could make the check out for eight hundred and fifty and give me fifty dollars cash on Monday please?"

"Sure, okay, I'll let my secretary know. Call around about three, okay?"

"Thanks."

I headed for the Duke Hotel. It was too early for Joe to be on duty, but Nasty was civil enough to give me a scribbled note that Joe had left for me.

"Contact me urgent—Hank." I read. There was a phone number. I looked for a phone on Sixth Avenue. I was now potentially affluent enough to be able to put a coin in a slot without imagining how much food or drink it would purchase. I phoned the number, out of town. Thirty-five cents! A full fathom of my lifeline clunked into the void.

"Hey, Tristan, howyadoin'?" Hank sounded excited.

"Oh . . . up and down. How're you, Hank?"

"Listen, Tristan, you get your goddam ass up here next week, yahearme?"

"Where is your place?" I had written a letter to Hank through a flying club address he had given me on *Star Rider*. He gave me the address.

"Hey, now listen carefully," he said. "There was a guy in my restaurant the other day . . . no one will ever believe this, Tris . . . an' he was from Texas an' he'd seen his name on my board-sign down on the goddam highway . . . He's got the same name as me, see? And curious, he came on in for lunch an' things were quiet and I told him I'd sailed with you and the guy is a sailor . . . yaknow, a yachtsman down in Texas, an' he's read somma your stuff. So I was telling him some of those crazy yarns you told me, you know, when you showed me your log-books 'cause I didn't believe you. Well, the guy is a shareholder in a publishing company in Kansas . . . and when he left he said he'd contact the directors . . . Well, one of the directors has been on the phone to me . . . He wants to meet you . . . His name's Jim Andrews and he's very enthusiastic about your god-dam book. When can you come up?"

"Wait a minute, Hank, I've got to think." My mind was reeling.

"Make it Monday."

I was going to collect the *Rudder* check on Monday.

"Tuesday okay?" I said.

"Okay . . . I'll phone Jim Andrews and ask him to make it Thursday but you get up here anyway, okay?"

"Okay. Hank, I'll be there." *"Halleluja, Halleluja!"*

"Right, seeya Toosday," Hank said. The phone clicked. Someone was waiting to use the phone. I staggered away and leaned against a handball-court fence. There were a hundred kids playing basketball. I didn't see one, nor did I hear the traffic on Sixth Avenue.

I sensed by the sun on my right shoulder that it was late afternoon. I stared at the brick wall on the far side of the courtyard. I heard the sounds of the sea, the gannets cry, and saw the wheeling of the petrels, the glide of the albatross, the sail's curve and the bow waves flash and crash, and the billion-starred sparkle of the wake in the night. The old sea gods had not abandoned me. I thought about some stranger from far away having the same name as Hank, driving a route out of his way . . .

"And they call it coincidence," I said to myself, over and over again. *"They call it coincidence."*

I recalled the tiny bird, unidentifiable, that had fluttered so suddenly out of the rainstorm off the Colombian Pacific coast. How *Sea Dart*, battered and tossed herself, had been over three hundred miles out when I picked up the pounding, gray-brown feathered little heart off the deck, where it had fallen. I had wondered how it could have possibly crossed my track out in all that gray wilderness with the clouds shredding apart and the wind moaning and bellowing like a bull being castrated. Was that coincidence, too? As I stared at the basketball court wall, I remembered how the bird had stayed only long enough to peck nervously at my meals and to sleep, a huddled ball of unimportant nothing, on the backstay brace until the following morning, when, as I watched him, he roused himself, fluttered his wings, and flew to his own destiny in the west, away to where the empty horizon was brighter. I had watched the bird until he disappeared, a tiny dot of life. It was as if he had taken part of me with him. Then I had shrugged off thinking about the bird and laid myself to, beating again against the cold, cheerless sadism of the Humboldt current, what, three years ago?

But why a publisher in Kansas City—about as far from the ocean as you can get—right in the very heart of the United States? Why? I decided, as I stared at the courtyard wall, that the answer would come to me, sooner or later. There was a design at work.

Suddenly I turned. The avenue lights were lit. It was night. It was raining. I must have passed a thousand people on my way back to the Uncle Sam. I didn't see them . . . the cold March rain blinded my eyes.

*   *   *

On the following Monday I took my first taxi ride for almost seven years—from Times Square to a bank in the Village. I arrived there only ten minutes before closing time, at 4:00 P.M.

Two hours later I had a room in a three-story walk-up in the Village. The only furniture was an old barber's chair. Black oil had oozed from the hydraulic cylinder all over the floor.

"Eets a ver' good room," said the Puerto Rican building superintendant. "Look . . . water an' everyt'ing." He turned on the tap over a tiny basin near the only door. With a spurt, a groan, and a gurgle, brownish water issued forth. I stared at it for a moment. I was actually having fresh water delivered to me! This was a miracle. No more buckets or jerry cans. No more mile-long rows in a dinghy.

"I don't have a bed," I said to the super. "*Una cama . . . no tengo.*"

He was about five foot six, chubby, with fair hair and blue eyes—the coloring of Galicia . . . distant Celtic relatives. He was dressed in an old gray jacket, a khaki shirt, bib-and-brace overalls, a flat cap, and straw sandals. He looked at me as if he had an excruciating toothache. "Huh . . . *que?*"

"A bed . . . *una cama,*" I explained.

"Ah, ze bed . . . no problen, my frien' "—he broke into a wide smile—"con wiz me." He marched out of the door into the stairway landing. He turned, half-bowed, and gestured like a bull-fighter waving his cape down in front of him. "Con on, I hav'a bed . . . I hav'a verree good bed for you!"

We went down the stairs, out into the courtyard. It was unkempt and littered, surrounded by the backs of other apartment houses. There were a couple of old, broken statuettes, and someone had once made an attempt to cultivate flowers and bushes where now a big motor-bike was parked. We went into a basement boiler-room. Inside, once my eyes became accustomed to the darkness, I saw old furniture piled. On top of all was a single mattress.

"You take," said the super. I passed him fifty cents. "Hokay . . . you slip verree good, eh?" he grinned, showing a fine double set of dentures. I carried the mattress up the stairs and into my abode. Then I borrowed a bucket and some detergent from the super and set to. I scrubbed the floor and the walls. Finished, I stood back and inspected my new home. It was twenty feet long by fifteen feet wide by twelve feet high. It had two windows, a tiny sink, a fireplace, a door, an old dentist's chair, and a mattress. Tomorrow I would fix up a table and a chair from the boiler-room. With these amenities I could write and finish my book. I walked around the room. I looked through the window. I could just see the White Horse tavern along Hudson Street. I tested the door lock. I turned the tap on and off again and again, in wonder. I sat back on the barber's chair and closed my eyes.

For the first time since 1938—since I had left Llangareth in Merionydd thirty-eight years before, I had a home of my own ashore.

*   *   *

I went to the Bowery early next day to collect my typewriter.

"Sock it to 'em, baby!" cried Peter.

"We all wish you the best of luck, Captain," said the Colonel, "for the futah."

"Yeah, give it ta them assholes!" muttered Maximum.

I made my way out into the street, with the Colonel and Maximum close behind me. "Hey, Cap'n," said Maximum, "hey, thanks for the . . ." he bent a closed fist on his wrist and waggled it and his eyebrows up and down. They shuffled off.

"That's okay, see you, fellas!" I walked toward the subway on Houston. I had given the Colonel's gang a dollar each; anything more would have been almost a death sentence on them. As it was, the car-washing was at a halt for the day, so they could celebrate my gains. I felt, for some reason I could not at first fathom, as if I were betraying my friends by leaving them. I thought about it for a moment, then I coughed, sneezed, took the short-term view, and braced myself to visit Hank. Thus the origins of class guilt.

*   *   *

I went to the publisher's uptown, to collect my manuscript.

Mzz Spielhummer was almost apologetic. "No, there wasn't enough time for any of our editors to get around to reading it. Anyway, good luck with it, and keep us in mind if you decide to write another book."

"Yes, sure, Mzz Spielhummer; of course I will."

"Did you have an interesting time in the city, Mr. Jones? It must be wonderful for you, seeing all the sights, Broadway shows, night clubs . . ."

"Oh yes, it's been very interesting, I learned quite a lot."

"Oh, come now, what could you learn in New York, after all those exotic places Mr. Geelunker told me you've been to?"

"Well, I learned one or two things, anyway." I smiled.

"You're leaving us?"

"Just going into the country for a few days to visit friends."

"Have a nice time . . . sorry we couldn't help you more."

"Thanks, I'll do my best."

God's bosun's chair descended as silently and fast as it had ascended. It was crowded and I just managed to figure out what I had learned by the time I was gently shepherded out of the elevator by the small posse of passengers as they rushed out for the building exit.

Alcoholism and probably drug or any other self-damaging addiction is a symptom of total rejection, conscious or subconscious, of values as they are sold to you or forced upon you. Alcoholism or addiction of any other kind are acts of defiance, but they are futile, because they are self-destructive. In this world the only real act of defiance can be in art expressed. Any art—even if it's only knocking a nail into a piece of wood, just as long as you are satisfied that it is what you have done your-self. Any art—even if it is only a prayer. And should the addic-tion persist after the cause of it is clearly recognized, then it is nothing more than a symptom of weakness . . . human weakness caused by fear. Fear caused by not realizing that fear is only the netherside of intelligence.

The lights turned green. I walked. Midtown Manhattan was crowded. On my way to the subway I thought of the Tate Gal-lery and the English fields of Kent. *"Was it only seven months ago?"*

On My Way Rejoicing

A wand'ring minstrel I—
A thing of shreds, and patches,
Of ballads, songs and snatches,
And dreamy lullaby . . .

. . . And dreamy lullaby!

FROM "A WAND'RING MINSTREL I," *The Mikado,*
W. S. GILBERT

I hear America singing, the varied carols I hear,
Those of the mechanics, each one singing his as it should be blithe and
    strong,
The carpenter singing his as he measures his plank or beam,
The mason singing his as he makes ready for work, or leaves off work,
The boatman singing what belongs to him in his boat, the deckhand singing
    on the steamboat deck,
The shoemaker singing as he sits on his bench, the hatter singing as he
    stands,
The woodcutter's song, the ploughboy's on his way in the morning, or at
    noon intermissions or at sundown,
The delicious singing of the mother, or of the young wife at work, or of the
    girl sewing or washing,
Each singing what belongs to him or her and to no-one else,
The day what belongs to the day—at night a party of young fellows, robust,
    friendly,
Singing with open mouths their strong melodious songs.

FROM "LEAVES OF GRASS," WALT WHITMAN. AT ONE TIME WHITMAN
PEDDLED HIS POEMS FROM A HANDCART ON EIGHTH STREET, SIXTH
AVENUE, AND SHERIDAN SQUARE.

Voices and Vectors

PASSING from the Bowery to Outurb was more of a cul-
ture-shock than had been shifting from the Virgin Islands
to the Bowery. In the Virgins I had still been in a loosely
knit shore-world of people who lived fairly close together and
who walked about, and who, in many cases, greeted each other
on the street. It was the same, though in a different way, in the
Bowery and the Village. It had been the same in most of the
ports of the world. This was the first time I had been inland in
the United States.

In Outurb everything was geographically spread apart—the
houses, the amenities such as the shops, the post office, the
library, the movie houses, the bars and eateries; and so, it follows, the people.

There was a tremendous sense of limitless space stretching
on and on into infinity. Yet it was not the sense of space that I
felt at sea, where I knew that conditions anywhere else might
be completely different than the spot I occupied. It was not the
same as being in the countryside elsewhere, where the land
seems to be anchored to the center of the world. Here I got the
impression that the land was only a few feet deep and almost
sinking under the weight of everything that man has put on it,
because everything above ground in Outurb looked much heav-
ier than the same thing would have done anywhere else. Everything was either big and moving, or big and squatting. The land
seemed *temporary*.

The scenery, in early March, was superb. The trees were
budding and the sun shone on the New York City reservoirs. As
I passed them I looked for likely boat havens along the banks.
Hank's hospitality was generous, the meals superb, the company civilized, but I soon knew that I could not stay in a place

that so heavily depended on the car. Public transport was very infrequent, and I could not impose on Hank or his family to drive six or seven miles into "town" every time I needed some stationery or stamps, or to send a letter or buy a typewriter ribbon. At least that's the excuse I made. The truth was that I also missed the energy in the city. For me to write, absorbing energy is a must. At sea, energy flows out of me; in the city, it flows into me from outside, from all the millions of souls around me, until it flows out into my work. In the country I sensed no flow of energy at all. I enjoyed looking at the grass and the trees and the sky, but it was, for me, a sterile enjoyment. In any case, I disliked cars. I realized that for some they were vital, but I dislike what they do to a lot of the people that drive them and what they do to the world around them. But this was 1976, and when I told the folks in Outurb what I thought—that the days of the tyranny of the automobile would come to an end in the next two decades, and that I couldn't wait for the day, they smiled at me and probably thought I was "quaint."

I was amazed, time and time again, at the way people's nature changed as soon as they got behind the wheel of a car. I was astonished, driving around Outurb with Hank, that parking space, in this land of limitless space, could cause so much anxiety, competition, and downright enmity. I tried to imagine how much human energy and emotion were being wasted at any given moment throughout the modern world in placing metal boxes on wheels over lumps of concrete.

The waste—the sheer amount of waste all around—but here I am not going to comment. That must have been observed and written about by people before me, and they came from lands that were already, to seamen's eyes, pretty wasteful themselves. Suffice it to say that the average Outurb household threw away more in a week than the average household in many parts of the globe uses in a year, I would guess. This is not a criticism— quite the reverse. For a castaway sailor, American suburban and city streets are lands flowing with milk and honey; the landscape burgeoned with largesse.

Preoccupied, I met with and signed the contract with Jim

Andrews, squared up, made my excuses to Hank, his family and friends, and returned to Manhattan.

In three days I had a room full of furniture—all off the street. I found a table—it had only three legs, but when it was jammed against the window-frame it held up well; an armchair—its upholstery was a bit tatty, but who looks at a chair back when he's sitting on it?—and an old rusty electric boiling ring that I soon fixed up, so I could make my own tea and cook a meal each day. Then I heaved the barber's chair out for any needy person to pick up off the street, set my battered old typewriter on the steady table from the boiler-house, and set to work, to do what I had returned to New York to do—write *The Incredible Voyage* and earn the money to free *Sea Dart*. Now I was no longer stranded ashore—now I was *based* ashore.

As soon as I had returned to New York with a three-thousand-dollar advance on the book, I paid off all the money I owed the shipping company for *Sea Dart*'s transportation from South America to England, for storage, and for insurance. This came to $1,323.00. I still paid nothing to them for the Customs tax.

There's an old Royal Navy saying—"If in danger or in doubt, sort the biggest bastard out"—in other words, aim for the top. In my bare room I sat down on the shaky chair and wrote a letter to Prince Philip. He was the admiral of the Royal Naval Sailing Association, of which I was (and am, at least until now) a proud member.

To His Royal Highness Prince Philip, KG, PC, KT, OM, GBE,
Sir,
You may recall that I last wrote to you from Lake Titicaca . . .

That done, I mailed the letter and got down to writing the book.

What to put into the book was not a difficult problem for me —the puzzle was what could be left out. In *The Incredible Voyage*, to have written about *all* I had seen and experienced in the six years would have been impossible to do in less than a million words. As it was, I cut it down to 120,000, written in three drafts. This took nine months of steady work, writing about twelve hours a day, every day.

The only day I took off was July Fourth—Independence Day. Then I went down to the West Side piers and watched the sailing ships of nine different nations wend their way up the river Hudson, and saw and felt how the power of their presence was transmitted to the thousands of city folk who watched them, and sensed the wave of goodwill pass through the throng like an electric shock as *Eagle* led the fleet majestically upstream. I watched, fascinated, hard hustlers' and cops' faces change and soften as the sailing ships passed by, and how people practically wept for joy to see the beautiful symbols of honest, clean, silent power send their bow waves rippling under the rusty, worm-eaten piers on the waterfront. I was a silent witness, and yet I knew that the proud bond I felt with those ships was felt, partly, perhaps in the main unconsciously, by everyone who was watching. I felt that they all knew, somehow, that sail and sailors had affected their destinies, and the destiny of their country, deeper than was evident in the hustle-bustle of their everyday lives. I tried to imagine how many of them knew that sail was making ready to come back into its own again—that plans were already afoot to launch three cargo sailing ships in 1979, and that by the end of the century there would be dozens of them plying the oceans? Probably very few of them.

As the great sailing ships moved slowly upstream, it was as if they were benignly displaying themselves to the crowds of people and the great city. It was as if they were saying, "Look how graceful we are, and clean, and beautiful—and think of where we come from, the sea. The boundless sea into which you pour your filthy waste. The sea, of which the fear-peddlers among you would have you afraid. The sea, which, should you choose, could give you and your descendants all the power you will ever need, and give it freely, from her tides, her waves, and her salt. If some of you sneer and say that we are anachronisms, that we are slow and inefficient, how is it that we are here, a score of us big ships and a hundred smaller sisters from every quarter of the globe, all gathered here on one day, in one harbor, to salute you, America?"

There was a gasp from the crowd as the sun broke through a cloud and the sails of the mighty ships quivered and shone. They said, "See how we can range the ocean roads and leave none of the muck and grime that you pour into the air, none of the oil, none of the coal, none of the nuclear danger. See what the sea offers you. See what we represent, here, before your eyes! And see how, when man works in accordance with nature, he creates beauty! You want food as well as power?—go talk to the farmers, tell them about sea-barley, which can thrive on salt-water! Tell them of cordgrass and orach, lamb's quarter and mallow!"

The sun was now behind the spars and sails, which moved in stately silhouettes, now downstream. "But most of all," they said, "think of how our beauty and grace was created by those who designed us, who built us, and who sail us, and think of love and loyalty and know for what you hunger!"

*   *   *

All summer and fall I worked in my room. When I went out I went out alone. I avoided the company of other writers. This was a kind of instinct. I felt they might obscure my view of the city, and perhaps in some way prevent me hearing some voices in New York clearly. It didn't make sense at the time. It's just beginning to now. New York is so vast—so varied, that it would take ten years to even know the surface currents—and by then they would have changed completely. You can only know them first hand.

Sometimes, if the work was getting me down, I took an hour off in the early afternoon to go to Julius's, one of the local bars just up the street, and seek out my good friend Saratoga. Julius's was the first bar (I was told) to open up in Manhattan after Prohibition was repealed in 1934. It looked as if it had never been cleaned above shoulder level since. It brought to my mind memories of the famous old Dirty Dick's public house, near Liverpool Street Station in London.

There was sawdust on the floor, and the bartender, Mick, was friendly and interesting to talk with.

Along the bottom of the bar was a brass footrail in the shape of a line of dachshunds. These had, over the years, been well stomped on and rubbed over by many famous, infamous, and aspiring literary feet.

Saratoga was a short, slight man with a craggy city face of Italian cast. He was about sixty, with curly hair, brown eyes, an infectious grin, and only one leg. He was, he told me, diabetic. He was nicknamed after the horse racetrack in upstate New York. Saratoga was a punter—the betting man *par excellence.* He always had a little transistor radio and a track-form paper with him.

He told me about his wartime days in England, when he was a U.S. Army corporal. He made it sound as if all he did over there was tour the racetracks and meet prominent people in racing. That he met them I have no doubt. He described Dorothy Paget, for example, who was at one time the owner of Aintree, and the Zulu chieftain who used to sell tips on Epsom Downs and shout *"I gotta horse!"* Listening to Saratoga's stories, it seemed that he met a goodly number of the titled people in the United Kingdom, and was even pretty close to marrying into their families a couple of times.

I asked him about his false leg, and we discussed other people we knew who had them. Suddenly Saratoga broke into a wide grin. Mickey also grinned. "Shall I tell him about Peggy?" Saratoga asked Mick.

"Yeah, go on, tell him," said Mickey.

Saratoga turned to me. "Dere was dis guy—buddy of mine—and Mickey's too, come ta dat, right, Mickey?"

Mickey nodded and grinned.

"So dey call him Peggy 'cos of his false leg, see, and one day he goes to Belmont—dat's a racetrack, too, 'case ya didn't know —an' Peggy wins fifty grand—fifty t'ousand bucks, see, but dese guys seen him, too . . . mobsters . . . an' dey pick Peggy up outside da track an' dey hustle him inna da car, see. Dey tear

off back inna da city, an' dey hold up Peggy for da dough, an'
Peggy tells 'em he ain't got no dough, see? So da heavy guy
who's inna back of da car wid Peggy, he says to da driver, 'He
says he ain't got no money wid him; he says he gave it to some
guy back at da track ta bring in for him!' "

As he spoke, Saratoga rocked his shoulders slowly as if he
were being driven in a car at speed. " 'Sonuvabitch' says da
driver. 'So what'r we gonna do wid him?' says da guy inna back
wid Peggy. So da driver's t'inkin', see? an' aftera while he says
to da guy inna back, 'Okay, take his goddam leg off an' t'row it
over da bridge!' "

Saratoga leaned over confidentially, "Deir passin' over
Queensborough Bridge, see? So da guy inna back takes off
Peggy's leg . . . an' when dey got it off da driver slows down da
car, an' dey t'row Peggy out onna da side of da road an' while
dey speed off dey t'row da goddam leg outta da car window an'
off da goddam bridge an' inna da goddam East River, an' as da
leg falls, fifty t'ousand bucks fall out ada leg 'n' go floatin' away
onna goddam breeze—'cos dat's where Peggy hid his money,
inside his leg, see? So da guys inna car are so goddam mad dey
swoive inna a fast hack. Dat bounces 'em off'n da goddam side
ada bridge—buttay gottaway. Jeese, dat bounce musta broke da
heavy guy's arm, buttay got clear . . ."

"What happened to Peggy?" I asked Saratoga.

"Ahh . . . he just lay dere for an hour'r two, 'til some guy
picked him up 'n' brought him back on inna da city . . . Hey, ya
wanna drink?"

I thought, as I took a drink with Saratoga, how all humor has
at its heart elements of tragedy. Most of the clowns—people
who purposely behaved in a funny way—were fundamentally
very sad. All those I had met whose life demanded the serious
calculation of grave risks had an acutely sharp sense of humor.
Every bigot I had ever known had no sense of humor. I wondered if, perhaps, animals have a sense of humor, or maybe that
is what made another difference between them and man? Perhaps humor proves that man does indeed have a soul? I could

not understand how anyone could possibly live long without humor, and I pitied the poor souls who lived out their existence in that particular circle of hell.

As Saratoga listened to the race results, I wondered how anyone could go through life without finding joy in the incongruous, the illusive, the unexpected, and (the arch-enemy of the "artist") the imperfect, when we ourselves are all, at times, just so, else we should sprout wings. I would rather die with a smile on my lips than a million pounds in the bank. If there were both then all the better. In that case my smile might not be any wider, though perhaps those of some others might.

I glanced at Saratoga. I could see by the lines on his face a little of what he had suffered, being dismantled bit by bit for the past few years. I asked myself if suffering creates a sense of humor, but according to what I knew of Saratoga from other people, of what he was like before his illnesses, that could not have been the case. No, it was his sense of humor that carried him through the suffering. Then I remembered how I had felt going to the Bowery a few months before: that worth only seems to be created through suffering. I saw the error of my conclusion. It was not suffering that caused worth. Beauty and worth were created *despite* suffering, and so made even more beautiful and worthy.

After some thought about suffering and my change of view, it appeared to me that the two conclusions were not "incorrect" and "correct"—they were both valid points of view. One from the angle of the impoverished and one from the angle of the more comfortably off, and both were true, yet each contradicted the other. Thus the root of class struggle? Perhaps.

*   *   *

By the end of October, the final draft of *The Incredible Voyage* was completed. I sent it off to the publisher in Kansas City. The next three or four weeks were spent writing six articles for *Motor Boat and Sailing*.

Jim Andrews, the editor-in-chief in Kansas, wrote to me. He wanted to see me. We met on December 6, 1976, for the second time. It was a gray, drizzly morning. I had spent nothing on clothes. I was still in my yellow oilskin and jeans, the same in which I had tramped the roads and streets, roamed the fields, slept in and voyaged in deep waters during the past eighteen months. With ear-splitting noises, great lumbering diesel trucks ground past and clattered in nerve-tingling *ker-lunks!* over the potholes. Buses and cars vied with each other for space. Noise and fumes roared and spewed into the air. Cars whizzed past, their driver's gray faces set in boredom, frustration, anxiety, or hostility, their yesterday weekend excesses showing in their glares, and pedestrians hurried, huddled against the cold northeast wind, to their rendezvous with destiny, each one.

Jim eased his portly frame out of a yellow cab. A boyish smile brightened his face. He greeted me with a drawling "Hi, Tristan!"

"Hello, Jim! I see you found your way, then. How are things in the great beyond?"

Jim pulled his blue raincoat together about him. "We goin' in here?" He gestured with his briefcase at a restaurant nearby—La Groceria.

"Fine."

La Groceria is about as authentic a Neapolitan coffee shop as can be found anywhere in Manhattan. Jim and I ordered coffee. We talked then for a while about *The Incredible Voyage,* which Jim thought was "just fine."

"How's the boat?" he asked me.

"I'm very concerned, Jim. The bloody Customs are still insisting that I pay the twenty-five percent import tax . . . look." I showed Jim some recent missives that I had selected out of a growing pile.

Jim's face fell serious.

"What are you gonna do?" he asked.

"I'm determined not to pay it, Jim. As you can see, I've been in touch with this member of Parliament—I think Prince Philip's aide passed the case on to him—and he took it up and has got the bloody Customs to reduce the tax to twelve and a half percent of the estimated value. But I still won't pay a tax for a British boat to enter Britain. It's just plain legalized highway robbery. Sod it, Jim. That boat went through purgatory. I never voted for the tax . . . the hell with the Common Market and all that crap . . . *no taxation without representation!* The damned EEC won't last in its present form, more than a few years anyway . . . I give it ten, maybe fifteen . . ."

"What'll you do if they seize the boat?" Jim asked me as he ordered another coffee.

"Before they do that I'll fly over and sail her out of the country . . . out of territorial waters."

"But she's not fit to sail, is she? I thought you said . . ."

"She's fit enough to hobble twelve miles out, Jim," I said. I looked straight into his blue eyes.

"Then what?"

"Then I'll burn her and scuttle her!"

"Aww . . . come on . . ."

"I'm serious, Jim. I've never been more serious in my life. Rather than pay that damned tax I'll destroy her before their eyes."

There was silence for a minute, then I said, "Of course, if I had another advance on the book, I could ship her over to America . . . Look, I've an estimate here from the Cunard Company . . . it'll cost two thousand dollars . . ."

"Just what I wanted to talk to you about," said Jim. He reached into his briefcase and brought out a wad of papers. He spread them on the table. "I've got a contract here for you for *three more books.* I'll advance you money on the first one right away!"

"Give me a pen, Jim . . . I'd sign a mortgage with the devil himself as long as it gets *Sea Dart* out of the maws of those bleedin' bureaucrats." I signed.

It was one of those moments when two humans are on the exact same wavelength.

"And . . ." Jim started.

"—wouldn't it be great," I joined in as we both said our thoughts.

"—if we could take the boat," Jim went on.

"—and haul her right across America to the Pacific," I added.

"—to promote *The Incredible Voyage*," Jim concluded.

"Give me your hand, Jim—I'll do it!" I said.

We parted outside La Groceria. It was raining. Black clouds rolled over Sixth Avenue, traffic screeched and roared, police and ambulance sirens wailed, but all I could sense was the trembling of little *Sea Dart*'s hull on the windswept jetty of Newhaven, four and a half thousand miles away, where the hard Channel blusters sweep in, and the gray swarming seas crowd in to pay their dying homage to the mighty white cliffs of England. All I could hear was the two-thousand-year-old defiant hymn of Wales.

As I walked down West Fourth Street, I reflected to myself that there was much more to all this than merely tilting a repaired lance at the sturdy, well-rooted windmills of bureaucracy. *Sea Dart* was my vessel. Not like any other piece of property. Not like the low, luxurious houses and long, shining automobiles of Outurb. When a mariner considers his vessel it is not, I am sure, with a feeling of ownership so much as of loyalty. In wooden vessels is this particularly so.

A wooden ship *lives*. I was certain that if *Sea Dart* had been made of plastic or steel I would have abandoned her long ago —probably up on Lake Titicaca. But she *lives*, and I owed her a debt beyond money for her past loyalty to me.

Wooden boats are made of the same stuff as we are, ourselves. They are born in the forests, in pine and oak, cedar and mahogany. In that form, they, like us, reach upright for the sky and the stars, the wind, and the rain. Each tree has a life of its own. Men choose them, and hew them, and cut them to beautiful shapes. Whoever works with wood to build a boat cannot but work with love and care, and this becomes part of the vessel, just as surely as do its knees and futtocks, its floors, and its keel. A wooden sailing boat, surely, is the closest that man has yet come to creating another form of life. Just like us, she will be the best she can be, but never will she be better. Between a mariner, his wooden boat, the sea, and the stars there is a communion like no other. Most wooden boats give their all and some boats take everything that you can give them and never stop wanting more. Most wooden boats are built with love and know it—affection pours out of them. Others never wanted to be built and you always know it.

I didn't despise the other boats—the impersonal boats of steel and plastic. I knew that for some folk a boat is a thing only to be enjoyed, and in their pleasure so I took mine. But I did wonder what they did with the time they saved in not having to care for their craft, and whether or not the time saved was put to creative use—to add to their own or the world's growing.

Some boats demand only someone's presence on board— most wooden boats demand love, care, and loyalty, the same as all other living things. I could not give *Sea Dart* care—but the love and the loyalty were there aplenty, and in this life, between two living beings, nothing else mattered. She had taught me a few things about defiance in the face of overwhelming odds. Now I would show her that the lesson had been learned.

This needed a celebration.

I headed for the Lion's Head in Sheridan Square. It was empty of customers.

"*Her Majesty's Customs,*" I silently toasted to myself as a noggin of Scotland's pride went coursing down my throat. "Bugger 'em!"

"Wazzat?" The bartender looked big, well fed, and very Irish.

"God save the Queen and bugger the Customs!"

"I'll drink to that!" he said. We both grinned. "'S long as you're savin' sump'n."

I left the bar, went to the bank, deposited the check, and sent two thousand dollars to the Cunard Line. Then I looked around me. It was time to meet some different people.

The fault is not in aiming and missing—the fault is aiming low.

Dream not then
Of named lands, and abodes of men!
Alas, alas, the lonliest
Of all such were a land of rest
When set against the land where I
Unhelped must note the hours go by! . . .

My feet, my love, shall wander soon
East of the Sun, West of the Moon!
Tell not old tales of love so strong,
That all the world with all its wrong
And heedlessness was weak to part
The loving heart from loving heart?

FROM "THE EARTHLY PARADISE" (*September*), WILLIAM MORRIS,
A WELSH-AMERICAN

East of the Sun,
West of the Moon

IF you have a place to live in winter in New York City—even though the heating breaks down for days at a time—if you have shelter, the first fall of snow in New York City is pure magic. I went to bed wrung out after another twelve-hour stint of writing. Next morning I was awakened by silence. It was as if the world slept. I looked through the window at an enchanted street. There were no heavy trucks lumbering past, and few cars. All the litter and dirt-laden street surfaces were covered by a foot and more of white peace, which looked as if it would —as if it should—stay with us forever. But city government seemed to be affronted by this cold charity that, like a quiet forgiveness, hid its sins. It set to work attacking the strangeness of beauty on the streets. Soon its henchmen in incredibly rowdy, fume-spouting snow-plough-rigged garbage trucks had restored "normality" and soon, undisturbed by the excitement of silence, I set to work again.

Sometimes, but rarely, I went down to the waterfront to watch the steamers and ice-chunks heading out for the ocean, and to view the low winter mist over the Statue of Liberty and the massive World Trade Center. There was silent hope for my aloneness and quiet consolation for my smallness. I was landward of the statue and I had sailed higher than the top story of the building.

Sometimes, on special occasions, when I reached the end of writing a particularly difficult part of the book, I went downtown to stroll around the South Street Seaport Museum. It was in a sad state. The old Cape Horn three-master *Peking* was down there, looking tired, a little shabby, and forlorn. Apart from a few devoted but mainly nostalgic sightseers, no one seemed to be much interested. The cars and trucks rushed past on the overhead East Side Expressway, uncaring. The huge blocks of stone and glass of the Wall Street finance district loomed over the site like Claudius Caesar resting his foot on brave, defeated, Caractus's head.

One fine day in March, I loafed on the South Street pier and watched the East River traffic and the traffic booming across Brooklyn Bridge. I wondered then if the thoughts that had been dawning on me during the winter were mistaken—that I had come to America to witness the rebirth of commercial sail, and perhaps, in my own way, to help it? Or was it a new birth of something else? Something even greater?

It seemed to me, from my conversations with different landsmen, that their views of the ocean were quite different from those of the seafarer. They seemed to view the sea as either an empty wilderness or a promising prairie. They seemed to think that if something could not be controlled, it ought to be exploited. They mostly, it seemed, thought of the ocean in terms of a "manifest destiny" and did not realize that destiny is the sum total of what is put *into* it, not of the total material-gain gotten *out of it*. Here, as I sat on a bollard, waiting for *Sea Dart* to join me again, I reflected on the differences in attitude to life and the world between the landsmen and the seafarers. They were, it seemed to me, the root cause of the conflict between modern man's behavior—his needs and aspirations—and the cavalier way he was treating his surroundings, the land, the air, and the sea.

Life for the landsmen is not the same as life for the seamen. The landsman, at base, is a farmer. The farmer works with, in the main, steady weather cycles. He improves the land. He tries to make things grow where they never grew before. Once that is done, he can, with judicious care, expect to harvest from the same land again and again, year after year, generation after generation.

Successful agriculture creates comfort for many and it allows capital—in the form of grain, for example—to be accumulated in good years and set aside against setbacks in poor years. At sea there has been and is yet no setting aside. The accumulation of wealth on land was the origin of those looming palaces of fortune on Wall Street that looked down on the poor old *Peking*. The farmer's grain-horde was the basis of all the rest of shore-culture, from class systems to standing military forces, art patrons and religious hierarchies to sanction the system. The tendency was to achieve security for the system and centralize control, whereas "control" at sea was fragmented—necessarily so, for survival. The creeping centralization of government has been steady throughout landsman's history. As population and land production increased, so the central control increased. Security, though shaky for everyone, was, however, not granted by the land's central control to innovators or deviators whose activities might interfere with the flow of irrigation water or the gathering of the harvest.

To the seafarer—the cargo carrier or the fisherman—such values as resulted from the landsman's system were anathema because they did not basically aid survival. All through the centuries the seafarer was, in and on the main, clear of the land, free of the landsman's control. The sea trader-navigator, from whatever culture, was of necessity cosmopolitan. In order to trade with people of other cultures, he had to be tolerant of their differences.

Camus tells us that we humans see the truth differently at night than we do in the light of noon. How much less, then, do landsmen see the truth about the oceans from the shore than seafarers do from the sea itself? Surely, whatever view of reality aids us to see the deep issues of life in the area in which we move is, for whomever, in whatever area, closer to the truth than any view that diminishes our sight of the issues?

To the mariner, even the concept of truth was different from the landsman's. The basis of his "truth" was "does it work at sea?" "*Will it aid survival?*" Very little else mattered to him fundamentally.

The innovator at sea, or he who strays from the beaten path, if his method or idea is found not to be valid, is looked upon by the seaman more as a fool than a sinner, as he is considered on land.

The mariner's world is unstable, naturally confused. The mariner was and is subject to storms from out of nowhere. The fish suddenly disappear for no obvious reason. Because of this the mariner did not try to control or to predict his environment. Instead, with learned skills, handed-down sea knowledge, and improvization, he moved through his world, *surviving*. There is at sea comparably little of the predictability and control in landsman's activities. His vessel could be insured—but it was insured ashore and the money was collected by landsmen, not by the seafarer. The peaceable seaman's survival depended upon his own wits, not a central control.

Inherent in the landsman's make-up was the delusion that you can be successful at anything as long as you follow the farmer's rule carefully and collect enough grain. That is, follow the old rules and collect enough power. The landsman's society tends toward centralized control, opportunistic (I'm not being derogatory) and manipulative attitudes toward land use and a principled systematic approach, sometimes called the "scientific method." Now, it was obvious that the landsman, in the advanced countries, and in some not so advanced, was wearing out the land, the waters of the land, the air; and the inshore sea waters. Now he was about to invade the ocean using the same philosophy and methods that had done so much harm ashore. This process was already in progress, for an ever-increasing number of the people who now organized and ran the navies (not the coast guards) and the great clumsy, dangerous oil-tankers were themselves operating as landsmen do. There were to be sure, among them, some older seamen, now confused, who yet remembered what it was to tie a Blackwall hitch or take a star sight from the salt-sprayed bucking bridge-deck of a tramp-steamer, but these were few indeed and being pensioned off or dying. With them the ocean—our ocean, your ocean— was in grave peril of dying too.

You would have thought that with so much of the landsman's surroundings in such a mess he would have turned to the mariner's inground philosophy of survival for lessons. But no—instead he turned his eyes to the ocean and directed his roaring garbage trucks to "clean up" one of the only pure snowdrifts we have left.

Now the landsman turned his capital and "sophisticated" technology onto the ocean. Modern materials, plastic and other oil-based products, monstrous ships, electronic navigation and control systems enabled push-button operators to "navigate" the time bombs that are super tankers through the waters of the deep, and management enterprises were set up exactly the same as nonmaritime organizations control not to *farm* the oceans, but to *hunt* them. To hunt so efficiently, with their farmer-and-shotgun mentality, that now it was slowly dawning on them that there were limits to natural fish breeding, to the number of whales. Now the farmers and the fishermen were at loggerheads, the one group frustrated, turning their eyes to grabbing the ocean minerals, and the other group exasperated —its way of life doomed and much of the centuries of hard-earned sea-lore doomed with them. The seafarers numbered *millions, millions,* and most of them were poor and had no voice, and if the plight of the sea was not heeded there would be none left in two generations!

Out in the coastal waters of many parts of the world the landsmen, with farmer's and land-exploiter's mentality, were planting oil rigs right, left, and center, making a nightmare for navigators and cluttering up the narrow seas with infernal devices capable of destroying every natural living thing within a hundred miles of each one.

Below the oceans, the more powerful farmers had sent forth something like two hundred sinister-looking nuclear submarines, all under push-button control, all under landsman's central authorities, loaded down with death-dealing missiles, gliding in the gloomy, beautiful depths like Mafia henchmen clustering for the kill.

The prospects for the ocean, I thought, as I sat on the wharf at South Street, communing with old storm-battered *Peking,* was, as the lass in the St. Marks' coffee shop would have put it, "the pits."

Yet there was a brightening, like the light purple glow over the ocean's black horizon at dawn. *The oil was beginning to run out.* To my mind it seemed that the ocean was bigger than anything that the landsman, with the depleting oilstocks, would be able to blindly pit against her. He would be forced, eventually, to come to terms with the ocean. He would be forced, eventually, to use what the mariners themselves had used for centuries before the Industrial Revolution, ever since the dawn of sea navigation, ever since the first tree dweller had shoved off from a river shore and held aloft a leafy branch to propel him away from his ferocious pursuers. He would return to the power of the sun and become mate again to the sun's offsprings, the winds. *And that meant sail.* It might not be the billowing spreads of canvas the old China tea-clippers had when they carved a memory of immortal grace over the moving waters, but it would be *sail*. It would be clean and it would be again a vision of delight, and again men would love their ships and glory in a sea passage.

I had been saying all this for two decades. For years I had been writing it in articles; for years I had been looked upon as an "eccentric." For years, when I entered a sailing club, say in Cape Town or Gibraltar or Panama, people moved away from me and looked at me very strangely when I told them, again and again and again, that we must turn our ideas and our eyes again to the wind and the sun. Even now, in 1976, here in New York, some landsmen were putting me in the slot they reserved for the "ancient mariner." Even now they said I was crying doom. Would they not cry, too, if their gardens and hills were being ruined bit by bit before their crying eyes? One thing was certain. Alone, no wilting wallflower was ever going to get landsmen to listen. The sea demanded work, work, and more work. She always did. I promised myself five years ashore and seven books to write; five for the symbols and seven for the stars.

I looked again at the old *Peking*. Then my eyes strayed to the cluster of financial fortresses rising in the sky, and the highway, and the rushing trucks, and the jet planes. I looked at them with the eyes of a seaman newly fetched into haven from ocean storms, and I remembered the sailor's old saying—"So big, so strong . . . so useless!" I tried to imagine what the old dowager *Peking* would look like alongside a modern oil-tanker; alongside one of those great brutish blind monstrosities; she would be as big as a bumboat in size, and under sail, a butterfly gliding by a dinosaur.

I imagined a ship like *Peking,* and yet not like her. Graceful in lines, built of treated woods, using modern methods, fitted with the latest electronic aids so she could dodge the storms and avoid lee shores, a hundred and fifty feet long, crewed by people who were at home on the sea and over the sea and in the sea. I imagined their cargoes, these sailing ships of the next century, and I saw great aquariums onboard for transporting live fish to the depleted fishing grounds near the high-population areas of the land. I saw living and growing animals and plants onboard, and the propagation of them onboard in solariums. I saw the ships at anchor off impoverished shores and in depleted rivers, sending life and instruction and hope ashore. I saw kids no longer blank-eyed, their skulls no longer numbed by bombardments of banality, going onboard as apprentices and students, and I saw them coming back down the gangway at the end of the voyage with firmer step, an air of purpose, and the certain knowledge that they were a part of something so great, so vast, so beautiful as to be almost beyond our understanding.

As I walked through the gate I imagined that many landsmen might see my vision as merely that: a vision, something beyond reason. But reason is not all. Sometimes reason may fail you. If ·you have reason to dream, then sometimes you must, in your dream, move away from reason. But if nature, the way of things, has any need of your dream, your vision, you will find that reason and reasonableness will be part of your dream.

Reason will come trotting along to take your dream in hand and make it come true. It is sometimes called "coincidence," it is sometimes described as grabbing an opportunity. It seems more to me like reason filling a void created by a dream. Nature abhors a vacuum.

The dream, I had thought, was to find something in America.

I had been mistaken. Something had sent me here, not to take, but to *give;* perhaps to help pass on a dream.

For me to go to other lands involved in the senseless grabs at the ocean—to go to the USSR or Japan, for example, would be as useful, I imagined, as a wolf baying at the moon. America is open to ideas, sometimes even if they are against the immediate interests of the country. The Americans might not listen very attentively at first, but even if they did think I was a raving madman the chances were they would not lock me away or throw me out. And if my concerns and anxieties about the ocean and man's treatment of it were valid, sooner or later America would not only listen, but more and more Americans would themselves see where things were leading and demand a turnaround. No one likes to be told that the course he has been navigating is in error, but I knew enough American mariners to be sure that they were just as familiar as I with the "180 degree change of course." Some of them knew that I was not coming from Britain, not from Wales, but from the ocean, which recognizes only one passport—hard experience—and only accepts only three stamps in that passport—love and respect for her and willingness to take on any odds to preserve *her* values. The ocean admires not full pockets but a full heart. She cares not one jot for anyone's self-pity; but for anyone's concern for her, for her threatening beauty, she salves the troubled mind and the heart breaking for her.

The more I thought about the "180 degree turn" back from the effects of the Industrial Revolution, the more I wondered if perhaps it might be more of a need to break forward through the mold in which we had been set, to the cleaner, brighter world that lies ahead in the future if the right paths are taken. It seemed to me that everything ashore was still set for the ways of the nineteenth century. Social structures, restrictive families, old laws, "left" and "right" politics, all these would, perhaps sooner than we think—*"and the sooner the better,"* I thought —join the dinosaurs, along with filth-emitting cars and muckspewing oil-tankers.

I started to walk up the jetty, back into the dirty streets of the city. I knew that there were landsmen who would scoff at me for a dreamer, an idealist. That was their privilege. The dream was there all right. So was the will to express the ideal and to give some substance to the dream. And *that was why* Sea Dart *was coming.* Now I had to find a way to direct my idea and my dream where it mattered—right to the main arteries of modern landsman's culture—business, industry, agriculture, communications, and government—right to the very heart of his control systems.

That there were organizations already pleading against the unthinking assault on the oceans I knew. By the very nature of my being, I could not join them, nor, because of my heavy work schedule, could I work with them. I was a loner. This message I would bring alone, with *Sea Dart*. It would be pointless for me to duplicate the sermons already being read by the environmentalists. As I saw it, my task was to try to make people think about the *folk* of the oceans—mariners—and about sail. My job was to try to make the landsman wonder—now if one man can do this, without using up the riches of the earth, what can we not do all together? What can we not do, with all the knowledge we have and are gathering daily? If one man, without any formal education, can overcome all these difficulties and hazards, what cannot the brains we have, all of us, overcome?

At the same time I knew that I would have to suffer, many times, the traditional landsman's attitude to the mariner—especially to the older, small-boat mariner. I would be, to them, either a "character"—an "old salt"—or a semi-lunatic. It seems that, to a landsman, the smaller a man's vessel, the smaller his brain, whereas the ocean knows differently. It would be several years and several books and I would have to let the landsmen think that I had strayed into their camp for life before I could hope to whisper in as many ears as would count. I hoped that some people would read my writings and recognize not only the humor and the enjoyment, but also the suffering, and not only the physical and mental suffering at sea and in struggle, but the suffering at the thought of what was happening to our world and especially to the ocean.

As I walked past the fish market on Fulton Street I tried to imagine the ocean we now had to tackle, *Sea Dart* and I, an ocean of seeming deafness to the plight of the oceans. I could not tackle it like Cousteau—I had no formal education or government and institutional funds behind me. I had no industrial or media complex backing me, like Heyerdahl or Chichester or many other well-known ocean sailors. All I had was a typewriter, a barely furnished room, and a little nineteen-foot boat battered almost beyond belief that was only now emerging from the dark clouds of seemingly unrepayable debt, and still four and a half thousand miles away, unknown, unhonored, and unsung, like a bit of jetsam washed up on some shore.

I knew I would have to play my part. It takes courage to be what you are—I would not be able to pretend to be anyone else but me. I would have to be the "old salt." But to gain people's ears and to talk urgently to them about the ruination of one of the last great comparatively unspoiled assets that the human race yet has, I would have walked on my hands and knees through broken glass in a clown's get-up, with a glowing red nose, all the way to Frisco and back.

Later, I expected, by the interests vested in despoiling the waters of the world I would be accused of exaggeration—even of megalomania, of riding hobby horses, but this would be, to me, like water off a duck's back. I might become unpopular with folk who use the sea merely for "status," but the score was even, for their motives were already anathema to me. There would be no love lost, and that, after all, is what really counts.

I had set myself five years ashore to do a job. It had already taken me over a year to merely secure a base and get my boat out of the tide-race into which, mainly through my own fault, she had been swept.

The pieces of the puzzle of destiny over which I had been racking my brains—to try to find some rhyme or reason to them —were at last beginning to fall into place one by one. I could almost hear them *thunking* into their slots. Now I suddenly saw it all clearly—*why* I had been guided to New York the previous year; *why* I had been forced to make the voyage in *Star Rider;*

why I had been yanked back to New York, almost as if by an unseen hand; and *why* the publisher of the coming book was to be in, of all the unlikely places, Kansas City, in the very heart of this most powerful nation. Still there was yet something missing . . .

I sat and dreamed for an hour or so, then I felt an irresistible urge. I made my way to the City Hall subway. I knew where I was bound, now.

*   *   *

I alighted at Sixty-eighth Street, and was soon ringing on the bell of the plush Explorers Club. I had, for some time, been in correspondence with the club. Inside the foyer, the walls were hung with pictures of famous men from the past and present— Teddy Roosevelt, Admiral Byrd, Thor Heyerdahl, Jacques Cousteau. There was a regal silence as I waited for whoever would turn up to greet me. I sat down on a well-placed, sturdy, all-leather sofa. Soon, a tall, slender man of about my age came up to me, smiling, his hand outstretched.

"Hi, Tristan Jones? Welcome to the Explorers Club and welcome to New York. I'm Russ Gurney; I'm a speleologist."

"A what?"

"A cave explorer."

"Good afternoon," I said.

"Looks like our lucky day, there's usually no members around during weekday afternoons. We've been waiting for you to show up for years, and especially since we heard from one of our members that you were in the Virgin Islands. Where have you been? Are you back from another intrepid journey?"

"Sort of . . . I'm here for a few months, got a book being published in June . . . writing three more," I explained.

"Where's your boat?" he asked me. "*Sea Dart,* isn't it?"

I explained what had happened with *Sea Dart,* and how she was now due to be shipped out to New York in April.

"What will you do then?"

"I'll keep her at the South Street Seaport—Frank Braynard has very kindly offered me a free berth until I'm ready to push off again."

"Where will you go then?" asked Russ.

"I haven't thought about it yet—there are some other things I want to do before I shove off on another voyage."

Russell studied me for a few moments. I was in my paint-bespattered jeans and I had my yellow jacket with me. Suddenly his face glowed.

"I've just had a helluvan idea," he said.

"What's that, Mr. Gurney?"

"Aww, call me Russ. Look, our annual Explorers Club dinner is slated for the middle of April. When's your boat due to arrive?"

"April ninth."

"Our dinner is on April fifteenth. You did say she was very small?"

"Nineteen feet, with the bowsprit unshipped."

"Wouldn't it be something if you could get her up to the dinner . . . There's a stage . . . We could have her as one of the display. Say, wouldn't it be just great? There'll be fifteen hundred of the most prominent people in America there . . . Mr. Rockwell, the electronics man, Lowell Thomas, Jimmy Doolittle, Lovell, the astronaut—"

I interrupted Russell. "Where?"

"You'd have to check that you can get her in there, of course. It's on the fourth floor, and right inside the building, well away from the elevators . . ."

"Where?" I insisted excitedly.

"The Waldorf Astoria Hotel."

Russell studied me as I weighed the prospects. The concept of dragging a full-blown ocean-going craft through the guts of one of the world's most famous hotels was staggering, but so was the task that I had already set myself—of dragging the plea of the precious oceans' plight to the land. If I failed, the landsmen might look upon me as a transgressor. The seamen, those who would not see my aim, would consider me a fool. Between the two—sinner and fool—there's not much difference to a sailor. If I failed, time would eradicate the fault for the landsmen, and for the real sailors, who can be a real mariner, or a real explorer, who has never in his life been a fool? And if I succeeded and detractors might later say that I was an egotist, infatuated with my own ideals—might I not reply to them, "Maybe so—but I overcame the difficulties and if I can so can you!" They might scoff that I had appointed myself as spokesman for the ocean, but how could I ever pretend to be that, I who knew so very little of her deep wonders, I who only knew and tried to describe not only her beauty and her beguiling charm, her high delight, but also her heart-wrenching terrors, her fury, her savagery, her gut-curdling cruelties? How could I claim that, who could learn from the veriest neophyte at any center for marine biologists? No, I could only claim to be a spokesman for myself and for some of the seafarers that I had known, and for the little, ever-changing circles of blue, gray, and green magic that had been my beloved home for so long, and perhaps try to hint, somehow, of the will, the discipline, the skill, and the respect that the ocean demands from each and every one of us. And if I should succeed in translating the sea-law for the landsmen, they would surely say, "But here is a voice from the past" and conjure up Melville, London, Slocum, and Conrad. Conrad and only the seafarers will know that it is a voice, too, from the present—a very present present—and only the seafarers who were conscious of what was to happen on the oceans and in the world would know that it was also a voice of and for the future, because the ocean knows not time. To her, eternity is but a moment, and every moment is an eternity—for her there is no "then"; there is, and always has been, and always will be, only "now." To her there is no "you" and "me"—only "us."

"But," my friends would say, "you will be telling them things they do not want to hear. They want the romance of the sea." And I would reply, "But don't you see, can't you see, this *is* her romance? *Save her!* Tell those who need her so much to respect her, court her, woo her—stop trying to rape her! Respect her, love her, care for her, and the ocean will give her all!"

And where else should I take a little heroine arriving in New York but to dinner in one of the best hotels?

I spoke at last. "What's the address? . . . I'll go round right now and spy out the land."

Russell laughed, "No, don't be too hasty, we'll have to fix up your visit with the hotel people first . . ."

Knowing all the while that the missing piece of the puzzle had fallen into place, I said, "I'll get her up there, Russell, if it kills me."

*   *   *

From the Explorers Club I went to call on good friends I had met in the West Indies. They lived on Sixty-ninth Street, in, I found, an apartment that was, to me, huge and luxurious.

"Where've you been?" they asked.

"Oh, knocking around—poking about and writing."

"Why didn't you come to see us before?" they asked.

I made my excuses, trite mumbles about being "too busy." How could I bruise their hospitality by telling them that I was in the habit of getting myself off the reef? I imagine, though, that they may have guessed how things had been, for they were even more helpful and considerate than I expected. Their two children were amused, too, evidently, by the sudden appearance out of nowhere of what they told me was a rather piratical-looking figure who didn't quietly tell them to stop when things were a little too rough, but bellowed out *"Belay there!"*

*   *   *

I went to the Waldorf Astoria the following week. I had no precise details of *Sea Dart's* dimensions, other than her length. Her specifications were still in the boat, and could not be obtained because she was "in bond" until she left England. No one was allowed onboard. I had a vague idea of her beam (width) and height, though, so, with a security man, I went through the route she would have to take, up the goods elevators (I was not certain she would fit in—she might do, if she was slanted across the floor), through the kitchens (she might make it, if she were only six-three wide, and not six-six), and through the very posh-looking ante-rooms and dance halls (she might just get through the doors if she were only seven feet high and not eight). Outside I phoned Russell. "She'll make it, Russ," I said.

When I got home to my room there was good news. *Quest* magazine had bought excerpts from *The Incredible Voyage,* and, as I had suggested to them, they were willing to pay for the haulage of *Sea Dart* from the New Jersey docks to the Waldorf Astoria, if I were willing to have their ads on display on the rig. Ads? To help the ocean I'd have displayed a hanging!

There was bad news, too. The ship bringing *Sea Dart* had been delayed. She would now arrive on the fourteenth of April. The big event was on the fifteenth. That left a one-day margin to shift all three tons of her from Bayonne to the Waldorf. I read the letter. *"Okay,"* I thought. My seaman's caution added, *"If all goes well."* Then I reflected that the sea gods would make sure of that.

On the fourteenth of April, bright and early, along with Don Holway, a photographer working for *Quest,* I waited at the dockside in Bayonne, New Jersey, for the Cunard freighter *Atlantic Champagne.* I looked into the morning sun, at the low mist rising around lower Manhattan and the Statue of Liberty. I thought of the other Bayonne, in France, so far away, so very different.

Don and I were early. The day crew was just coming into the dock gates. We waited, watching. We saw the ship materialize out of a gray shadow in the Hudson mist. We watched her come bows up to the landing ramp.

"Whattaya waitin' for, fellas?" We were addressed by a rotund little man of around forty, very dark hair and bushy mustache. He was wearing a working suit and the obligatory protection helmet, as were Don and I, by the dock regulations.

"We're waiting for *Atlantic Champagne* to unload," said Don.

"Ya got materials onboard to ship outta da docks?"

I replied, "I'm waiting for my boat—she's being landed off the ship this morning." There was a thirty-six-hour margin before she was due for dinner.

"Where ya takin' it?" he nodded. "I'm da foreman 'round here . . . name's Eddie."

"Manhattan." The Waldorf was about twenty miles away by our route.

"Yer outta luck, fellas . . . dere's a cargo handlin' strike just been called. I'm da foreman here . . . Da stevedores will allow da ship to land da stuff, but dey ain't gonna be handlin' nuttin' from den on . . . She goin' inna water right away or what?"

"No, we're putting her on the back of that truck," I said. I pointed to the huge boat-hauler that my publishers had arranged.

"Too bad, fellas, da crane drivers won't handle it . . . 'S against union orders," announced Eddie.

"How long do you think the strike will last?" asked Don.

"Oh . . . maybe a week, maybe ten days . . . Who da hell knows . . ."

I broke in, feeling rather idiotic, "But she's supposed to be in the Waldorf by tomorrow afternoon!"

We all three stood and watched the great bow-doors of the freighter open slowly. Impatiently, I waited for my first sight of *Sea Dart* since we had parted company on that bitter day in Newhaven twenty months before. Twenty months . . . and a lifetime.

"Too bad," said Eddie, "can't buck da union."

There is no frigate like a book,
　To take us lands away,
Nor any coursers like a page
　Of prancing poetry.

This traverse may the poorest take
　Without oppress or toll;
How frugal is the chariot
　That bears a human soul!

EMILY DICKINSON

The Traverse

THE northerly breeze stabbed bayonets of cold through my new Welsh jersey on the docks of Bayonne, New Jersey.

Eddie side-looked a glance at me as I shivered, not only with cold.

"You from around here, fella?" he asked me, offhandedly.

"No, I've come over from Manhattan," I said, not knowing whether or not to apologize for feeling superior. It was my first visit to New Jersey.

"Naww . . . I mean, you some kinda limey, aintcha?"

"Yeah, something like that . . . I'm Welsh."

"Dat anywheres near Iddaly?"

"Italy? Well you could say that . . . It's about as near as say Florida is from New Jersey . . ."

"Dat's where my folks 'r' from," said Eddie. "Howya like Noo Joisey?"

It was my first visit. "Great," I said. Anywhere I could rejoin *Sea Dart* had my affection for life.

"We get t'ings done in Joisey . . ." said Eddie. Don grinned at me. I kept a straight face. I decided to cultivate Eddie.

"Do you know that New Jersey is named after an Italian?" I asked him.

"How come?" asked Eddie, as he glanced at the unloading team boarding the ship. "Ain't it named after some limey island? Dat's what dey loined me when I was a kid, anyways."

"Well, that's right, Eddie, but the limey island of Jersey was named for an Italian in the first place."

"How come?"

"Well, when the Romans conquered Britain and the other

247

islands around, they named one island after Julius Caesar—
Caesaria—but the Celtic tribesmen couldn't pronounce the
name, and so after a while it became 'Jersey' . . ."

"Zattso?" said Eddie. Don raised his eyebrows as he gazed
at me.

"True as I'm standing here, Eddie."

Eddie was silent for a moment or two. "Allus knew dem limeys was pretty dumb!" he said, grinning at me.

I was going to tell him that we had to be dumb to export
spaghetti to Italy—about half of what's eaten there—but
thought it better to hold my tongue.

As we waited, silently now, a dozen cars were driven out of
the bows of the cargo-freighter *Atlantic Champagne*. They
were followed by some racing yachts, all fiberglass and new-
looking. They belonged to the Cruising Club of America and
they were returning from a visit to European waters. They were
sleek and loaded with expensive equipment. Don and Eddie
were impressed.

"How much ya reckon dat one's worth?" asked Eddie as a
scarlet ocean greyhound trundled by, her stainless steel gear
flashing in the morning sun.

I weighed her up. "At a guess, about eighty thousand dollars
. . . perhaps one hundred thousand dollars."

"Jesus H. Christ!" whispered Eddie. He walked over and
inspected the hull as it waited to be hauled off. He tapped it. It
was, to me, huge; all of fifty feet long. "Those guys go ta sea in
dis t'ing?" he asked me.

"Oh, yes, she's an ocean-cruising vessel."

"She's American?"

"Right."

"Guess dere must be some dumb Americans, too!"

Another half-dozen sea machines were dragged out of the
guts of the ship on their trailers. Then I saw *Sea Dart*, a tiny,
shabby unmistakable shape, in the corner gloom of the hold. I
wanted to board the ship and go to her, but it was not allowed.
I stood silent, staring at her dim shape, for a good ten minutes.
The two men with me must have sensed the holy moment.

Neither of them said a word. Then it was her turn to arrive. The bumptious tractor was hooked on to her trolley and she was dragged ashore so fast that she bounced on her trailer as it heaved over the unloading ramp. Swiftly, she was parked alongside the Cruising Club boats. She looked like an old blind pit pony that had strayed into the royal paddock at Ascot.

She was filthy. Her tarpaulin cover was in tattered shreds. Her sides still showed the battering of the Plate Estuary storm almost two years before. The great gashes on her rubbing strake, her wounds from the Wild Paraná, were now weather-cured, the splintered oak below she wore like Boadicea's crown of oak leaves. On her stern a tiny tatty remnant of her old red ensign still fluttered as she saluted America.

Don and Eddie must have sensed what I was feeling. They let me walk over to her side alone. She sat there on her three keels—and she grinned. I went right up to her. I put my hand on the patched-up stern that I had repaired for her in Montevideo. I ran my fingers over the rough patches. Then I slapped her stern and said quietly, just for her: "You bloody little bitch . . . you made it!" To me, she seemed to tremble, but maybe it was the ground shaking as another loaded trailer rumbled past. I looked up at my two new-found friends, but they were, it seemed, in a misty haze. I looked at her again, and ran my hand over her strakes, to reassure myself that she really was here, safe.

Don was wandering around, taking pictures. Eddie just stood, gazing from me to *Sea Dart* and back to me, looking incredulous.

"Everything okay, Tristan?" called Don.

I had to clear my throat before I could speak. "Looks okay topsides, Don, but some thieving bastard has swiped her sheet winches. It must have been while she was delayed in Southampton docks—she was more or less under guard the rest of the time. It must have been some bleeding wharf-rat in Southampton—Look, they ripped the winches right out of her . . . Must have been done in a hurry . . ."

Eddie spoke. "Goddam sonuvabitch!"

"You can say that again, Eddie. I hope the bastard, whoever it was, gets his bloody balls caught in his sheet-ropes."

Eddie shook his head. "Naww," he said. "I mean . . . is this the goddam boat ya gonna take ta da Waldorf?"

"Yes, like I was telling you, she's invited to appear for a reception there tomorrow . . ."

"Ya mean ya go ta goddam sea in dis?"

"She's a bloody good seaboat, Eddie, got everything . . . a kitchen . . ."

"Ya gotta bed in dere?"

"Sure, three."

"Goddam . . ." Eddie removed his helmet and scratched his head. "Waddaya do wit' yaself all goddam day at sea?"

"Oh, work, navigate, repair the sails . . . read," I said.

"Ya mean ya gotta library in dere?"

"Well, there's a little bookshelf."

"How many books ya got?"

"Oh, about thirty, forty, something like that, but they're probably all moldy by now."

Eddie shook his head. Silently he turned around and walked over toward a group of striking dockers standing near the office building. "Hey, youse guys!" he bellowed. The loafers looked up at him, lackadaisically. "Come on over here—dis youse fellas gotta see, goddam!" The group of dockers, all helmeted, ambled over.

"Take a look at dat, guys," Eddie told them. "You ain't gonna see dis more'n oncet inna lifetime, goddam it . . . dis guy goes ta sea innat poky li'l bucket . . . an' here I am scared shitless ta go out fishin' in Bozo's fifty-footer off da Joisey shore!" Joe turned to me. "Lissen . . ." he whispered hoarsely, "us guys . . . we ain't s'posed ta do dis, but we's gonna fixya up, fella."

Eddie turned to one of his cohorts. "Charlie, drag dat goddam boat outta here, down ta da parkin' lot downna road. Jimmy, ya gonna drive a goddam crane outta da gate an' follow dat heap an' load it onna da goddam truck!" He turned to me. "We gotta get ya outta here fast, 'fore anyone sees . . . but before ya go, you an' your buddy come an' have a cuppa cawfee wid me, inna awfice, 'cos I got sump'n for ya . . . fromma old country, see?"

In minutes the boat had been hauled down the road and lifted onto the back of the boat-hauler's low bed. Don and I returned to the foreman's office. Eddie poured us coffee, then he disappeared into an inner office. In the silence I gazed through the office window. For a moment the mist in the distance lifted. A dark gray shape was revealed. "Ship?" asked Don, laconically.

"Statue of Liberty," I said.

"Oh, yeah, that's right, we're practically underneath it here," he observed.

"Practically," I said.

There was something in the view out the window. Something that seemed to be calling to me, a presence born out of a strength that I could feel, whose cry my whole being recognized, a password? Pride? Hope? Compassion? A feeling of desire passed through me, a wanting to do good, to do what was right. It was as though I could reach now through the mist over the water around the statue, out to the wide, rolling Atlantic Ocean itself, feeling in her own heart a never-ending need, an immeasurable longing, an almost hopeless wanting.

Minutes later Eddie was back again. "Here y'are, fella . . . fromma old country . . . f'ya bookshelf." Eddie grinned shyly as he handed me a bulky brown envelope. Then he said to both Don and me, "Chees . . . somma da guys innere, dey got wangers like a goddam donkey, anna boobs on somma da broads innere . . ." He cupped his hands palms down above his chest, then swept them out and down. "Chees, somma dem babes . . ." He shook his head. " . . . dey musta hadda goddam ball inna old country . . ."

I opened the bulky envelope. Inside was a big book. A coffee table book. I read the title: *Erotic Art of Pompeii.*

That book is still among my few treasured possessions. One day I shall take it to Pompeii, when I go to visit the "guys" and the "broads" of twenty centuries ago, and give them Eddie's regards, for they will recognize him, too.

* * *

As they used to say in Pompeii, *tempus fugit*. Time flies and so did we, up through Jersey City, over the George Washington Bridge, to the boat-hauler's yard in The Bronx. I do not describe the journey—there are more than enough guide books and films to do that. New Yorkers know it—those who have never visited Babylon-on-Hudson can envisage it. *Sea Dart* was well bowsed down onto the truck and travelled as well cosseted as any beloved should.

At the yard, with *Sea Dart* and her truck well locked up and guarded, we left her for the night. I gave her a goodnight tap and took off, with Don, for Manhattan.

* * *

Next day, the fifteenth of April, with Don being driven in his car to shoot pictures, the truck trundled through the garbage-strewn grime and over the potholes of upper Manhattan. By 3:00 P.M. the hauler had skillfully maneuvered his leviathan close into the loading bay of the Waldorf Astoria. By 4:00 P.M. a heavy fork-lift had unloaded *Sea Dart* and her trolley, all three tons of them, off the truck and onto the sidewalk, with Don taking pictures and helping where he could. Soon the hauler ground off, his job (and a fine job, too) done. The fork-lift disappeared as magically as it had arrived. Don and I were left with the boat.

"What do we do now, Tristan?" asked Don.

"Shove her inside the elevator," I replied, putting my weight onto her stern. "I've got exactly three hours to get her onto the stage in the ballroom," I told him to the fascination of a dozen passers-by who had stopped in their tracks at the sight—unusual even for Manhattan.

"You're going to need some help," Don observed.

"Let's get her in the elevator first, Don, give us a hand here," I puffed. Don looked at me nonplussed for a moment.

"The old *fait accompli*," I explained.

"The what?" Don grinned. He was getting to know me by now.

"Latin for 'here it is, mate—and here it stays.' " I heaved my heavy lever again.

It took Don and me about half an hour to lever the trolley into the elevator foyer. I was concentrating all my energy now, mental as well as physical, into inching *Sea Dart* closer to her goal. Someone tapped me on the shoulder. A voice demanded, "What the hell *is* this?"

Without looking round to face my inquisitor I grunted, "It's a boat . . . going . . . to . . . the ballroom."

"A what . . . goin' where? . . . I'm hotel security."

I let go of the great wooden lever. I turned to face him, breathing hard.

He was a tall, hefty man of about my age, silver haired, wearing spectacles and a gray business suit. "I'm hotel security," he repeated. He showed me a badge of some kind. "An' that thing isn't going inside this hotel."

"But she's due for the Explorers Club dinner!" I expostulated.

"That's neither here nor there," said the security officer. "It isn't going in—for one thing . . ." He stood back to inspect her. ". . . it's too damned big to get into the elevator, an' for another it's going to create a hazard, an' for another if you get it inside it's going to cause a lotta damage . . ."

I was getting riled now. "Do you know the chief maintenance engineer?" I asked him.

"Why, sure . . . but . . ."

"Can you contact him, please?"

"What for? He can't spare any staff to help . . ."

"I don't want any help . . ."

"Waddaya want?"

"I want two electric saws . . ."

"Saws?"

"Yes . . . because this boat's come four thousand miles to attend this function and she's going in, even if I have to cut her up into little pieces and stick her together again inside!"

The security officer studied me. I stood with one foot in front of me and one hand on *Sea Dart*'s gunwhale. He was silent for a moment, then he said quietly, "Hey, you're some guy, ya know that? Wait here a minute . . ." He disappeared into the receiving office and picked up a phone.

While the security man was away, Russell Gurney showed up. In a second he had his coat off (America! America!) and he, too, was heaving at another lever. Now there were three of us shoving the boat. In minutes the security man, with two hotel-staff, all in their shirt sleeves, without saying a word, were grunting and pushing along with us.

Govannon entered me. I grabbed the guardrail stanchions, one-inch-thick rods of cast-steel that made her too high to enter, and bent them over like putty with my bare hands. I severely strained my stomach muscles doing it, but I consoled myself that what will bend can always be straightened again. (The rails took a week—my stomach two years.)

How we—by now eight of us (the reception office staff had been drawn into *Sea Dart*'s magic vortex—got her into the elevator was a miracle. When the job was finished, she was positioned diagonally athwart the machine's floor. Fore and aft, when the doors shut there was no more than a sixteenth of an inch to spare. Between the top of her doghouse and the heavy wire-netting roof of the elevator, you could not have inserted a cigarette paper sideways. As we got her ready to slide into the elevator, the hotel staff stared.

The fit in the elevator was so tight that only one person could go up the four stories with the boat.

"Skipper's job," Russell puffed.

"The very man himself," I said as I wedged myself horizontally onto her foredeck in the dark with an eighth of an inch to spare.

When the elevator stopped and the gates opened, I struggled down from my perch and stretched myself. Then I walked around a tight corner and went to reconnoiter the track through the great kitchens. I was as quick as I could, but not quick enough. When I returned from checking that the way was clear through the Cavendish Room, into the kitchen, the sight that met my eyes was *remarkable*.

All around were steaming vats and stainless steel ovens. The air was warm, but not oppressively so. Through it wafted a dozen delicious cooking aromas. Scullery hands rushed around, there was a noisy clatter of utensils. Chefs and their assistants in their varieties of curious tall white headgear were stirring their concoctions and mixing their magic, now and then gazing, astonished, at the sight of a seagoing sailing boat moving slowly but surely right through their kitchen with only a fraction of an inch to spare on either side of her. It was *surrealistic*. I hesitated for a moment, taking in the sight, fixing it in my memory. *Sea Dart* was enjoying all this attention and cosseting. She was like a crochety old queen being wheeled through the castle kitchen to check on the expenditures. I grinned at her, then grabbed the rope on the forward end of her trolley and heaved with all my might.

She passed through the doorways from the kitchens into the inner corridors with hardly a paint-coat's thickness to spare each side of her after we had removed the doors from their hinges. Above her, the space between her doghouse roof and the door lintels was less than a thirty-second of an inch. When her full height was passing through you could not see daylight between her and the door cross-beam. Tavan and Govannon were still with us. Dagda's caldron was just ahead. It was as if someone were pushing the doorposts apart and lifting the lintels to let her pass.

Heaving, shoving, and pushing, by now there were a dozen Americans all puffing, blowing and shouting to each other in English, Spanish, and French (four sous-chefs, going off duty, had fallen under *Sea Dart*'s spell), all helping her to her destination.

By six o'clock she was in the Cavendish Room. Here, again the scene was out of this world. The room was a spacious chamber, half as big as a football field, all carpeted and hung with tapestries. Around the walls sat silver-painted furniture upholstered in red. In the center of the molded ceiling hung a chandelier with more than a hundred lights—and under the chandelier a dozen men danced attendance on an unbelievably battered old nineteen-foot ocean sailing boat's hull. She *loved* it.

Russell measured the last remaining doorways between the boat and the ballroom. There had been an afternoon function. We had not been able to get to them since the operation commenced. Soon he was back with a serious face. Behind us, as *Sea Dart* had passed, the way back was now closed off, with all the doors replaced and the kitchens going at full blast for dinner. Russell used a phrase that I thought was colorful. "We've painted her into a corner, Tristan," he said. "She's too high to go through into the ballroom. We'll never take her off the trolley."

"Too high?"

"Yes, by two inches." It was now six-thirty. We had half an hour to spare. "And it looks like we're not going to be able to manage it. There's no way we can lift her without a big car jack —and that's going to put too much strain on the floor in one place ... It looks like she'll have to stay out here ..." His face was glum. "I guess the guests will just have to be content seeing her out here, outside the ballroom ..." All around us sweaty faces saddened. There was silence except for an almost apologetic shuffle of embarrassed feet.

Seafarers see things differently from landsmen. A vessel is not a thing ... she is the sum total of all her voyages, past, present, and future, and every emotion that ever goes into her ... love, strength, care ... *determination* ...

I looked at the security officer. His shoulders dropped a little. I turned to Don—he was studying me, waiting. I looked at the others who had spent their free time helping *Sea Dart*. It was as if they were all trying to read my thoughts.

"She promised to get to the stage, Russ," I said, finally. "Can you get me a saw?"

"What . . . you're not going to cut her up?" Russell exploded.

"Don't say anything, please . . . Just get me a saw."

While Russ was gone to his car there was a wondering silence among the crew. Then one French-American sous-chef, still in his white kitchen gear, climbed down from the cockpit, where he had been inspecting the cabin, peering inside, murmuring "wonderfool—wonderfool, ze workmansheep!"

"Treestan," he said. He was very young, perhaps twenty or so. "You cannot cut up all zat beautifool wood in zere . . . ze workmansheep . . ." He was almost crying. "'Ow can you own a boat like zees and cut into 'er?"

"I know," I said, "it's like cutting into my own heart—but her destination is just as much a part of her as her doghouse. Her destination cannot be repeated or replaced—her doghouse can."

The logic appealed to the Frenchman in him. But he still stood back and shook his head and murmured, *"Putaine! foutre le camp!"*

At a quarter to seven, the doghouse was sawn away from the deck. At seven *Sea Dart* was on the five-foot-high stage behind the curtains. By seven-thirty I had her sails hauled up, by seven-forty I had showered and changed into the requisite tuxedo, and by eight o'clock the function commenced.

*   *   *

There was a self-serve buffet for hors d'oeuvres. There was lion loin from Uganda, niblets of hippopotamus, buffalo sausages, wild boar pâté, elk, deer, wild goose, the hump of a Lake Titicaca llama, musk ox, bear-meatballs, moose, caribou, walrus, kangaroo, red deer, ibex, Alaska salmon, elephant, and oryx meat, all set out on long tables. I had some salmon, having more of an affinity with things that come out of the water, and when you're dressed in a tuxedo you can afford to be finicky.

The guests and the other guests-of-honor were an American galaxy of achievement, power, influence, and plain old money. Fifteen hundred stars and I sat down to fish soup and roast wild boar, praline soufflé and peaches flambé. It was the best meal

I'd had in a month of Sundays, and the wine was much better than Irish Rose, I found. The guests-of-honor sat on the high table—all twenty-three of them and me. Among the diners below I could see my publishers, eyes a-twinkle. The ladies were all graciously dressed in evening dresses, their jewelry shining under the bright lights. Their escorts, of all ages, from nineteen to ninety, were all dressed to the nines, all in formal wear, but it was nowhere near as stuffy an atmosphere as a similar function might have been in Britain, at least, a few years ago.

Apart from Russell Gurney and a very few others, none of the guests knew that *Sea Dart* was near—or they did not know what *Sea Dart* was.

The evening's program was to be on the theme of exploration —from the "brave old sailing days" to the space shuttle.

With *Sea Dart* only yards away from it, even the microphone behaved perfectly from the very first opening bars of the "Stars and Stripes." After this the speeches commenced, introduced by James Lovell, who made, I thought, an eloquent job of it.

"The past two centuries have been the scene of an explosion of geographic discovery. The vast unexplored continents have been travelled, the polar regions explored, the seas traversed, and the highest mountains climbed. Space travel is now a reality and man has now set foot on the moon. Tonight we pause to look back at some of the great accomplishments of this century through the eyes of some of the men who contributed to these discoveries. Their zeal, enthusiasm, and courage exemplify the spirit that brought about the great explorations of past years, and we salute them and their fellow explorers who have given us this heritage.

"We also look to the future and hope that the inspiration of past accomplishments will stimulate the youth of today to continue on the trail that has been so brilliantly blazed by these eminent men."

As I applauded James Lovell, with all the others, I breathed to myself, "Amen to that last bit."

There were five other main speakers, including yours truly.

Then came Professor Robert Jastrow, chairman of the gradu-ate program in space physics at Columbia University. He was deeply concerned with making space understandable to the general public and was the author of several books on the sub-ject. He spoke fascinatingly about contacting other cultures in space.

Willard F. Rockwell was next. He took us into the realm of the coming mini-computers, and chips so small that the whole of Shakespeare could now be stored in a piece of material no bigger than your thumbnail. Very useful in small craft.

Elie Rogers, a lecturer at George Washington University, took us all through the wonders of microscopic photography, showing us slides of such beautiful objects as a fly's hair mag-nified until it was twelve feet high on the slide screen.

Then came Lowell Thomas, too well known for comment by me. Now in his eighties, the author of fifty-three books, he showed us a film he had taken on his recent honeymoon in Tibet. It was a highly original film, full of joy and color and the zest for life. Lowell had vigorously shaken my hand.

Even while Lowell's films were still showing, Russell nudged me. "You're on next, Tristan," he said. I walked quietly around behind the stage curtains. *Sea Dart* looked as pretty as she could in the circumstances. I had draped little flags of all the countries visited during *The Incredible Voyage*—all thirty-six of them—over the worst of her scars, and her sails, in the spotlights, looked reasonably clean and wind-worthy. I had fixed her now-loose doghouse back in place and re-shipped her bowsprit.

Someone placed a microphone cord around my tuxedo collar. I stood slightly to one side of *Sea Dart* and waited. I felt the same trembling inside as I do before a voyage.

Suddenly there was a *zizz* overhead. The curtains silently opened. There were blazing lights aimed at the stage. In the glare I could see nothing of the audience. There was a momen-tary dead hush, then, like an Atlantic sea breaking on the eternally beaten rocks of Llanfihangel, fifteen hundred American souls gasped. It was so loud it was like the swoosh of a katabatic wind.

"Good evening, ladies and gentlemen . . . and sailors." My voice, as if disembodied, spoke.

The great game again was afoot. The chips were down. Another voyage was under way.

* * *

After the show was over, many well-known people visited *Sea Dart* as she sat on the stage.

James Lovell peeped into the cabin. "Hey," he said in a slight drawl, "this is even smaller than Apollo—I don't know how you do it."

"Slower, too, Captain," I suggested. He gave me a boyish grin. "Bounces around more," I said.

"I'll bet she does," allowed the astronaut.

"And she bumps when she hits the ground," I concluded.

"I'll bet she does that, too, Tristan," he said, and laughed. It was only later that I realized he had been talking about the space vehicle—I had been talking about H.M.S. *Apollo,* the old mine-laying cruiser.

* * *

The New York papers did not pick up the story. They were busy with the "Son of Sam" murder case, but *The Washington Post* reported it. The New York papers missing it was a disappointment, but disappointments are for ditching overboard, not for cargo. They never aided any voyage.

There were farmers in the audience—I met some, from Iowa and Kansas, after the show. They told me they had never thought of the sea as being anything but "just water" before.

* * *

Sea Dart had to be out of the Waldorf by 8:00 A.M. the following day, to make way for the next function. At midnight she was lowered delicately, like an invalid lady, from the stage, by thirty-two American socialites, men and women, all in evening dress. By 3:00 A.M. she was out on the sidewalk on Park Avenue and I was locked away in my own berth, sleeping inside her for the first time since our parting in the Montevideo docks twenty months before. I was woken a couple of times by awestruck voices, but no one attempted to board her.

"I just don't b'lieve my *eyes*, man . . . goddam it, now I know . . . I just seen *everything!*" The voice faded away and I snuggled my head again on the Bolivian flag *Sea Dart* had brought down from the Andes.

Only false pride can feel threatened. I slept.

Oh Shenandoah, I love your daughter,
Oh away, you rolling river!
Oh Shenandoah, I love your daughter,
Away, I'm bound to go, 'cross the wide Missouri.

'Tis seven long years since last I've seen thee,
Oh away, you rolling river!
'Tis seven long years since last I've seen thee,
Away, I'm bound to go, 'cross the wide Missouri.

"SHENANDOAH." A MID-NINETEENTH-CENTURY HALYARD CHANTY, IT HAS
THE MOST HAUNTING MELODY OF ALL THE CHANTIES. IT WAS USUALLY
SUNG AS SHIPS HOISTED THEIR SAILS TO MAKE THEIR DEPARTURES.

Avowed Intent

I DON'T SUPPOSE that one in ten thousand New Yorkers, should you ever need to be courageous enough to ask them, would be able to tell you where there is a horse-stable in Manhattan. There is one—on West Fifty-second Street, two stories up in an anonymous-looking nineteenth-century building.

That's where the boat-hauler took *Sea Dart* from the Waldorf entrance, after a lot of energy and huffing and puffing to get her back onto the low-loader. Below the stables she was lifted off the truck body and gently lowered onto a float. To the float were harnessed three mules. Not the mules you see in third-world countries, not beaten, scrawny, half-starved animals. Chubby American mules, each one eager, willing, and strong enough, as I soon found, to haul the rig all alone. This was arranged by *Quest* magazine. In exchange for publicity for their magazine, and for the excerpt of *The Incredible Voyage* in the current issue, they agreed to transport the boat from the Waldorf to the South Street Seaport.

For three days we rambled around Manhattan. Not too fast, not in any hurry. We ambled through Times Square, and up Sixth Avenue and through Central Park. I let the kids scramble up onboard everywhere—East Side, West Side, all around the town. The kids loved it.

"Hey, mister!" This was aimed at me by a small elf-faced laddie of about nine years.

"Hello!"

"Is that boat for real?"

"Sure . . . here, climb up the ladder, have a look inside."

The kid hesitated. "Does it really sail?" he asked, doubtfully. "Does it really go to sea . . . is it a *real* boat?"

Jake, the mule driver, from somewhere in the South, answered him, "She sure does."

"Aww, I don't believe it," said the kid.

"Why not?" queried Jake. "You kin see the sails inside."

"'Cos I ain't seen it on television, that's why . . ." said the tyke.

I looked at Jake. He was about thirty, dressed in Western style, with a Stetson hat. He had red hair and a relaxed air about him. He returned my look in silence for a minute, while the boy briefly glanced inside the boat. Then the kid climbed back down again. "Well, maybe . . ." he said.

Jake said, "Where to now, Cap'n?"

"CBS studios," I said. "That's one complaint we'll scotch."

* * *

During the three-day cruise around Manhattan I would, at a wild guess, say that *Sea Dart* passed around a half-million people and around two thousand kids climbed onboard her deck.

I treat children as what they are, rather small people. It seems to me that the child (and perhaps the childish adult) has two main fears. The first fear is that of being manipulated by someone else, and the second one is a fear that something is being hidden from him. I was quite open with them. I told them what I was doing and why, to focus some attention on the sea. I think most of them over the age of five understood and appreciated it. I got a few strange looks from the adolescents now and then, but I had had those same looks from adolescents of all ages for so long that it bothered me not one jot.

Sometimes mothers would wonder about the danger of their child climbing the ladder and I would reassure them that it was no more dangerous than the ladder he was already four rungs up simply by reaching the age of six or whatever it was. The unruly ones (and God knows, there are enough of them in New York City) I gave a smart quiet tap on the funny-bone; this had a wonderfully quieting effect on them, but I doubt if any of them ever concluded that I valued them less for their silence.

How can anything that has been at fault and been corrected be less valuable than what has not been put right?

Even the most ill-behaved of the kids, the most foul-mouthed, the most restless of them, had something true, something naturally true, about him, at least to me. I think they knew that by instinct, and many a little fiend became a little friend. Then they delayed me for hours at a time, as they put it, "rappin' 'bout storms an' pirates 'n' stuff, man."

If you want to learn about expression, ask a little New York City kid how his strawberry ice cream tastes on a hot, muggy June afternoon on Tompkins Square! The only beautiful things about the square were the kids. The ones under five; the ones that cynicism hadn't been thrust at too much, up to then.

When I was thirteen years old I went to sea. My first skipper knew men who had been at sea with old sailors who had served at the battle of Trafalgar as powder-monkeys in 1805! Now, here in New York City I was conscious that I was chatting with some of the folk of the future. I was talking with people who will belong to a culture where it might very well be possible to choose to remain alive for a hundred—two hundred—five hundred years! To think that I was a link in a human chain of only three people—my old skipper, me, and the child—yet spanning over a possible six centuries; it was impossible for me not to love and respect every child I clapped eyes on. Among them were, highly likely, some who will reach the stars! That thought was enough to make the most hard-boiled old salt a little humble, even though I knew that humility never clawed anyone off a lee shore.

Like seafarers' vessels, children are the sum total of all our voyages, past and present, and all our hopes for the future. Like destiny, it is what we give them that counts, not what we expect of them. Every time a little boy or girl grabbed *Sea Dart*'s tiller and swung it with a whoop, every time a little lad or lass gazed at my tiny (to them, sensible size) galley with delight, so my heart sang as *Sea Dart*, high and dry, trembled slightly under children's feet.

It was noon: "Hey, Cap'n!" (Why do Americans use titles so much?) He was no more than nine or ten, bronze face and wide brown eyes.

"What's that, mate?"

"D'ya think I can ever go out on adventures like you?"

"Sure, why not?"

"Aww . . . the world's all discovered now . . ."

"They used to say that when I was your age, too."

"Where'dya think we can go?" He was excited now, bouncing up and down.

"Much, much farther than we did." I looked over at the reddish-blue heat-smog-haze over Roosevelt Island ". . . To places where noon is mazarine . . ."

"Hey, that's neat . . . Hey, yawannsom popcorn?"

"Give it to one of the mules . . . they love it," I told him.

"Hey . . . thanks, Cap'n."

"And help your sister down the ladder."

"Aw, she's okay, she's older'n me."

"Then tie your shoelace up. You look like a bloomin' midshipman!"

*   *   *

On the eighteenth of April *Sea Dart,* after spending an hour berthed alongside the steps of the New York Stock Exchange, finally arrived at her resting place for the next three months, until she was due to depart on the journey arranged for her by the publishers of *The Incredible Voyage.* She was to be hauled right across the United States, from Boston to Seattle. She would touch the Canadian border in the north, she would, it was intended, sail down the Mississippi from Minneapolis to St. Louis, and she would touch the Mexican border in the south. She would visit thirty-six cities en route, and a probable twenty thousand Americans, kids and adults, would visit her. When the three mules hauled her onto the South Street Seaport museum jetty thus far had the plan progressed.

There was a large sailing ketch lying tied up to the jetty as Jake unhitched the mules. We had seen no one yet except the

jetty-foreman, who had indicated where he wanted *Sea Dart,*
on her float, placed.

Suddenly, from the ketch there rose an irate female voice.

"You brutes should be ashamed of yourselves, letting those
poor animals have to haul that thing around!" By now Jake and
his team had disappeared out of the small dockyard. The
woman, about thirty-five, I would guess, medium height,
dressed in jeans, pants, and black jersey, with spectacles and
very black hair, glared at me aggressively.

"They're very well fed, and Jake only lets them haul for half
an hour at a stretch . . ." I started to explain.

"You should be ashamed of yourselves . . . you *chauvinists*
. . . You're exploiting those poor dumb beasts . . ." she ranted
and raved and screeched at me in a high-pitched voice. She
lectured me, in front of a dozen deck-hands who looked on
expressionlessly, for a good twenty minutes. As she shouted I
remembered the *human* beasts of burden I had seen, the sweat-
ing cargo-loaders of Mombasa, the little Andes Indian kids lug-
ging a hundredweight of potatoes up vertical cliffs, the convicts
on Gorgona at their cruel labor of shifting seventy-five-pound
stones from one end of the beach to the other and back again;
the effort squeezed out of so many poorly fed *human* frames the
world over. Most of her tirade was, to me, like daisies in the
mouth of a bull. What hurt me most was calling me a "chauvin-
ist" . . . and then mostly because Chauvin was, I recalled as I
seethed, a Napoleonic demagogue, a Frenchman, not even a
Breton . . . She left me wondering who had been cruel to whom.
But cruelty itself is a human trait, and so at least I allowed that
she was, after all, human.

I said nothing. I let her rant. I did think about what Dr. Sam-
uel Johnson said to James Boswell about a dog walking on its
hind legs once, but I held my tongue. I was not in eighteenth-
century Harwich—this was twentieth-century America. I stood
there, a dumb beast too, while she accused me of cruelty to
animals and just about every other evil persuasion under the
sun. Then she tired, and silently marched back onboard the

vessel. I was informed, later, that the vessel she was aboard was used for concerts given to support environmentalists! Well, as my friend Saratoga says, "Ya can't win 'em all!"

*   *   *

From April to June I worked hard on *Ice!*, the next book, due to be published in the following year, 1978. On the few days I took off from writing, I made my way to the South Street Seaport, to work on *Sea Dart*, patching her up, painting her a little, cleaning out her cabin. One day in May I had started work onboard the boat when, to my disgust, the rain started to fall. I packed up my tools, locked her cabin, and took off for the Village again. I was crossing over Front Street in my yellow oilskin and cap. A young woman, in a raincoat, quite good looking, but with nothing particular to distinguish her, about twenty-one, suddenly called out to me.

"Hey!"

I stopped. I looked around me, in case I had dropped something. She ran up to me. She gasped, "I know who you are! I read your stuff in *Quest*—say, can you do me a favor?" she said, smiling at me.

"Well . . . what's that?"

"I wanna shake your hand . . . I just wanna shake your hand . . . You've given me something to base my dreams on!"

It was the first time I had ever been recognized by someone who was not a mariner or a magazine editor. I was too flabbergasted to say anything. I shook her hand and she walked away. The rain was easing off. I looked back at the dock gate. I saw in my mind's eye *Sea Dart* sitting forlorn in the rain, with still much to be done for her. *"Bugger it,"* I said to myself and headed back to her. The sun broke through the clouds fifteen minutes later and the rest of the day was fine. I cleaned out her bilge.

*   *   *

The day for our departure on the haul across America finally came around in early June. It was hot and clammy in New York City. The publishers had arranged for a brand-new Ford truck, all gleaming white, to haul the boat, and a driver from Kansas, who contacted me in the Village. I guided him to the Seaport. One of the biggest mobile cranes I ever saw in my life trundled up to load *Sea Dart* onto the Ford with amazing delicacy and accuracy. Kansas and I soon had the boat tied down. We were due at a press reception at the Explorers Club at 1:00 P.M. before setting off with the boat for important shopping centers on Long Island. Important because they were in the center of a great yachting area.

"Where to?" asked Kansas. "Which way?" He was twenty and had never been to New York before. He pored over a city street map.

"Up Broadway and onto Sixth Avenue," I said. We set off. We only had half an hour to get to Seventy-second Street, but we made it in time for the reporters to ask questions and take photographs. Walter Cronkite, the television newsman and an avid yachtsman, turned up, and he and I sat in *Sea Dart*'s cockpit for a while, talking of boats and the ocean. He had missed the Explorers Club dinner, and was taking the opportunity to visit with us. Quite a few of the other members showed up, but we were pressed for time. With everyone wishing us farewell and Godspeed, *Sea Dart* was hustled away past the trees along the street and round the corner into Lexington Avenue.

"So long, Tristan, take care now!" called Walter.

"Where now?" asked Kansas, his eyes glued to the road.

I had the street map on my knee as I sat beside him in the cab.

"Keep on down Lexington and go on down the Bowery. Turn left when we get to Delancey—we'll head across the Williamsburg Bridge into Brooklyn and Long Island."

Driving a truck for the first time in your life, among Manhattan drivers for the first time in your life, is not the easiest thing in the world, but somehow Kansas held his own. The comments from cab-drivers flew thick and fast each time we stopped at traffic lights.

"Waddaya got dere, a QE Two?"

"C'n I take dat home 'n' put it inna bathtub?"

The truck shook its way down Lexington, a bit of juggling

around Gramercy Square, and then on down Third Avenue and the Bowery. I remembered well the last time I had been in this area a year before, and wondered if the Colonel's gang would be at the lights on Houston. Sure enough, there they were, except the Colonel and Hot Shot were missing.

"Pull up here a minute," I said to Kansas. We stopped by the lights—right under them, in the middle of the road, with all the traffic honking and cursing its way around us. Kansas, a quick-witted lad, ran to the hood and opened it, so it would appear we had a breakdown.

The Colonel's gang, Jimmyjo, Big Bluey, the Denver Kid— looking even older and more gaunt than ever—and Maximum all stood there with cleaning rags in their hands, not much rag-gier or dirtier than the clothes on their backs. They all stood there gaping at me, the truck, and the boat.

"Hey . . . Jesus Christ! . . ." Maximum was the first to speak. "Where 'da fuck ya *goin'*, Cap'n?" His crew-cut was now a shaggy mop, but he was still as hefty as he had been a year before.

"Long Island and Boston," I said, grinning at the Denver Kid. "And Denver."

"Well . . ." Big Bluey was staring wide-eyed at the boat. "Don't that just beat *all* . . . godDAM! . . . uhm . . . *uhhm!*"

I offered, "Clean her up, fellers! We gotta be quick before the cops get down on our case."

Maximum laughed. "You goddam sonuvabitch . . . you god-dam limey . . . if Coinul could only see *this* . . ."

"Where is he?" I asked Maximum. "And what's with Hot Shot?"

"Gonna Florida fora summer . . . Miami Beach . . . Hot Shot's gone wid him . . ."

In a flash, as the honking traffic sped by on each side, four of the window-cleaners were wiping every surface within reach, squirting cleaning fluid from aerosol cans over the truck and the boat.

Maximum stood back to supervise and chat with me.

"How's things going, Maximum?" I asked him.

"Fuckin' lousy." He was, it was plain to me, a bit over-whelmed.

"What's with you?"

"Ahh . . . da goddam Bowery . . . da Welfare's lousing every-thing up. The flop-joints'r' closin' down . . . da Uncle Sam, da Clover, most of da others dey're all gonna close," Maximum shouted over the roar of the traffic. "Soon it's gonna be like we don't get a goddam two-dollar bed no more. Da Welfare is doin' a lotta harm, Cap'n . . . it's fuckenup da ciddy!"

"How come?" I asked him.

"Too many goddam junkies 'n' transients . . . not enough hon-est bums anymore . . . Dey're all movin' out, all over da goddam ciddy . . . Dey're movin' away ta da SROs . . ." [single-room oc-cupancy hotels] "them that ain't too bombed ta manage 'a rent. Dey're all . . . all da honest bums 'r' movin' up ta da Upper West Side. It's gettin' like dere ain't no more decent drunks ta drink wid no more. 'At Welfare is a crocka shit, Cap'n." Maximum turned to bellow at Big Bluey, "Hey, don't forget 'a goddam back window ada cab!" Big Bluey grinned and clambered up to clean the window, rushing to beat the lights.

Maximum turned again to me. "An' 'a goddam suburban kids 'at's comin' in wid dere old man's money an' settin' 'emselves up as artists . . . Da goddam Bowery is gonna be more middle class 'n' 'a goddam Village!"

A police siren sounded a few blocks away. Kansas went rigid. I pressed four dollars into Maximum's hand. "A buck apiece," I said. "We gotta split."

"Hey, okay," murmured Maximum. Kansas and I clambered into the cab.

"Hey all *right!*" Jimmyjo shouted.

"So long, Cap'n . . ." The Denver Kid waved his rag and screwed up his face.

"So long, fellas!" called Jimmyjo from behind his spunyarn beard.

Kansas reved up the engine. Maximum bellowed above the noise, "Now you watch them goddam coppers in L.A., Cap'n. They're real sonsubitches . . . yahearme?"

"Send us a card from Denver!" croaked the Kid, through his toothless gums.

"I'll send you a book!" I shouted back.

"When?" Maximum and Jimmyjo chorused. Kansas shifted gears.

"When I've something to write about!" The lights changed. *Sea Dart* moved her message forward. We were off, on a new trail, the American trail.

EPILOG

I have tried to write Paradise

Do not move
    Let the wind speak
        That is paradise

Let the Gods forgive what I
        have made
Let those I love try to forgive
        what I have made.

CANTO 120, *The Cantos,* EZRA POUND